Pit Boss
Smoker

Cookbook for Beginners

2500-Day Pit Boss Pellet Smoker Recipes Assist You to Master the Versatile
Grill & Smoker and Cook Multiple Items at a Time

Christine Cowell

Table of Contents

Introduction

Do you want to become the finest pitmaster in your family? Do you relish grilling and smoking savory foods and tender meat cuts at home? Then here is a recipe book and a handbook for the Pit Boss wood pellet grill that will make pro at grilling, smoking, and barbecuing practically every delicacy you want to enjoy on your BBQ night. This recipe collection is all about providing the best ideas for using the high-quality pit boss wood pellet grill and smoker. You can now use your pit boss grill griddle for cooking our extensive selection of beef, lamb, chicken, turkey, vegan, and dessert meals. This master pit smoker is designed to produce controlled heat and perfect sear so that the user can enjoy the juiciest steaks or evenly grilled veggies or meat every time.

Fundamentals of Pit Boss Wood Pellet Grill & Smoker

Since the BBQ season is upon us and we all are looking for fine recipes to cook luscious BBQ menus for family and friends. If you want to grill tough meat cuts, juicy steak, and smoke whole chickens and turkeys, then you definitely need a premium quality grill and smoker in your backyard. A great cooking station makes the entire process simple, practical, and enjoyable. The wood pellet grills made by Pit Boss are famous for doing the same. The Pit Boss grill and smokers are easy to operate and effective at cooking huge quantities of food. The recipes featured in this book serve as a short pit boss wood pellet guide for all beginners and are the ideal place to start using this grill.

What is Pit Boss Wood Pellet Grill & Smoker?

Pit boss pellet grill is an all-in-one cooking station that combines the features of charcoal-gas grills, smokers, and ovens in one place. Pit Boss Pellet Grills provide both direct and indirect heat since its fuel source is 100% all-natural hardwood pellets.

The Pit boos Pellet grill provides its users the option to smoke food, but they differ from conventional smokers in a few important ways. For example, pellet grills use an automated fuel and air supply system, making temperature control simpler than for conventional smokers. Traditional smokers make it challenging to regulate the heat and fuel source. When smoking food, pellet grills can handle this task, enabling you to "set the temperature and forget it." To appreciate the culinary benefits of smoking, you don't have to be an accomplished BBQ pitmaster.

Benefits of Using It

The reason why the Pit Boss grills are recommended for home-based or professional grilling is the smart functions of this grill. If you have the Pit Boss grill, you can easily manage cooking multiple items at a time. It is all possible only because of the following special features of this cooking appliance.

Multipurpose

Pit Boss Pellet grills allow you to combine a variety of cooking methods into a single appliance. A standard smoker only smokes, so if you want to grill, bake, or roast your meal, you'll need to buy a smoker separately. However, the pit boss grill, with its various cooking accessories and a broad cooking surface, lets you cook in different ways as you need.

Great Built

Every Pit Boss wood pellet grill is constructed of heavy-duty steel and features two huge metal wheels for convenient mobility. It has a High Temp Powder Coat Finish and a hopper lid side shelf. A stainless steel thermometer and a sturdy bottom shelf are also included in this package.

Advanced Grilling

The best feature of this Pitboss grill is its temperature sensor and the probes that come with it. They enable you to keep an eye on the food while it is covered and grilled. The sensor indicates the temperature inside the grill, and the probes are used to read the internal temperatures of the meat cooked inside. In this way, it gets easier to manage the temperature.

Easy Cleaning:

Easy and convenient cleaning is something we all secretly wish for. Because when you are done cooking, you need a few simple steps to clean your appliance and keep it ready for the next session. And Pit Boss grill and smoker guarantee quick and easy cleaning due to its smart structure. You can easily remove the chimney cap, grill drum, grilling grates, grease tray, and bucket to clean them well

Before cooking on your Pit Boss grill for the first time, we recommend that you "burn off" the grill to rid it of any foreign matter. Light and operate the grill on HIGH with the lid down for 30 – 40 minutes. Your "Pit Boss" Pellet Grill should always be a minimum of 12 inches away from any wall or structure around the entire grill. Your grill does come with wheels, so the smoker and chimney stack can be turned away from the wind resulting in better temperature output. If you are able to shelter your grill from the wind, this will also aid in temperature output, heat retention, and heat recovery time when opening the lid.

Understanding the Control Board

Pit Boss Temperature Dial

One of my favorite features of the Pit Boss digital control board is how simple it is to use. Even if you've never used one before, it's simple to operate. You'll have control over the following, depending on the model:

• Temperature • Off Setting • Smoke Setting • High Setting
• LCD Screen • "P" SET Button

Hit the power button to turn the grill on or switch it off. When the grill is connected to a power source, the power button will glow blue.

Temperature

Both the set and actual temperatures are shown on the control board. This allows you to quickly determine whether the grill is operating hotter or colder than it should be without having to raise the top.

Off Setting: The Off Setting on the Temperature Control Dial is the off mode for the unit. The unit will not function on this setting.

Smoke Setting: The Smoke Setting on the Temperature Control Dial is the start-up mode for the unit. The grill operates at the lowest temperature, without the fire going out.

High Setting: The High Setting on the Temperature Control Dial is the highest heat level for the unit. The grill operates at the highest temperature. When the lid is open, the grill will run at this speed to compensate for the loss of heat in the barrel.

LCD Screen: The LED Screen is used as the information center for your unit. The LED screen will display your desired cook temperature (SET), actual cook temperature (ACTUAL), and the "P" setting selected ("P" SET).

"P" SET Button: The "P" SET Button is used to select one of the eight temperature fine tunings. Use this feature to change the "P" setting to accommodate to your cooking style and cooking environment, as preferred. With a short push of the recessed button, the setting increases from P0 to P7, then repeats. Adjustments are best made when the Temperature Control Dial is set to Smoke, which allows for manual control of the pellet feed system. Default setting is "P4".

Understanding the P-Setting

The P Setting Control Button's main advantage is that it enables you, the Pit Master, to fine-tune your Pit Boss Pellet Grill to account for environmental variables like wind, humidity, ambient temperatures, and pellet fuel kind and quality. Every time, a World Championship result is guaranteed.

The auger goes on, delivers fuel for 18 seconds, and then shuts off when the Temperature Dial is set to Smoke Or High. The smoke control push button, which shows a "P" setting, sets or modifies the Off-Time. When the Smoke Control Button is pressed, the LCD panel briefly shows the corresponding "P" setting. Eight "P" settings, from P0 to P7, are available.

This helps you customize your Pit Boss Pellet Grill to your specific requirements. If you enjoy hot smoking and prefer a stronger smoke flavor, you can increase the "P" setting while in the smoke mode to extend the interval between auger feeds. As a result, your cooking will take longer to complete and produce a "Smoke Ring" with a deeper color and more flavor.

In the High setting, you can decrease the "P" setting to shorten the time between auger feeds if you prefer to Grill Or Sear. As a result, the temperature output and pellet consumption go up, but you can acquire "Steak House Sear" markings and cook food more quickly.

As the "P" setting is raised, the fuel feed rate decreases (heat output). The smoke flavor will be stronger because the grill's output temperatures are lower and fewer pellets are being used. Raising the "P" setting must be done with caution, as doing so increases the likelihood of extinguishing the flames.

As the "P" setting is lowered, the Fuel Feed Rate rises (heat output). As a result, both the temperature of the grill's output and the quantity of pellets used will rise. Avoid lowering the "P" setting too much to avoid overfeeding the pellets, which could lead to incomplete combustion or the production of creosote.

Lighting Your Grill

It is recommended practice to always clean your burn grate after every 1 to 3 uses. This will ensure proper ignition and many happy grilling experiences. Light as per instructions found in detail later in this manual. Should your auto igniter refuse to ignite the wood pellets, it is easy to light your grill manually with a match and lighting agent.

Preheating

It is extremely important to always allow your grill to preheat before cooking. This allows the grill and cooking grids to heat up quicker, and the grill is able to maintain its cooking temperature once your food is placed in the cooking area. If you do not allow the grill to preheat, you will find that it takes a longer period of time to bring both the grill and the food to cooking temperatures. Always preheat your "Pit Boss" Grill and smoker with the lid closed. Once your grill has started to burn, shut the cover and, depending on the weather, set the temperature control knob to HIGH for 10 to 15 minutes. It also serves as the last step in cleaning your cooking grids. This provides you ample time to get your food ready for the grill.

Lid Position

Always cook with the lid closed. Not only does this keep the temperature even, but the food will also cook faster, using less fuel. A closed lid also helps to create a smokier flavor. You can slow down your cooking by propping up the lid.

Automatic Use

Make sure the Grill's Power switch is in the "OFF" position. Connect the Power Cord to a grounded 110V outlet. A non-grounded outlet or extension cable should NOT be used, nor should the ground end of the cord be cut off.

Make sure the plug is at least 15 amps when using a GFI. Try plugging the appliance into a surge-protected power bar first, as lower-grade GFIs may trip. Release the Hopper Lid. Make that the hopper and Auger feed system are Free of any extraneous objects. Put dry, naturally scented wood pellets in the hopper. Open the cooking lid. The main lid must be open while the system is starting up and cooling down. Set the Smoke temperature dial. The start-up cycle is triggered by this. The fan will start to blow air into the fire pot, the feed system will start to rotate, and the Igniter will start to glow.

During the start-up stage, your grill will start to create smoke. Once the smoke has subsided, the pellets have ignited. To confirm, you hear a torch-like roar and feel some heat being produced with your stove lid still open. Set the temperature dial to High and give the appliance 15 to 20 minutes to preheat. Turn the feed control down if there is an excessive amount of flame visible, such as when the tasting plate is burning red.

Now that the preheating is finished, you may benefit from the pellet grill. Keep in mind that cooking at lower temperatures results in more flavor and fewer flare-ups. The temperatures you cook at will vary according to the type of wood pellets you use, the outside temperature, and the weather. The control's settings are approximate.

Manual Use

Ensure that the temperature dial is set to "OFF." Connect the POWER CORD to a grounded 110V outlet. A non-grounded outlet or extension cable should NOT be used, nor should the ground end of the cord be cut off. As lower-grade GFIs could trip, try first plugging the equipment into a surge-protected power bar. Flip the hopper lid out. Make sure there are no extraneous things in the hopper or hopper of the auger feed system. Put wood pellets that are dry and naturally fragrant in the hopper.

Take away the cooking grids, grease tray, and flame diffuser to reveal the burn pot. Fill the burn pot with lots of pellets. Add a thin layer of solid fuel fire starter, such as those manufactured from sawdust and wax or wood shavings, or squirt-gelled fire starter or another acceptable pellet starting over the top of the pellets.

Add a small number of pellets over the fire starter. Light the starter using a long fireplace match or a long lighter. Give the starting 3 to 5 minutes to burn. Replace the flavor/grease plate and cooking grids quickly and carefully. Set the Smoke temperature dial.

The start-up cycle is triggered by this. The fan will begin to blow air into the

fire pot when the feed system turns. During the start-up stage, your grill will start to create smoke. Set the temperature dial to High and give the appliance 15 to 20 minutes to preheat. Set the temperature dial to High and give the appliance 15 to 20 minutes to preheat.

You don't have to quit grilling just because the vividly colored leaves are gone, and the golf clubs are stored for another season. The heavenly aroma of cooked food and flavorful wood pellets, along with the crisp, fresh air, may be just what the doctor prescribed to heal your winter blues. Holiday grilling also leaves more room in the oven for other crucial meal items. Listed below are some ideas for using your barbecue during the cooler months:

Straight from the Store

Pellets used in the pit boss grills are made of natural wood. The auger transfers the pellets into the firepot after they've been fed into the pellet hopper, where they catch fire and grill the food in the cooking area. Several Pit Boss models, unlike normal barbecue grills, have the multifunctional cooking capability; thus, it's no surprise that it's the second most popular grill. You can smoke, grill, sear, roast, bake, and dehydrate using your pit boss wood pellet grill.

Ignitor
On any pellet grill, the ignitor is one of the essential components. The ignitor is what ignites the fire in the firepot by lighting the pellets. If the ignitor fails, you may still use the grill, but you'll have to ignite the firepot using a propane torch.

Combustion Fan
When you switch on the Pit Boss grill, one of the first things you'll notice is how loud the combustion fan is. It's quite normal for your pellet grill to make an engine-like noise when it initially turns on. Throughout the cooking period, the induction fan remains on. It works by circulating hardwood smoke around the cook chamber, allowing for convection cooking.

Auger
The auger is a large screw used to feed the fire pot with the wood pellet fuel. The P-setting on the control board may be used to regulate the flow of pellets. The auger will pause longer with a higher P-setting, delaying the pellets it feeds into the firepot. Learning how to alter the P-setting on the Pit Boss takes patience. You'll learn how to utilize the grill as you use it more.

Firepot
The pellets and ash residue in the grill are collected in the firepot. The pellets are ignited on fire by the hot rod after the fire pot contains enough pellets. The induction fan then stokes the fire, resulting in the well-known induction heat.

Hopper
It's the large pellet storage box that's connected to the grill. The hopper's only purpose is to retain the wood pellets that the auger feeds into the cooking chamber. Before starting your Pit Boss grill, make sure the hopper is filled with enough pellets to last the whole cooking session.

Top Rack
The top shelf on most Pit Boss versions is detachable. Consider the upper shelf as the additional cooking area. For example, if you're cooking 18 burgers on the bottom level and you're running out of room, you may utilize the upper shelf. Just keep in mind that because the foods on the top shelf are further away from the fire, they may take longer to cook. Many individuals indicate they haven't observed a change in cooking time while utilizing the top shelf on internet forums. Even so, a thermometer should always be used when cooking on the Pit Boss. It makes it simpler to ensure that meats are cooked to the correct internal temperature.

Cooking Surface
The main cooking surface of the pit boss grill is made up of removable grates, and here is where the majority of your meals are prepared in the pit boss grill. It sits right on top of the flame broiler, allowing the food to sear fast. Depending on the model, the actual size of the cooking area will vary. The cooking area of a stainless steel 2-burner gas grill is 267.8 square inches. The cooking area of a Pit Boss 7-series Vertical Smoker is 1,853 square inches. The cooking space will vary depending on the model you purchase.

Flame Broiler
Flame broiling is simple with the flame broiler. Cover the fire with the sliding plate for direct flame grilling. It sears burgers, steaks, hot dogs, and other foods like nothing I've ever seen before. It's also beneficial when using a cast iron pan for cooking.

With little maintenance, your "pit boss" pellet grill will provide you with many years of delightful use. A crucial step is to run the grill on high temperature for 5–10 minutes after each usage, allowing the grill and cooking grids to "self-clean." turn the temperature dial to High once you're done grilling. Allow your grill to run for 5 to 10 minutes so it may perform its typical cleaning process. It is best to let the grill burn for an additional 10 to 20 minutes if you have been cooking exceptionally fatty meats. This will lessen the possibility of a "flare-up" while cooking your subsequent delicious meal. When finished, just open your grill's cover and turn the temperature dial to the smoke position.

Before switching to the off position, turn the grill to the smoke position and let it run for a little while. Your grill will automatically begin the "shut down" process. After the auger system stops feeding fuel, the flame will go out on its own, and the combustion and cooling fan will continue to operate for an extra five minutes. Upon completion of this procedure, the fan will turn off. Once it has cooled, just close the lid and cover the container to ensure safety.

When it comes to keeping the grill clean, there are two extremes. Those who insist on cleaning the grill completely after each usage, both inside and out, and those who believe that doing so just ruins the flavor of the food.

Ensure that the grease collection area is always clean and debris-free. Check the grease bucket. Cleaning it up as needed, and be mindful of the kind of cooking you perform. If you do use heavy-duty aluminum foil to line the grease tray, make sure to replace it after each use. Regularly clean the internal surfaces of the grill, the grease drain tube, and the grease catch areas.

Clean up the grease tray of any grease or debris buildup, as this can inhibit grease run-off and eventually cause an unwelcome flare-up. When the grill is warm, it is simpler to remove built-up grease.

Maintenance of painted surfaces and paint are not covered by warranties. This is a component of general upkeep and maintenance. Do not clean the outer surfaces of the grill using oven cleaners, abrasive cleaners, or abrasive cleaning pads.

After each use, clean your grill with a warm, moist cloth dipped in soapy water. It is strongly advised that you use a cover to keep your grill safe! While the cooking grids are still heated, clean them of any food or buildup with a long-handled grill cleaning brush made of brass or another soft metal. Take out the flavor plate and cooking grid twice or three times a year, and clean the area surrounding the burn pot. The shop vac comes in handy for this task. Ensure that the grill is totally cold.

What to do if the grill does not light or if fuel runs out in the unit?

The Temperature Dial should be set to OFF. Cooking Grids, Grease Tray, and Flame Diffuser can be removed by opening the lid. Clear the Fire Pot of all unburned pellets and ash. AVOID touching the Igniter. Burns can result from this item's extraordinarily high temperature. Once everything is cleaned, set the temperature dial to SMOKE. Look over the following:

• Visually check to see if the Igniter is blazing red and getting hot.
• Check Pellets are falling into the fire pot visually from the auger.
• Check the fan is operational.
• Never grill in an area that isn't well-ventilated!

You should put an outdoor thermometer close to your cooking area so that you can monitor the weather. This will aid in estimating the amount of time your dish will need to cook.

You might want to keep a record of what you cooked, the outside temperature, and the outcomes. Later on, you'll be able to use this to decide what to cook and how long it will take. It is preferable to increase your preheating time by at least 20 minutes when cooking in chilly weather.

How often do I need to lift the grill lid?

Lifting the grill lid more than is necessary should be avoided. The temperature of your grill might be completely reduced by chilly wind gusts. Be flexible with your serving time; each time you open the cover, allow an additional 10 to 15 minutes for cooking. Always check the interior temperature of your food with a meat thermometer. It is a good idea to operate in a lit environment or to keep a lamp or flashlight close by during the colder months because the nights approach earlier. Prepare a warming platter and perhaps a cover in advance to keep your meal warm throughout the return trip inside.

Simple-to-prepare items like roasts, whole chicken, ribs, and turkey are some of the best options for winter cooking. You may prepare meals even more quickly by including vegetables and potatoes.

How should my Pit Boss Grill be turned on?

Start the grill on the smoke setting with the lid open for ten minutes. (The temperature range for the smoke setting is 80-100 C/180-210 F.) Once your temperature is set to the desired setpoint, close the lid. To prevent the firepot from becoming filled with pellets, start the grill on the smoke setting.

By leaving the lid open, you can avoid overfilling the barrel with smoke and avoiding a backdraft inside the appliance. Food can be added to the grill when it has reached the ideal cooking temperature. A Prime Button is present on a lot of our Pit Boss grills. To push the pellets to the fire pot while the Igniter is still hot, your grill will need to be primed if it has never been used or has entirely run out of pellets.

After the first five minutes, the Igniter doesn't cool off on its own. On the initial usage, it typically takes longer for the pellets to move from the hopper to the firepot. Holding the Prime button keeps the auger from pausing, hastening the delivery of the pellets. (Pressing and holding the Prime button does not make the auger spin more quickly.) Even with priming, your grill will probably need to be turned off and back on again to restart the Igniter for the first five minutes once the pellets reach the fire pot.

Tasty Grilling Tips and Tricks

Food has been prepared over fire since the dawn of time. Consequently, grilling is essentially the first way to cook. Even if modern fire cooking techniques are a little more advanced, the principle remains the same. When meats and vegetables are grilled over hot coals, the outside of the food is given a lovely sear while the interior remains juicy and delectable. These grilling hacks, tips, and techniques will rapidly make you a grill master, regardless of your experience level.

Always make sure your grill is hot

When food is added to a hot grill, the meal will get a lovely sear on the outside while still remaining perfectly juicy inside. It is crucial for cooking safety and will stop food from sticking to the grill. Bacteria can be killed by placing meat on a hot grill. Always heat your grill with the lid closed to ensure that it reaches the proper temperature quickly. Plan ahead because it can take up to 15 minutes to heat up a grill, depending on the grill and the temperature. So, what degree do you desire? Depending on what you're grilling, use this chart to determine the appropriate temperature.

Low heat: Grill's temperature should range from 250 to 300 degrees Fahrenheit. Medium Heat: Grill temperature should be between 300 and 350 degrees Fahrenheit. Medium-High: Grill temperature should be between 350 and 400 degrees Fahrenheit.

High Heat: Grill should be at a high temperature of 400 to 450 degrees Fahrenheit.

Clean the grill

This will prevent flavors from blending from what you just finished cooking on the grill and allow the flavor of whatever you're making to stand out. Additionally, it aids in avoiding food adhering to the grill.

I advise using a strong brush to clean the grill while it is still hot. Small pieces from your most recent grilling session are much simpler to remove when they heat up. I advise cleaning the grill right away after each usage, before turning off the fire, to keep a clean grill. Lacking a grill brush? Clean the grill using a piece of foil that has been rolled up. Hold the foil ball with tongs to wipe the grill while it's hot to prevent burning your fingers!

Oil the grill grates

This will lessen the likelihood of lean meats adhering to the grill. I advise avoiding using cooking spray on the grill because it can lead to flare-ups. Instead, squirt oil onto a paper towel and massage the towel with tongs over the grill grates. Place a piece of non-stick foil made for grills on the grill and cook your meal there if you want to cook without using any oil. Rest assured that the food will still get those wonderful grill marks that we've all come to appreciate. Cutting a potato in half and rubbing the cut side on hot grill grates is an interesting grilling trick that will make the grill naturally non-stick.

Don't move food around, and don't open the lid on the grill!

The majority of foods just require one flipping when cooking. While the meal cooks, moving it around the grill can result in uneven cooking and lengthen the cooking time. Since you only need to flip your food once, the lid of your grill should remain down when you're not flipping anything. This shortens the cooking time, ensures that the grill stays hot enough to sear your food, and keeps food from drying out. Additionally, it avoids flare-ups by reducing the amount of oxygen entering the grill.

Use an instant-read meat thermometer

Food safety is a top priority. Always check that the food on the grill has reached a safe internal temperature. Make sure the meat is cooked to the right temperature on the grill by using an instant-read thermometer.

• **Beef rare 125°F**   • **Beef well done at 160°F**   • **Ground beef burgers 160°F**   • **Pork: 145°F**   • **Poultry:** 165°F

Take into account carryover cooking when taking cooked meat from the grill because it will increase in temperature by 5 to 10 degrees after you remove it.

Let the meat rest

Before cutting into the meat, let it rest for anywhere between 5 and 15 minutes, depending on the type of meat. More resting time is required for a large piece of meat like a tri-tip than for a smaller steak like a tenderloin. A piece of meat that has been rested will be juicier and more tender since the juices will have been redistributed throughout the meat. To keep the meat warm as the juices are redistributed, I advise tenting it with a piece of foil while it rests.

Know whether to cook your foods directly or indirectly

Smaller pieces of meat should be grilled over the direct fire if they take 20 minutes or less to cook, whereas larger pieces of meat should be grilled over indirect heat if they take longer. While ribs should be cooked with indirect heat, a New York strip should be prepared over direct fire. So what exactly does "cooking using indirect heat" mean? This indicates that only the top half of your grill will be heated. The meat will be placed on the unheated side and cooked inadvertently on the hot side.

For indirect cooking, the grill's temperature should be close to 350 degrees Fahrenheit. While cooking indirectly, it's crucial to avoid opening the grill more than once or twice. Regularly opening the grill can considerably reduce the indirect temperature, and sudden variations in temperature during the cooking period can make the meat dry.

At the end of the grilling procedure, add sauce to the meat.

If the entire cooking time is shorter than 30 minutes, always baste the meat with a sauce or glaze in the final 5 minutes of cooking. Additionally, if cooking takes longer than 30 minutes, during the final 15 minutes of cooking, if you use a glaze or barbecue sauce too early in the cooking process, particularly one that contains sugar, your meat may burn and adhere to the grill.

4-Week Diet Plan

Week 1

Day 1:
Lunch: Grilled Cheese Garlic Potatoes
Snack: Smoked Beer Cream Cheese Dip
Dinner: Smoked Citrus Seafood Ceviche
Dessert: Grilled Cinnamon Peaches

Day 2:
Lunch: Smoked Cheese Potatoes
Snack: Simple Grilled Sweet Potato
Dinner: Juicy Teriyaki Salmon
Dessert: Tasty Pimento Cheese Cornbread

Day 3:
Lunch: Smoked Devilled Eggs
Snack: Thai-Style Chicken Wings with Peanuts
Dinner: BBQ Garlic Chicken Breasts
Dessert: Smoked Bourbon Pumpkin Pie

Day 4:
Lunch: Roasted Crispy Lemony Potatoes
Snack: Sweet & Spicy Cashews
Dinner: White Wine-Braised Shrimp Scampi
Dessert: Blueberry Cheesecake Skillet Brownie

Day 5:
Lunch: Smoked Macaroni Carrot Salad
Snack: Thai-Style Chicken Wings with Peanuts
Dinner: Sweet & Spicy Chicken Drumsticks
Dessert: Grilled Honey Apricot with Gelato

Day 6:
Lunch: Spiced Pumpkin Soup
Snack: Sweet & Spicy Cashews
Dinner: BBQ Chicken Wings
Dessert: Classic Red Velvet Cake

Day 7:
Lunch: Delicious Smoked Ratatouille
Snack: Smoked Beer Cream Cheese Dip
Dinner: Smoked Whole Turkey
Dessert: Homemade Strawberry Rhubarb Pie

Week 2

Day 1:
Lunch: Smoked Asparagus
Snack: Simple Grilled Sweet Potato
Dinner: Grilled Lamb & Apricots Kabobs
Dessert: Maple Bacon Donuts

Day 2:
Lunch: Baked Cinnamon Sweet Potatoes
Snack: Smoked Cheese Chicken Stuffed Jalapeño Poppers
Dinner: Grilled Lemony Lamb Skirt Steak
Dessert: Smoked S'mores Marshmallow Cake Bars

Day 3:
Lunch: Smoked Cheese Stuffed mushrooms
Snack: Seared Lemon Buttered Scallops
Dinner: Herbed Leg of Lamb Roast
Dessert: Smoked S'mores Marshmallow Cake Bars

Day 4:
Lunch: Grilled Cheese Stuffed Zucchini
Snack: Simple Grilled Sweet Potato
Dinner: BBQ Cheese Chicken Stuffed Bell Peppers
Dessert: Baked Molten Chocolate Butter Cake

Day 5:
Lunch: Herbed Mashed Potatoes with Cream
Snack: Artichoke Parmesan Stuffed Mushrooms
Dinner: Smoked Garlicky Leg of Lamb
Dessert: Caramel Bourbon Bacon Browni

Day 6:
Lunch: Baked Supreme Cheese Pepperoni Pizza
Snack: Roasted Sweet Cinnamon Almonds
Dinner: Grilled Lamb with Ginger-Sugar Glaze
Dessert: Baked Molten Chocolate Butter Cake

Day 7:
Lunch: Crispy Asparagus Fries with Balsamic Mayo Sauce
Snack: Baked Bacon Wrapped Cheese Jalapeno Poppers
Dinner: Garlicky Lamb Skewers
Dessert: Grilled Honey Apricot with Gelato

Week 3

Day 1:
Lunch: Grilled Asparagus with Honey-Glazed Carrots
Snack: Loaded Cheese Chicken Nachos
Dinner: Smoked Mustard Rack of Lamb
Dessert: Tasty Pimento Cheese Cornbread

Day 2:
Lunch: Roasted Cinnamon Root Vegetables
Snack: Smoked Beer Cream Cheese Dip
Dinner: Citrus Grilled Lamb Chops
Dessert: Blueberry Cheesecake Skillet Brownie

Day 3:
Lunch: Roasted Cauliflower with Garlic Parmesan Butter
Snack: Sweet & Spicy Cashews
Dinner: Maple BBQ Pork Tenderloin
Dessert: Grilled Cinnamon Peaches

Day 4:
Lunch: Tasty Smoked Cheddar Cheese
Snack: Crispy Sweet Potatoes with Lime-Mayo Sauce
Dinner: Smoked Garlicky Porchetta
Dessert: Blueberry Cheesecake Skillet Brownie

Day 5:
Lunch: Grilled Garlicky Broccoli
Snack: Pit Boss Chex Party Snack Mix
Dinner: Smoked Sweet Bacon
Dessert: Smoked Bourbon Pumpkin Pie

Day 6:
Lunch: Cheese Bacon Loaded Portobello Mushrooms
Snack: Thai-Style Chicken Wings with Peanuts
Dinner: Smoked BBQ Pork Ribs
Dessert: Baked Coconut Chocolate Cookies

Day 7:
Lunch: Buttered Corn on the Cob
Snack: Spicy Lemony Cashew
Dinner: Grilled Sweet Pork Ribs
Dessert: Homemade Strawberry Rhubarb Pie

Week 4

Day 1:
Lunch: Vegan Bacon & Green Beans
Snack: Roasted Potatoes with Bacon
Dinner: Smoked Mustard Pork Loin
Dessert: Honey Cornbread Cake

Day 2:
Lunch: Braised Garlicky Collard Greens
Snack: Grilled Rosemary Olives
Dinner: Pulled Pork & Egg Breakfast Burritos
Dessert: Maple Bacon Donuts

Day 3:
Lunch: BBQ Quinoa Stuffed Bell Peppers
Snack: Smoked Cheese Popcorn
Dinner: BBQ Pulled Pork Sandwich
Dessert: Grilled Peaches with Cream Cheese

Day 4:
Lunch: Grilled Sweet Potato & Marshmallows Casserole
Snack: Buffalo Ranch Spicy Chicken Wings
Dinner: Honey Smoked Ham
Dessert: Honey Cornbread Cake

Day 5:
Lunch: Gluten Free Celery & Carrot Stuffing
Snack: Buffalo Sriracha Chicken Wings
Dinner: Smoked Beef Burgers
Dessert: Grilled Peaches with Cream Cheese

Day 6:
Lunch: Parmesan Cheese Crusted Smashed Potatoes
Snack: Smoked Honey Chicken Kabobs
Dinner: Bacon Wrapped Beef Tenderloin
Dessert: Smoked Bourbon Pumpkin Pie

Day 7:
Lunch: Braised Garlicky Collard Greens
Snack: Crispy Kale Chips
Dinner: Pumpkin Spice Grilled Pork Ribs
Dessert: Baked Coconut Chocolate Cookies

Chapter 1 Beef Recipes

Beef Chuck Roast Sandwiches

Prep Time:10 minutes | Cook Time: 9 hours | Servings: 4

Ingredients:

4 hoagie rolls, sliced lengthwise
3 cups beef stock, divided
1 yellow onion

Lone Star Brisket Rub, to taste
2 lbs. chuck roast

Preparation:

1. In a glass baking dish, place the chuck roast. Cover with plastic wrap and chill overnight after seasoning with Lone Star Brisket Rub. 2. Remove the chuck roast from the refrigerator the next day. Set your temperature to SMOKE mode and fire up your Pit Boss with the lid open. 3. Preheat the Pit Boss Wood Pellet Grill to 225°F once the fire is ignited. If you're going to use a gas or charcoal grill, make sure it's set to Low, indirect heat. 4. Arrange the chuck roast on the Grill Grate, cover, and smoke for 3 hours, spraying every hour with 1 cup beef stock. 5. Arrange the onions in a cast iron skillet and slice them, then pour the remaining cup of stock over them and place the roast on top. 6. Cook for an additional 2½ - 3 hours, or until the internal temperature reaches 165°F, at 275°F. 7. Cover with aluminum foil and cook for another 2½ to 3 hours. 8. Using tongs, remove the chuck roast from the Pit Boss Wood Pellet Grill. Allow 10 minutes for the roast to rest before removing it from the skillet and shredding it. 9. With braised onions, serve pulled roast beef in a hoagie roll.

Serving Suggestions: Serve with the dip of your choice.

Variation Tip: When selecting ground chuck, look for a cut that is dry to the touch and smells well.

Nutritional Information per Serving: Calories: 733 | Fat: 22.3g | Sat Fat: 8.1g | Carbohydrates: 46.7g | Fiber: 7.6g | Sugar: 5.1g | Protein: 87.3g

Cheesesteak Sandwiches

Prep Time:10 minutes | Cook Time: 10 minutes | Servings: 4

Ingredients:

2 tbsps. butter, divided
2 tbsps. olive oil
8 slices provolone cheese, sliced
1 yellow onion, sliced

4 hoagie rolls, sliced lengthwise
2 tbsps. Pit Boss chop house steak rub
2 lbs. rib-eye steaks, thinly sliced

Preparation:

1. Preheat the Pit Boss Wood Pellet Grill to 375°F once the fire is ignited. If you're going to use a gas or charcoal grill, make sure it's set to MEDIUM heat, indirect heat. 2. Melt 1 tablespoon each of olive oil and butter on a griddle. With a serrated knife, slice rolls ¾ of the way through, then place upside down on griddle and toast until golden. Keep aside. 3. On the griddle, melt the remaining tablespoon of butter and olive oil. Cook for 2 minutes, or until faintly caramelized, after adding the sliced onions. To keep warm, move to the griddle's lower-right corner. 4. Season steak with Pit Boss Chop House Steak Rub generously, then cook for 3 minutes on griddle, flipping to brown all sides. Add the caramelized onions to the mix. 5. On the griddle, divide the steak and onions into four sections, then top each with two slices of provolone cheese. 6. Allow cheese to melt slightly before using a bench scraper or metal spatula to transfer on a toasted hoagie roll. Serve immediately and enjoy!

Serving Suggestions: Serve with your favorite dip.

Variation Tip: Wrap the steak in plastic wrap and freeze for about 20 minutes, or until firm but not frozen. This will make cutting with a sharp knife much easier.

Nutritional Information per Serving: Calories: 538 | Fat: 30.7g | Sat Fat: 15.3g | Carbohydrates: 47.8g | Fiber: 7.6g | Sugar: 5.5g | Protein: 24.7g

Smoked Rib Meat Chili

Prep Time:15 minutes | Cook Time: 30 minutes | Servings: 4

Ingredients:

1 tbsp. chili powder
1 can beer
1 can black beans, rinsed and drained
½ tbsp. cumin
1 tbsp. olive oil
1 can kidney beans, drained and rinsed

1 can tomato sauce
2 cups leftover rib meat, pulled from the bone
½ white onion, diced
1 can corn kernels, drained
2 tbsps. Louisiana grills pulled pork rub

Preparation:

1. Switch your Pit Boss to SMOKE mode. Set your Pit Boss Wood Pellet Grill to 250°F once it's hot. In a skillet with 1 tablespoon of beer, sauté your diced onions until they develop a mellow yellow color. 2. Combine the sautéed onions and the remaining ingredients, including the leftover beef rib meat, in a disposable aluminum pan. 3. Mingle all of the ingredients in a large mixing bowl and cover securely with aluminum foil. 4. Close the top and place on the Pit Boss Wood Pellet Grill. Allow for 2 to 3 hours of smoking time, or until the chili is bubbling and tender.

Serving Suggestions: Serve over the bed of rice.

Variation Tip: The richer the flavor, the lower the temperature and the longer it takes to cook your chili.

Nutritional Information per Serving: Calories: 449 | Fat: 5.6g | Sat Fat: 0.9g | Carbohydrates: 74.6g | Fiber: 17.3g | Sugar: 6.6g | Protein: 23.7g

Grilled Tri Tip Roast with Cajun Butter

Prep Time: 2 hours | Cook Time: 20 minutes | Servings: 2

Ingredients:

1 stick butter, unsalted and softened
4 tbsps. beef and brisket rub
1 garlic clove, minced
⅓ cup soy sauce
⅓ cup brown sugar
2 tbsps. olive oil

4 pounds trimmed tri tip roast
Juice from 1 orange
2 tbsps. Worcestershire sauce
½ tsp. cayenne pepper
1 tbsp. paprika, powder

Preparation:

1. In a resealable plastic bag, merge the orange juice, brown sugar, Worcestershire sauce, soy sauce, and minced garlic. Place the tri tip in the bag, seal it, and massage the meat to help the marinade coat it evenly. Allow the tri tip to marinade in the bag for 2 hours in the refrigerator. 2. Remove the bag from the fridge and drain the marinade. Using paper towels, blot the steak dry after removing it from the bag. 3. Combine the softened butter, 2 tablespoons Beef & Brisket Seasoning, cayenne, and paprika in a small mixing basin. Mix in the butter until it is completely smooth. Keep aside. 4. Splash the olive oil over the tri tip and generously season with the leftover Beef and Brisket Seasoning. 5. Preheat your Pit Boss Wood Pellet Grill to 450°F. Set the Pit Boss Wood Pellet Grill to HIGH heat if you're using a gas or charcoal grill. Place the steak on the Pit Boss Wood Pellet Grill with a temperature probe inserted into the thickest part of the meat. Sear the tri tip for 3 to 5 minutes on one side, turning over and sear for another 3 to 5 minutes on the other. 6. Lessen the heat to 250°F and carry on grilling the tri tip for another 15 minutes.

Serving Suggestions: Serve with the mashed potatoes.
Variation Tip: Fill your hopper with Mesquite Hardwood Pellets for even more spiciness.
Nutritional Information per Serving: Calories: 568 | Fat: 46.5g | Sat Fat: 29.1g | Carbohydrates: 37.1g | Fiber: 1.9g |Sugar: 31.2g | Protein: 4.1g

Lime Chuck Roast Chili

Prep Time: 15 minutes | Cook Time: 2 hours 30 minutes | Servings: 4

Ingredients:

⅓ cup chili powder
1 cup beef stock
2½ lbs. chuck roast, cut in 2-inch cubes
2 tbsps. green chili peppers, diced
1½ tsps. kosher salt
1 tbsp. olive oil
½ tsp. chipotle powder
1 tbsp. cumin, ground
1 jalapeño, minced

1½ tsp. oregano, dried
15 oz. crushed tomatoes
Jalapeño, to taste
Sour cream, to taste
½ tsp. black pepper
Cilantro, to taste
3 garlic cloves, minced
1 lime, zest & juice
1 red onion, diced

Preparation:

1. Preheat your Pit Boss Wood Pellet Grill to 400°F by turning it on SMOKE mode and letting it run with the lid open for 10 minutes. Set the Pit Boss Wood Pellet Grill to MEDIUM-HIGH heat if using a gas or charcoal grill. Allow a deep cast iron skillet or Dutch oven to warm on the Pit Boss Wood Pellet Grill. 2. Season cubed chuck roast with salt and pepper in a shallow pan. 3. Heat the olive oil in a huge pan and brown the steak on all sides. Remove the seared steak from the pan and set it aside. 4. Add the garlic, onions, and jalapeño to the pot and stir to combine. Season with salt and pepper after stirring. After 3 minutes, press all of the onions to the sides of the saucepan, leaving a hole in the middle. Combine the chili powder, cumin, oregano, and green chilies in a mixing bowl. Cook for 1 minute and drag the onions back in. Bring the beef stock to a boil, then reduce to a low heat. 5. Stir the seared beef back into the Dutch oven to coat it. Place a single layer of smashed tomatoes on top of the beef. Reduce the Pit Boss Wood Pellet Grill temperature to 300°F and cover the pot. Cook for about 2½ hours, while waiting for the beef to be finely tendered. 6. Remove the pan from the heat and add the lime zest and juice to mix.

Serving Suggestions: Serve hot with your favorite chili toppings.
Variation Tip: To balance out the chili's fiery and smoky flavors, serve it over cornbread.
Nutritional Information per Serving: Calories: 2753 | Fat: 106.4g | Sat Fat: 37g | Carbohydrates: 27g | Fiber: 10.4g | Sugar: 8.9g | Protein: 399.4g

Smoked Beef Brisket

Prep Time: 10 minutes | Cook Time: 8 hours | Servings: 12

Ingredients:

Pit Boss Chop House Steak Rub, as needed   1 (10-12 lb.) whole beef brisket

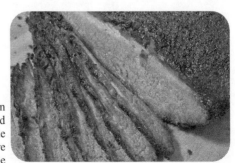

Preparation:

1. Set your Pit Boss Wood Pellet Grill to SMOKE mode, wait for the fire to catch, and then lower the temperature to 250°F. 2. Trim unwanted fat from the brisket while the Pit Boss Wood Pellet Grill is heating up and season with Chop House Steak Rub. 3. Place your brisket fat side up on the Pit Boss Wood Pellet Grill grates and cook for 8 hours until the internal temperature acquires 190°F. 4. If the meat is not probe tender, continue cooking until the temperature probe slides into the meat readily with little to no resistance. 5. Remove from the Pit Boss Wood Pellet Grill and set aside for 30 minutes to rest. 6. Enjoy by slicing against the grain.

Serving Suggestions: Serve topped with mint leaves and apple chunks.
Variation Tip: Choose a brisket that is either choice or prime for the highest quality meat.
Nutritional Information per Serving: Calories: 1456 | Fat: 119.3g | Sat Fat: 46.8g | Carbohydrates: 0.2g | Fiber: 0g | Sugar: 0g | Protein: 88.8g

Garlicky Bacon Wrapped Steaks
Prep Time:10 minutes | Cook Time: 15 minutes | Servings: 4

Ingredients:

3½ tsps. chives, chopped
½ tsp. black pepper
¼ cup olive oil
3 tbsps. butter, unsalted and melted

Kosher salt, to taste
4 (6-7 ounce) 1-inch thick steak, beef
12 large peeled garlic, cloves
½ tsp. dried thyme, fresh sprigs

Preparation:

1. Preheat your Pit Boss Wood Pellet Grill and set the temperature to HIGH. Check that the Flame Broiler Plate is not closed. 2. In a bowl, merge the olive oil, melted butter, chives, garlic, kosher salt, pepper, and thyme while your Pit Boss Wood Pellet Grill is heating up. 3. Wrap the bacon over the sides of steaks and secure it with a toothpick. 4. Using a basting brush, baste the top and bottom of the steaks with the mixture. 5. Cook the steak for 5 minutes on each side on a hot Pit Boss Wood Pellet Grill. 6. When the internal temperature reaches the appropriate level of doneness, remove the steaks. Rare: 120°F; Medium Rare: 130°F; Medium: 140°F; Well Done: 160°F. 7. Keep the steaks aside for 5 minutes after taking them from the pan.
Serving Suggestions: Serve with the stir fried vegetables.
Variation Tip: Marinate the steaks in marsala wine for up to 24 hours, covered in the refrigerator, for juicier results.
Nutritional Information per Serving: Calories: 533 | Fat: 31.9g | Sat Fat: 11.3g | Carbohydrates: 0.4g | Fiber: 0.2g | Sugar: 0.1g | Protein: 51.9g

Caramelized Onion & Cheese Stuffed Beef Burgers
Prep Time:10 minutes | Cook Time: 1 hour | Servings: 4

Ingredients:

½ lb. cheddar jack, cubed
8 bacon slices
1 jalapeno pepper, minced

10 oz. barbecue rub
1 white onion, caramelized
2½ lbs. ground beef

Preparation:

1. Preheat your Pit Boss Wood Pellet Grill to 300°F. Set the Pit Boss Wood Pellet Grill to MEDIUM-LOW heat if using a gas or charcoal grill. 2. In a bowl, season ground beef with barbecue rub and combine by hand. Form four 10-ounce balls, then press a can (any 12-ounce aluminum can would suffice) through the center of each ball to make a little beef bowl. To make a beef bowl, press along the sides and roll to make a 3½ inch tall meat bowl. 3. Wrap two pieces of bacon around the beef, then stuff with cheese, caramelized onion, and minced jalapeño. 4. Fill a big cast iron pan halfway with burgers, then put to the Pit Boss Wood Pellet Grill. Cook the patties in the skillet for 25 minutes before transferring them to the top shelf of the grill. 5. Raise the temperature to 325°F and continue cooking for another 25 to 30 minutes, rotating halfway through. 6. Remove from the grill, top with the remaining jalapeño, and let aside for 5 minutes before serving warm.
Serving Suggestions: Top with extra jalapeños before serving.
Variation Tip: Start the burgers on SMOKE mode for 60 minutes, then increase the temperature to 300°F to finish them.
Nutritional Information per Serving: Calories: 2965 | Fat: 109g | Sat Fat: 44.6g | Carbohydrates: 8.4g | Fiber: 0.7g | Sugar: 1.3g | Protein: 389.3g

Smoked BBQ Beef Ribs
Prep Time:15 minutes | Cook Time: 15 minutes | Servings: 4

Ingredients:

½ cup Kansas City maple & molasses BBQ sauce
3 lbs. beef ribs, bone-in

½ cup Chicago BBQ rub
¼ cup olive oil

Preparation:

1. Preheat your Pit Boss Wood Pellet Grill to 250°F by setting it to SMOKE and letting it run with the lid open for 10 minutes. Preheat the Pit Boss Wood Pellet Grill to MEDIUM-LOW heat if using a gas or charcoal grill. 2. Remove the membrane from the ribs' undersides. Using a butter knife, slit the membrane open. Pull and remove the entire membrane with a paper towel once enough has been pulled up. 3. Splash olive oil over the racks of ribs. This will serve as the dish's binder. 4. Generously season both racks with Chicago BBQ Rub. Ensure that you get all of the sides, as well as the top and bottom. 5. Allow 20-30 minutes for the meat to soak up the seasoning before cooking. 6. On the smoker, place the racks of ribs, meat side up, over indirect heat. 7. Cook until the ribs are fork tender. Alternatively, until the temperature hits 205°F. 8. Before removing the ribs from the Pit Boss Wood Pellet Grill, lightly baste them with Kansas City BBQ sauce. 9. Allow 30 minutes for the meat to rest before serving.
Serving Suggestions: Serve with yogurt dip.
Variation Tip: Brown the meat well to get a head start on the flavor development.
Nutritional Information per Serving: Calories: 787 | Fat: 33.9g | Sat Fat: 9.8g | Carbohydrates: 11.3g | Fiber: 0.2g | Sugar: 8.1g | Protein: 103.2g

Cheese Spinach Stuffed Steak Rolls

Prep Time:20 minutes | Cook Time: 10 minutes | Servings: 4

Ingredients:

1¼ lbs. flank steak
4 (oz.) cream cheese, softened
Pit Boss chop house steak rub
1 tbsp. sun dried tomatoes, minced
2 tbsps. olive oil

1 cup spinach, chopped
¼ cup sour cream
¼ tsp. fennel, ground
6 slices provolone cheese, sliced

Preparation:

1. Preheat the Pit Boss Griddle to HIGH. 2. Place the flank steak on a chopping board and cut horizontally across it to open it up without cutting through it completely. If necessary, pound the meat to an equal thickness with a meat mallet. 3. Evenly season both sides of the meat with Pit Boss Chop House Steak Rub. Remove from the equation. 4. In a bowl, blend sour cream, cream cheese, sun dried tomatoes, and fennel with a hand mixer. 5. Layer the cream cheese mixture on the steak, then top with spinach and provolone cheese. Roll the steak and tie it every 2 inches using kitchen twine. To divide the steak into individual parts, slice it between the ties. 6. Carefully pour oil onto the griddle top and heat. Add the steak rolls and cook for 5 minutes on each side. 7. Remove the steaks from the Pit Boss Wood Pellet Grill and set aside for 5 minutes to rest. Warm the dish before serving.

Serving Suggestions: Serve with your favorite sauce.

Variation Tip: If you want to cook on a pellet grill, preheat it to 400°F, open the sear slide, and sear the steaks for about 5 minutes per side.

Nutritional Information per Serving: Calories: 621 | Fat: 43.1g | Sat Fat: 21.2g | Carbohydrates: 3.4g | Fiber: 0.3g | Sugar: 0.4g | Protein: 53.1g

Beef Chili Mac and Cheese

Prep Time:10 minutes | Cook Time: 25 minutes | Servings: 6

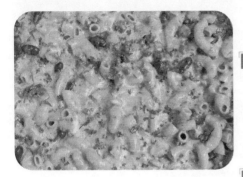

Ingredients:

2 tbsps. fresh parsley leaves, chopped
4 cups beef stock
1½ tsps. cumin
Salt and black pepper, to taste
¾ cup cheddar cheese, shredded
2 garlic cloves, minced
¾ cup kidney beans, drained and rinsed

1 tbsp. Pit Boss Sweet Heat Rub
8 oz. ground beef
1 onion, diced
2 tsps. chili powder
10 (oz.) elbow macaroni
1 tbsp. olive oil
1 (14.5-ounce) tomatoes, canned and diced

Preparation:

1. Preheat your Pit Boss Wood Pellet Grill to SMOKE mode for 5 minutes with the lid open until a fire forms. Preheat it to 350°F. Set the Pit Boss Wood Pellet Grill to MEDIUM heat if you are using a charcoal or gas grill. 2. In a cast iron pan over MEDIUM-HIGH heat, heat the olive oil. Cook until the onion, garlic, and ground beef are browned, about 5 minutes. With a large wooden fork, break up the beef while it cooks. 3. Combine beef broth, tomatoes, beans, Sweet Heat Rub, chili powder, elbow macaroni and cumin in a large mixing bowl. Season to taste with salt and pepper. Simmer on low heat before adding the pasta. 4. Cover the saucepan and place it on the prepared Pit Boss Wood Pellet Grill. Cook for 20 minutes, until the pasta is al dente. Eliminate from the heat and sprinkle with shredded cheese, then cover for 2 minutes to enable the cheese to melt.

Serving Suggestions: Serve garnished with fresh parsley.

Variation Tip: You can mix in the crispy grilled bacon.

Nutritional Information per Serving: Calories: 443 | Fat: 11.4g | Sat Fat: 4.6g | Carbohydrates: 55.8g | Fiber: 6.8g | Sugar: 4.5g | Protein: 29.5g

Grilled Flank Steak & Bell Pepper Fajitas

Prep Time:1 hour | Cook Time: 30 minutes | Servings: 1

Ingredients:

1 onion, diced
1 green bell pepper, sliced
1 red bell pepper, sliced
3 tbsps. olive oil

1 (16-oz) steak, flank
8 corn tortillas
Pit Boss Sweet Heat Rub
1 yellow bell pepper, sliced

Preparation:

1. Brush flank steak with Pit Boss Sweet Heat Rub and 1 tablespoon olive oil. Let it refrigerate for 1 hour after covering and marinating. 2. Splash a little olive oil over the peppers and onion. 3. Preheat your Pit Boss to 400°F. Grill the onions and peppers for 5 minutes on each side. Keep an eye on the peppers and onion to make sure they don't burn. 4. Remove the peppers and onion from the Pit Boss Wood Pellet Grill and toss briefly in a medium mixing dish with the remaining olive oil. Slice the peppers and onions into strips on a cutting board. Set aside. 5. Place the flank steak on the Pit Boss Wood Pellet Grill directly. Cook until the meat is medium rare (165°F internal temperature). 7. Transfer the flank steak to a chopping board after removing it from the Pit Boss Wood Pellet Grill. Keep the meat aside for 5 minutes before slicing it into strips against the grain.

Serving Suggestions: Serve immediately with warm tortillas, guacamole, salsa, sour cream, shredded cheese, iceberg lettuce, or your favorite fajita toppings.

Variation Tip: Marinate the flank steak for at least 24 hours in the refrigerator to make it more tender.

Nutritional Information per Serving: Calories: 1837 | Fat: 71.2g | Sat Fat: 14.8g | Carbohydrates: 122.3g | Fiber: 19.8g | Sugar: 15.2g | Protein: 180.1g

Butter Seared Ribeye Steak
Prep Time:1 hour | Cook Time: 20 minutes | Servings: 2

Ingredients:

1 tsp. olive oil
4 tbsps. butter, room temperature
1 tsp. parsley, chopped

1 ribeye steak, 1 to 1.5 inch thick
Pit Boss Chophouse Steak Rub, to taste

Preparation:

1. Season the steak with Pit Boss Chophouse Rub and chill for an hour. 2. In a small bowl, mash butter and 1 teaspoon Pit Boss Chophouse Rub with a fork. Put the butter on a sheet of parchment paper, roll it up. Then place it in the refrigerator for 1 hour. 3. Eliminate the steak from the refrigerator and lay it on the Pit Boss Wood Pellet Grill in a covered cast iron skillet. 4. Set your Pit Boss Wood Pellet Grill to SMOKE mode and let it running for 10 minutes with the lid open. 5. Preheat your Pit Boss Wood Pellet Grill to 400°F and allow it to warm up. Set the Pit Boss Wood Pellet Grill to MEDIUM-HIGH heat if using a gas or charcoal grill. 6. Take the skillet's cover off. Slide the sear slide open. Char the steak for 2 minutes per side after adding the oil. 7. Baste the steak with 3 tablespoons butter, 12 to 1 tablespoon at a time, tilting the pan and using a spoon. 8. Continue to sear for another 3 to 5 minutes, adding and basting with butter. 9. Remove the steak from the skillet and set aside to rest for 5 minutes before serving warm with more compound butter and fresh herbs.

Serving Suggestions: Serve alongside the mashed potatoes.

Variation Tip: Cook the steak on SMOKE mode for 45 minutes before beginning this dish for even additional smokiness. Depending on your preferred temperature of doneness, you may need to reduce the cook time on the sear.

Nutritional Information per Serving: Calories: 314 | Fat: 31.6g | Sat Fat: 14.9g | Carbohydrates: 0.7g | Fiber: 0.1g | Sugar: 0.1g | Protein: 8.1g

Smoked Apple Beef Short Ribs
Prep Time:15 minutes | Cook Time: 6 hours | Servings: 4

Ingredients:

1 cup apple juice
1 cup apple cider vinegar
4 tbsps. olive oil

2½ pounds (or 6 large) beef short ribs
4 tbsps. Pit Boss Beef & Brisket Rub

Preparation:

1. Preheat your Pit Boss Wood Pellet Grill to 225°F. 2. Combine the apple cider vinegar and apple juice in a food-safe spray bottle. Remove from the equation. 3. Remove the thick membrane from the bone side of the beef short ribs and discard. Scrub the short ribs generously with olive oil and Beef & Brisket Rub. 4. Arrange the beef ribs in the center of the oven. Smoke the short ribs for about 2 hours, or until they've grown a crust and are a rich lacquered brown. 5. Remove the beef short ribs from the smoker after 2 hours, place in a heat-proof baking dish, and pour in the apple cider vinegar and apple juice. 6. Cover securely with foil and continue to SMOKE for another 1½-2 hours, or until the ribs are fall-apart tender and the internal temperature reaches 200°F. 7. Remove the meat from the smoker and serve right away.

Serving Suggestions: Serve with the topping of whipped cream and caramel sauce.

Variation Tip: Try dry brining the ribs with the Beef and Brisket Rub for 30 minutes before starting this recipe for even more tender ribs.

Nutritional Information per Serving: Calories: 2602 | Fat: 121.4g | Sat Fat: 42.9g | Carbohydrates: 7.6g | Fiber: 0.1g | Sugar: 6.2g | Protein: 343.9g

Cocoa Chili Crusted Grilled Flank Steak
Prep Time: 15 minutes | Cook Time: 10 minutes | Serves: 6

Ingredients:

1 tablespoon cocoa powder
2 tablespoons chili powder
1 tablespoon chipotle chile powder
½ tablespoon garlic powder
½ tablespoon onion powder
1½ tablespoons brown sugar

1 tablespoon kosher salt
½ tablespoon black pepper
1 tablespoon cumin
1 tablespoon smoked paprika
3 pounds flank steak
2 tablespoons oil

Preparation:

1. In a bowl mix cocoa powder, chili powder, brown sugar, chipotle chile powder, onion powder, garlic powder, salt, black pepper, cumin, and smoked paprika. 2. Brush the steak with oil then rub it with the cocoa mixture. 3. Preheat your Pit Boss Wood Pellet Grill to 500 degrees F. 4. Cook the steak for about five minutes per side. Let the steak rest for about 10 minutes before slicing. 5. Serve and enjoy.

Serving suggestion: Serve this Frank steak in tacos.

Variation Tip: Reduce the chili and cumin if you don't want it too spicy.

Nutrition-Per Serving: Calories 335 | Fat 12g |Sodium 1319mg | Carbs 7g | Fiber 2g | Sugar 3g | Protein 50g

Grilled Butter–Mustard Basted Porterhouse Steak

Prep Time: 5 minutes | Cook Time: 40 minutes | Serves: 2

Ingredients:

4 tablespoons melted butter
2 tablespoons Worcestershire sauce
2 tablespoons Dijon mustard
20-ounce porterhouse steaks cut into 1-inch

thick pieces
1 tablespoon prime rib rub
1 rosemary sprig

Preparation:

1. Preheat your Pit Boss Wood Pellet Grill to 225 degrees F. 2. In a bowl whisk the butter, Worcestershire sauce, and mustard. 3. Brush the steak with the seasoning mixture then coat with the prime rib rub. Layer the steak on the grill and cook for 30 minutes. 4. Remove the steak from the grill and raise the grill temperature to 500 degrees F. 5. Place the steak on the grill. Grill for 3 minutes on each side. Let the steak rest for 3 minutes before slicing. 6. Garnish the steak with rosemary and serve.

Serving suggestion: Serve the butter-basted porterhouse steak with some green salad.
Variation Tip: Add a splash of Guinness for a coffee hint.
Nutrition-Per Serving: Calories 869 | Fat 67g | Sodium 702mg | Carbs 4g | Fiber 0.5g | Sugar 3.1g | Protein 60g

Smoked Coffee Cowboy Tri–Tip

Prep Time: 15 minutes | Cook Time: 4 hours | Serves: 6

Ingredients:

3 pounds tri-tip
⅛ cup coffee, grounded

¼ cup beef rub

Preparation:

1. Preheat your Pit Boss Wood Pellet Grill to 180 degrees F with the lid closed for 15 minutes. 2. Rub the meat with coffee and beef rub until well coated. 3. Place the meat on the grill grates and smoke for 3 hours. 4. Remove the meat and increase the heat to 300 degrees F. 5. Double wrap the meat and place it on the grill. Let cook for 45 minutes or until the internal temperature reaches 130 degrees F. 6. Let the meat rest before slicing and serving.

Serving suggestion: Serve the cowboy tri-tip with sautéed veggies.
Variation Tip: Use dried herbs and spice of choice in place of beef rub.
Nutrition-Per Serving: Calories 421 | Fat 22g | Sodium 1640mg | Carbs 1g | Fiber 0g | Sugar 1g | Protein 50g

Teriyaki Skirt Steak

Prep Time: 15 minutes | Cook Time: 4 hours | Serves: 8

Ingredients:

3 cups soy sauce
2 cups brown sugar
3 garlic cloves

inch ginger, diced finely
1 tablespoon sesame oil
4 pounds skirt steak

Preparation:

1. Add all ingredients to a blender except for the steak. Blend until smooth. 2. Trim any excess fat from the steak and slice into ¼ inch slices. Add the marinade and the steak in a ziplock bag, mix well and place in the fridge overnight. 3. Preheat your Pit Boss Wood Pellet Grill to 160 degrees F for 5 minutes. Arrange the steak on the grill grate without overlapping. 4. Cook for 5 minutes. Remove from the grill and let it cool before serving. Enjoy.

Serving suggestion: Serve beef jerky with sunflower seeds and teriyaki sauce.
Variation Tip: Use ginger and low sodium soy sauce.
Nutrition-Per Serving: Calories 670 | Fat 25g | Sodium 5573mg | Carbs 43g | Fiber 0.8g | Sugar 37g | Protein 70g

Tasty Smoked Ribeye Steak

Prep Time: 15 minutes | Cook Time: 35 minutes | Serves: 1

Ingredients:

½ pounds ribeye steak

Steak rubs of choice

Preparation:

1. Preheat your Pit Boss Wood Pellet Grill to 180 degrees F for 30 minutes. 2. Sprinkle the steak with rub and smoke it in the grill for 25 minutes. 3. Remove the steak from the grill and increase the temperature to 400 degrees F. 4. Sear each side of the steak for 5 minutes or until the internal temperature reaches 125 degrees F. 5. Wrap the steak with aluminium foil and let sit for 10 minutes. Slice and serve.

Serving suggestion: Serve the ribeye steak alongside grilled carrots.
Variation Tip: Use dried herbs and spices of choice.
Nutrition-Per Serving: Calories 756 | Fat 37g | Sodium 1496mg | Carbs 65g | Fiber 3g | Sugar 4g | Protein 36g

Beer-Braised Pulled Beef

Prep Time: 15minutes | Cook Time: 5 hours | Serves: 6

Ingredients:

3 pounds beef sirloin tip roast
½ cup BBQ dry rub
2 cans of amber beer

1 bottle barbecue sauce
6 buns

Preparation:

1. Trim excess fat from the beef roast and coat it with the BBQ dry rub. 2. Preheat your Pit Boss wood pellet grill to 180 degrees F. 3. Place the beef roast on the grill and smoke for 3 hours turning it after every 1 hour. 4. Place the beef in a braising pan and add the beer. Braise the beef on the grill for 4 hours. 5. Remove the beef from the pan and shred it with a fork. Return the shredded beef into the pan and stir in the barbecue sauce. 6. Serve and enjoy.

Serving suggestion: Serve the pulled beef with pasta.
Variation Tip: Use dried herbs and prime meat.
Nutrition-Per Serving: Calories 829 | Fat 46g |Sodium 181mg | Carbs 4g | Fiber 0g | Sugar 0g | Protein 86g

Grilled Flank Steak

Prep Time: 10 minutes | Cook Time: 20 minutes | Serves: 6

Ingredients:

1 tablespoon salt
½ tablespoons onion powder
¼ tablespoons garlic powder

½ tablespoons coarsely ground black pepper
3 pounds flank steak
Basil for garnishing

Preparation:

1. In a bowl, mix salt, onion powder, garlic powder, and black pepper. 2. Rub the steak with the seasoning mixture. 3. Preheat your Pit Boss Wood Pellet Grill to 225 degrees F. 4. Place the steak on the grill and cook for about 4 hours until the steak is 125 degrees F. 5. Remove the steak from the grill and turn the grill temperature to 500 degrees F. 6. Place the steak on the grill and grill for 3 minutes on each side. 7. Serve and enjoy.

Serving suggestion: Serve the flank steak with a pat of butter.
Variation Tip: Use fresh onion and crushed/ minced garlic.
Nutrition-Per Serving: Calories 112 | Fat 5g |Sodium 737mg | Carbs 1g | Fiber 0g | Sugar 0g | Protein 16g

Smoked Brisket Cheese Nachos

Prep Time: 15 minutes | Cook Time: 30 minutes | Serves: 2

Ingredients:

2 shallots, diced
2 tbsp bacon grease
4 cups leftover brisket, chopped
1 bottle (12 oz.) dark beer
¼ cup coffee
5 oz. can tomato sauce
3 tbsps adobo sauce
¾ cup pinto beans
Tomatillo and Tomato Salsa
3 tomatillos, chopped
1 large tomato, chopped
3 jalapeno peppers, sliced
Remaining Nachos Ingredients
½ cup cheddar cheese, shredded
½ cup smoked provolone cheese, shredded

¾ cup black beans
1 tbsp chili powder
1 tbsp cumin
1 tsp cayenne pepper
½ tsp smoked paprika
¼ tsp cinnamon
½ tsp Kosher salt

½ cup green onions, chopped
Juice from ½ lime

½ lb bacon fried and chopped
BBQ pork rinds

Preparation:

1. Heat bacon fat in a cast-iron skillet and add shallots. Cook until the shallots are softened. 2. Add leftover brisket and cook for about 3 minutes, or until the leftover brisket is browned. Bring the beer to a low simmer for 5-8 minutes. 3. Combine the coffee, tomato sauce, adobo paste, chilli powder, cumin, smoked paprika, cinnamon, salt, cayenne pepper, and pinto and black beans in a large mixing bowl. Turn off the heat after thoroughly mixing everything together. 4. Place cast-iron skillet into the smoker for 30 minutes at 300 degrees F. 5. Mix the tomatillos, tomato, green onion, jalapeno, and lime juice together to make the salsa. 6. Place the nachos directly on the grill grate and cook for about 10 minutes or until cheese is melted and chips are crisp. 7. Top with shredded cheese and then place back on the Pit Boss Pellet Grill and cook for 15 minutes. 8. Remove nachos from the grill, add some chopped bacon and top with the salsa.

Suggested Wood Pellet Flavor: Hickory.
Serving Suggestion: Serve the smoked brisket nachos with a refreshing drink.
Variation Tip: Use pork.
Nutritional Information per Serving: Calories 435| Fat 23.7g |Sodium 613mg | Carbs 31.3g | Fiber 7.6g | Sugar 4.6g | Protein 25.7g

Smoked Steaks with Herb Butter

Prep Time: 10 minutes | Cook Time: 55 minutes | Serves: 2

Ingredients:

¼ cup butter at room temperature
2 cloves garlic, minced
1 tsp horseradish
1 tsp Dijon mustard
¼ cup olive oil
1 tsp fresh parsley, minced

2 tbsp pepper
¼ cup red wine
1 tbsp rosemary sprigs, Springs
4¾ lbs steak, bone-in ribeye
1 tbsp vinegar
1 tbsp Worcestershire Sauce

Preparation:

1. Combine olive oil, red wine, rosemary, vinegar, mustard, pepper, Worcestershire sauce, and garlic; add steaks and seal in a plastic bag. Refrigerate the marinade overnight. 2. Start your grill on "smoke," with the lid open until a fire is established in the burn pot (3-4 minutes). Leave on "smoke" mode. 3. Take the steaks out of the bag and throw away the marinade. 4. Place on the grates of your grill and smoke for 40 minutes. 5. Combine butter, parsley, and horseradish in a bowl while the steaks are smoking. Set aside. 6. Remove the steaks from the grill after 40 minutes of smoking. Open the Flame Broiler Plate and crank up the temperature to "HIGH". 7. Let the grill preheat for about 15 minutes. Return the steaks to the grates and sear both sides until the internal temperature reaches 205 degrees F.

Suggested Wood Pellet Flavor: Use Competition Blend Hardwood Pellets.

Serving Suggestion: Serve the steaks with sauce of your preference.

Variation Tip: Use pork for a different taste.

Nutritional Information per Serving: Calories 830| Fat 52.7 g |Sodium 213mg | Carbs 9.3g | Fiber 2.6g | Sugar 1.6g | Protein 65.7g

Smoked Texas Beef Brisket

Prep Time: 15 minutes | Cook Time: 7 hrs | Serves: 4

Ingredients:

1 brisket flat, 4 to 6 pounds
1 cup apple cider vinegar
Texas Rub
¼ cup kosher salt

¼ cup black pepper
2 tbsp. garlic powder
1 tbsp. paprika
½ tsp cayenne powder

Preparation:

1. Preheat the smoker to 225 degrees F. 4–5 wood chunks should be tossed into the fire. Combine salt, pepper, garlic powder, paprika, and cayenne powder in a medium-sized mixing bowl. Break up any clumps with your fingers. Season the brisket on all sides with the dry rub. 2. Put the brisket on the grill. Cook for 4 hours or until the internal temperature of the brisket reaches 160 degrees F. 3. Fill a spray bottle with apple cider vinegar and spritz the brisket every hour. 4. Take the brisket out of the smoker, then wrap it in butcher paper and put it back in the smoker. Cook for 2 to 3 hours, or until the internal temperature reaches 205 degrees F. 5. Remove the brisket from the smoker and set it aside to rest for 30 minutes. Cut into slices and serve.

Suggested Wood Pellet Flavor: Use 4-5 oak, pecan or hickory wood chunks.

Serving Suggestion: Serve with smoked sweet potatoes fries.

Variation Tip: Use pork.

Nutritional Information per Serving: Calories 125| Fat 7.1g |Sodium 7513mg | Carbs 9.3g | Fiber 1.6g | Sugar 1.6g | Protein 6.7g

Juicy Mustard Rack of Ribs

Prep Time: 15 minutes | Cook Time: 30 minutes | Serves: 2

Ingredients:

One rack of ribs
¼ cup of apple cider vinegar
¼ cup of brown sugar
3 tbsp of ketchup
1 tbsp hot sauce

2 cups apple juice
¼ cup of honey
2 cups yellow mustard
7 tbsps rib rubs

Preparation:

1. First, combine the mustard, vinegar, ketchup, sugar, honey, sauce, and rib rub in a large mixing bowl. 2. Mix well and refrigerate it until the mixture is ready. Remove the peel from the ribs and prepare the ribs. 3. Next, generously coat the ribs with the mustard and sprinkle the rub over it. 4. Preheat your Pit Boss pellet grill to 275 degrees F. 5. Place the ribs on the grill for 2 to 3 hours to cook. Fill the spray bottle halfway with vinegar and spray it constantly for a few minutes. 6. After that, spray every hour or 45 minutes Cook for another 2-3 hours after you've attained a deep color. 7. Remove the grill and brush it with the mustard and serve it.

Suggested Wood Pellet Flavor: Use a hickory pellet.

Serving Suggestion: Serve the carolina mustard ribs with chili lime sauce and mashed potatoes.

Variation Tip: Use pork ribs for a different taste.

Nutritional Information per Serving: Calories 421| Fat 11.7g |Sodium 513mg | Carbs 59.3g | Fiber 4.6g | Sugar 3.6g | Protein 25.7g

Grilled Marinated Beef

Prep Time: 15 minutes | Cook Time: 30 minutes | Serves: 4

Ingredients:

1kg thick steak
2 tbsp gluten-free Worcestershire sauce
3 garlic cloves, crushed
Juice of 2 limes
2 tbsp red wine vinegar

1 tbsp cumin seed
1 tbsp chilli flakes
1 small onion, grated
2 tbsp olive oil, plus extra for drizzling
Salt and pepper to taste

Preparation:

1. Preheat the grill, then reduce slightly to 425 degrees F. 2. Cut the meat into 6 or 7 chunks. 3. Combine the Worcestershire sauce, garlic, lime juice, vinegar, spices, onion, and olive oil in a small bowl. 4. Season the meat on both sides with salt and pepper, then set it in a non-metallic baking dish or baking pan. Refrigerate for up to 1 day after covering with the marinade. 1 hour before grilling, bring to room temperature. 5. Place the steaks on the grill. Sear each side, flipping every few minutes. 6. Grill until desired doneness, then remove from grill. Place on the serving plates and top with warm vegetables.

Suggested Wood Pellet Flavor: Hickory / Mesquite / Whiskey.
Serving Suggestion: Serve Cumin & Onion Marinated Beef with sauce.
Variation Tip: Use mushrooms or turkey for a different taste.
Nutritional Information per Serving: Calories 155| Fat 2.7g |Sodium 513mg | Carbs 29.3g | Fiber 4.6g | Sugar 3.6g | Protein 5.7g

Grilled Ribeye Shish Kabobs

Prep Time: 20 minutes | Cook Time: 15 minutes | Serves: 6

Ingredients:

2 cup packed flat-leaf parsley leaves
¼ cup fresh oregano
6 cloves garlic
Black pepper
Kosher salt
1 cup olive oil

¼ cup red wine vinegar
1 teaspoon red pepper flakes
3 whole (1-inch-thick) rib-eye steaks, cut into
1 inch cubes
2 small red onions, quartered
2 cups cherry tomatoes

Preparation:

1. Add parsley, oregano, and garlic to a bowl and finely chop. Mix in the red wine vinegar, olive oil, and pepper flakes. Set aside on the counter after seasoning with salt and pepper. 2. Using wood skewers, skewer onions, ribeye, and tomatoes until all are used. Season with salt and pepper after brushing with olive oil. 3. Preheat the Pit Boss Wood Pellet Grill to high for 15 minutes when you're ready to cook. Place the skewers on the hot grill. Cook for 8 minutes on one side, then flip and cook for another 8 minutes. 4. Remove from the grill and serve with a side of chimichurri. On the side, serve the remaining chimichurri. Enjoy!

Suggested Wood Pellet Flavour: Use Cherry Pellets.
Serving Suggestion: Serve the Grilled Ribeye Shish Kabobs with Chimichurri Sauce with salad.
Variation Tip: Top loin roast.
Nutritional Information per Serving: Calories 415 | Fat 38.7g | Sodium 525mg | Carbs 7.9g | Fiber 2.8g | Sugar 2.6g | Protein 13g

BBQ Tomahawk Rib–Eye Steaks

Prep Time: 105 minutes | Cook Time: 60 minutes | Serves: 4

Ingredients:

1 (32 ounces) bone-in tomahawk rib-eye, 2 inch thick
Kosher salt

Pit Boss 9.0 ounces Chicago BBQ Rub
3 tablespoons butter, preferably high-quality

Preparation:

1. Season the meat generously with Kosher salt on all sides. Allow one hour for the steak to come to room temperature. 2. When ready to cook, set Pit Boss Wood Pellet Grill temperature to 225°F and preheat, lid closed 15 minutes. For optimal flavour, use Super Smoke if available. 3. After an hour, properly rinse the steak to remove all salt and pat it dry. Season both sides of the steak with Pit Boss 9.0 ounces Chicago BBQ Rub. (I prefer to season one side first and then lay it aside for a few minutes.) After that, flip the steak and rub the other side.) 4. Directly onto the cooking grate, place the meat. Don't touch it, don't turn it over, and don't spritz it. Cook the steak until it reaches a temperature of 120°F on the inside. Depending on the thickness, this should take 45 minutes or so. 5. After the steak has reached an internal temperature of 120°F, remove it. Allow 10 minutes for the steak to rest, lightly tented with aluminium foil. 6. Place a cast iron pan on the grill grate while the steak is resting. Preheat the grill to 500°F. Allow it to heat up to its maximum temperature. 7. Place the meat on a dry cast iron griddle and sear for one minute. Sear the other side of the meat for 1 minute. This should bring your steak to a temperature of no more than 130°F on the inside. 8. Remove the steak from the pan and smother it in butter. Due to carryover cooking, the steak will continue to cook for another 5 to 7 minutes as the butter melts on top. We're aiming for an interior temperature of 130°F to 135°F, which is a great medium-rare. 9. Allow 10 minutes for the meat to rest. Cut and savour!

Suggested Wood Pellet Flavour: Use Mesquite Pellets.
Serving Suggestion: Serve the BBQ Tomahawk Steaks with salad.
Variation Tip: Use top loin roast.
Nutritional Information per Serving: Calories 557 | Fat 32.7g | Sodium 2013mg | Carbs 0g | Fiber 0g | Sugar 0g | Protein 61.7g

Smoked BBQ Cheese Meatloaf

Prep Time: 15 minutes | Cook Time: 30 minutes | Serves: 2

Ingredients:

2 lbs ground beef, pork, sausage
1 jar (2 cups) BBQ sauce
1 cup panko bread crumbs
1 egg

½ cup onion, minced
½ cup parmesan, grated
½ cup (3.5 oz.) fresh mozzarella, diced
Plowboys BBQ Bovine Bold Rub

Preparation:

1. Preheat the grill, then reduce to SMOKE or 180-225 degrees F. 2. Combine the ground meat(s), egg, 1 cup BBQ sauce, panko, onion and cheeses in a bowl, mix well by your hand. Place the mixture on a work surface and form into a loaf shape. Season well with Plowboys BBQ Bovine Bold Rub. 4. Smoke the meatloaf on the second shelf of the smoker. Cook for 45 minutes, or the internal temperature reaches 100 degrees F. Increase the grill temperature to 350 degrees F and glaze the meatloaf with the remaining Plowboys BBQ Bean Buddy. 5. Cook until the internal temperature reaches 160 degrees F. Remove from the grill. Slice to serve.

Suggested Wood Pellet Flavor: Hickory / Competition / Apple.
Serving Suggestion: Serve the BBQ meatloaf with salad.
Variation Tip: Use tofu if you are vegan.
Nutritional Information per Serving: Calories 582| Fat 18.7g |Sodium 503mg | Carbs 23g | Fiber 1.6g | Sugar 4.6g | Protein 76g

Spicy Brisket

Prep Time: 15 minutes | Cook Time: 15 hrs | Serves: 4

Ingredients:

Rub
2 tbsp garlic powder
2 tbsp onion powder
2 tbsp paprika
2 tsp chili powder

⅓ cup Jacobsen salt or kosher salt
⅓ cup coarse ground black pepper, divided
Main
1 (12-14 lb) whole packer brisket, trimmed
1 ½ cup beef broth

Preparation:

1. When ready to cook, preheat the Pit Boss to 225 degrees F with the lid closed for 15 minutes. 2. For the Rub: Mix together garlic powder, onion powder, paprika, chili pepper, kosher salt and pepper in a small bowl. 3.Season the brisket on all sides with the rub mix. 4. Place the brisket, fat side down on grill grate. Cook the brisket until it reaches an internal temperature of 160 degrees F, about 5 to 6 hours. When it reaches a temperature of 160 degrees F, remove from the grill. 5. Double wrap meat in aluminium foil and add the beef broth to the foil packet. Return brisket to grill and cook until it reaches an internal temperature of 205 degrees F, about 3 hours more. 6. Once finished, remove from grill, unwrap from foil and let rest for 15 minutes. Slice against the grain and serve.

Suggested Wood Pellet Flavor: Use Hickory / Competition pellets.
Serving Suggestion: Serve the brisket with a sauce of your taste.
Variation Tip: Use pork.
Nutritional Information per Serving: Calories 155| Fat 4.7g |Sodium 1813mg | Carbs 19.3g | Fiber 4.3g | Sugar 1.6g | Protein 15.7g

Sirloin Steak with Chimichurri Sauce

Prep Time:15 minutes | Cook Time:45 minutes | Serve: 2

Ingredients:

2 tablespoons chili pepper flakes
½ cup extra-virgin olive oil
1 garlic, cloves
2 tablespoons oregano, leaves
¼ teaspoon paprika, powder
2 cups lightly packed parsley, leaves

1 teaspoon Pit Boss Smoked Salt & Pepper Rub
¼ cup red onion, chopped
1 ½ pound steak, sirloin
6 tablespoons vinegar red wine

Directions:

1. Start your Pit Boss Wood Pellet Grill on Smoke, leaving the lid open, until a fire forms in the burn pot (3-7 minutes). Preheat the grill to 250°F. Season both sides of your steaks to taste with the Smoked Salt & Pepper Rub. Place on the preheated grill grates. Cook the steaks until the internal temperature reaches 130°F (for medium-rare). 3. If you want to cook your steak done, use the following internal temperatures: 125°F is extremely rare. 130°F for medium rare. 140°F is considered medium. Finished: 160°F. It will take about 45 minutes to cook your steaks medium rare. 4. While the steaks are cooking, in a food processor, combine parsley, garlic, red onion, oregano, paprika, and chili pepper flakes and pulse to combine. 5. Continue to pulse for another 20 seconds, or until the mixture is chunky but combined, with the salt, vinegar, and oil. 6. When the steaks have reached the desired internal temperature, remove them from the grill and set aside for 15 minutes to rest. 7. Meanwhile, turn on your flame broiler and heat the grill to high. Sear the steak for about 1 minute on each side. 8. Thinly slice the steak and drizzle with the chimichurri sauce. Enjoy!

Serving suggestion: Serve the steak with bread.
Variation tip: Add some other sauce of your choice on steak.
Nutritional Value (Amount per Serving): Calories 939 | Fat 58.13g | Carbs 6.87g | Sugar 1.67g | Protein 97.1g

Juicy Cheese Beef Hamburgers

Prep Time: 15 minutes | Cook Time: 30 minutes | Serves: 4

Ingredients:

2 lbs ground beef or buffalo
3 tsp All-Purpose Seasoning
2 eggs, room temperature
2 cups bread crumbs

6-8 Hamburger / Kaiser Buns
6-8 cheese slices
2 tbsp butter

Preparation:

Preheat the grill to 400-500 degrees F. 2. In a mixing dish, combine the meat, seasoning, eggs, and bread crumbs. 3. Divide the meat into parts and carefully shape them into patties. The patties should be roughly 1.9cm or 3-4 inches thick. 4. Cook the patties on the grill. Grill the meat for six minutes per side, being careful not to press patties down on it. Using a meat thermometer, check for doneness; the interior temperature should reach 160 degrees F. 5. The meat may turn pink on the outside due to smoking. 6. Brush the buns with butter and lightly brown on the grill in the last few minutes of grilling. When the burgers and buns are done, remove them. Serve the burgers with melted cheese on top.

Suggested Wood Pellet Flavor: Use Hickory/Competition.
Serving Suggestion: Serve the hamburgers with French fries.
Variation Tip: Use ground turkey.
Nutritional Information per Serving: Calories 715| Fat 42.7g |Sodium 803mg | Carbs 29.3g | Fiber 16g | Sugar 3.6g | Protein 53.7g

Smoked Corn Beef Hot Dogs

Prep Time: 15 minutes | Cook Time: 35 minutes | Serves: 4

Ingredients:

6 whole uncured all beef hot dogs
Corn Dog Batter:
1 cup cornmeal
1 cup flour
3 tablespoons sugar

1 tablespoon baking powder
½ teaspoon salt
1 cup milk, plus more as needed
1 large egg
4 quarts grapeseed oil

Preparation:

1. When ready to cook, set Pit Boss Wood Pellet Grill temperature to 165°F and preheat, lid closed for 15 minutes. For optimal flavor, use Super Smoke if available. 2. Place hot dogs on Pit Boss Wood Pellet Grill and smoke for 30 minutes. 3. To make corn dog batter, combine all dry ingredients in a large bowl. Whisk in the egg and milk until all combined. Add up to a ¼ cup more milk if needed to thin out. Pour batter into a tall glass to make coating the hotdogs easier. 4. Fill a large saucepan halfway with oil, being careful not to overfill. Heat oil to 350°F on the stovetop. 5. Place a popsicle stick through the middle of the hot dog lengthwise. Coat hotdogs in batter by dipping into the glass and turning the stick to evenly coat. Carefully lower the corn dog into the oil and deep fry until golden brown in batches, taking care not to overfill the pan. 6. Serve with your favorite condiments and enjoy!

Suggested Wood Pellet Flavour: use Mesquite Pellets.
Serving Suggestion: Serve the Smoked Corn Dogs with sauce.
Variation Tip: Use turkey sausage.
Nutritional Information per Serving: Calories 580 | Fat 28g | Sodium 937mg | Carbs 63g | Fiber 3.2g | Sugar 13.6g | Protein 21.3g

Smoked Prime Rib Roast

Prep Time: 15 minutes | Cook Time: 30 minutes | Serves: 12

Ingredients:

lb prime rib roast
Plowboys Bovine Bold Beef Rub
tbsp flour
¼ cup duck fat
2 cups beef broth

¼ cup red wine
1 tsp horseradish
1 tbsp garlic salt
1 tsp black pepper

Preparation:

1. Season the prime rib on all sides with the Bovine Bold Beef Rub. 2. Preheat your Pit Boss Pellet Grill to 200 degrees F. Increase the temperature to 250 degrees F after 1 hour. 3. Then increase the temperature to 300 degrees F after another hour. You can get additional smoke flavor by cooking at lower heat for the first couple of hours. 4. Cook until the prime rib's core temperature reaches 120-122 degrees F for medium-rare. Make the Au Jus while the prime rib is resting. 5. Add any drippings from the prime rib to a sauce pan over medium heat. 6. Melt the duck fat, then add the flour and stir well until the flour is completely absorbed. 7. Add the beef broth and the remaining ingredients. Simmer for 5 to 10 minutes. Let the prime rib rest for about 15 minutes, slice and serve.

Suggested Wood Pellet Flavor: Combination of cherry, maple and hickory pellets.
Serving Suggestion: Serve smoked prime rib with salad.
Variation Tip: Use pork for a different taste.
Nutritional Information per Serving: Calories 645| Fat 42.7g |Sodium 1513mg | Carbs 9.3g | Fiber 0.6g | Sugar 0.6g | Protein 42.7g

BBQ Citrus Shredded Beef Tacos

Prep Time: 15 minutes | Cook Time: 4 hours | Serves: 4

Ingredients:

Beef Roast:
1 (4-6 pounds) chuck roast
¼ cup Pit Boss Beef Rub
3 cloves, garlic
1 small yellow onion, diced

1 orange, juiced
2 lime, juiced
2 cup beef stock

Pico De Gallo:
½ cup cherry tomatoes, halved
1 small red onion, diced
1 Jalapeño, chopped
4 tablespoons cilantro, finely chopped

1 lime, juiced
1 tablespoon extra-virgin olive oil
Salt
Black pepper

Main:
12 flour tortillas
1 avocado, sliced
4 tablespoons crumbled queso fresco, for

serving
Cilantro, finely chopped

Preparation:

1. Set the Pit Boss Wood Pellet Grill to 225°F and preheat for 15 minutes with the lid closed when you're ready to cook. If Super Smoke is available, use it for the best flavour. 2. Season chuck roast generously with Pit Boss 12.0 (oz.) Prime Beef Rub. 3. Place the chuck roast directly on the grill grates. Then, close the lid and cook for 45 minutes. 4. Add the garlic, onion, orange juice, lime juice, and beef stock to a large Dutch oven. Remove the roast from the grill and place it in the braising liquid in the Dutch oven. 5. Cover the Dutch oven and place it directly on the grill grates, close the lid. Cook for 2-3 hours or until fork-tender. 6. Make the Pico De Gallo. In a small bowl, add the tomatoes, onion, jalapeño, cilantro, lime juice, and olive oil. Stir to combine, and season with salt and pepper. 7. Remove the Dutch oven from the grill and remove the roast from the braising liquid. Shred using two forks and pour a little bit of the braising liquid back onto the meat. 8. Build the tacos. In the tortillas, add the shredded beef, top with Pico De Gallo, queso fresco, avocado, and garnish with cilantro, as desired. Enjoy!

Suggested Wood Pellet Flavour: Use Apple Pellets.
Serving Suggestion: Serve the BBQ Shredded Beef Tacos with salad.
Variation Tip: Use pork.
Nutritional Information per Serving: Calories 1050 | Fat 38.8g | Sodium 707mg | Carbs 13.5g | Fiber 2.8g | Sugar 5.6g | Protein 153.7g

Grilled Sirloin Steak with Sweet Onion & Peppers

Prep Time: 15 minutes | Cook Time: 30 minutes | Serves: 4

Ingredients:

1 lb steak, top sirloin
2 tsp Pit Boss Steak Rub
5 medium sweet onions (chopped coursely)

2 whole bell peppers chopped)
4 tbsp soy sauce
4 tbsp olive oil

Preparation:

1. Preheat the grill to 245 degrees F. 2. Rub the spice or rub on both sides of the steak. Refrigerate for at least 1 hour after covering. 3.Place the onions and bell peppers in an aluminium foil-covered tray. Drizzle the soy sauce and olive oil mixture over the tray. 4. Season with salt. Completely close the foil packet. Cook for 10–15 minutes, or until the vegetables are soft and delicious. Remove from the grill and cover. 5. Arrange the steaks on the grill. Sear each side for a few minutes before flipping. Cook until done to your liking, then remove from the grill. Serve on serving dishes with heated vegetables on top.

Suggested Wood Pellet Flavor: Hickory / Mesquite / Whiskey.
Serving Suggestion: Goes well with sauce and salad.
Variation Tip: Use lamb.
Nutritional Information per Serving: Calories 425| Fat 12.7g |Sodium 913mg | Carbs 19.3g | Fiber 4.2g | Sugar 7.6g | Protein 44g

Smoked Beef Burgers

Prep Time: 15 minutes | Cook Time: 2 hours | Serves: 8

Ingredients:

2 pounds, ground beef
1 tablespoon, Worcestershire sauce

2 tablespoons, Pit Boss 11.5 ounces Lonestar Beef Brisket Rub

Preparation:

1. Mix ground beef with Worcestershire sauce and Pit Boss 11.5 ounces Lonestar Beef Brisket Rub. 2. Form beef mixture into 8 hamburger patties. 3. When ready to cook, set Pit Boss Wood Pellet Grill temperature to 180°F and preheat, lid closed for 15 minutes. For optimal flavour, use Super Smoke if available. 4. Place patties directly on the grill grate and smoke for 2 hours. After 2 hours, remove from grill and serve with your favourite toppings. Enjoy!

Suggested Wood Pellet Flavour: Use Mesquite Pellets.
Serving Suggestion: Serve the Smoked Burgers with salad.
Variation Tip: Use ground chicken breast.
Nutritional Information per Serving: Calories 336 | Fat 12g | Sodium 210mg | Carbs 155g | Fiber 210g | Sugar 1g | Protein 52.5g

Sweet & Spicy Beef Jerky

Prep Time: 15 minutes | Cook Time: 30 minutes | Serves: 4

Ingredients:

2 lb London broil beef roast
2 tsp garlic powder
3 tsp dried ginger
1 cup Sriracha
½ cup brown sugar
2 tsp Kosher salt
2 tsp black pepper

3 tsp Dijon mustard
3 tbsp honey
¼ rice vinegar
2 tsp black pepper
¼ cup soy sauce
2 tbsp lime juice
5 tbsp Worcestershire sauce

Preparation:

1. Beef should be sliced into ¼ strips. 2. Combine all the ingredients in a large mixing bowl, cover, and refrigerate for at least 24 hours. 3. Remove the beef strips from the marinade the next day and pat dry with paper towels. Your time in the smoker will be extended if you do not pat dry. 4. Using your favorite wood pellets, heat the Pit Boss to 190 degrees F. 5. Place the meat strips on the Pit Boss grates, leaving some room between them. 6. Smoke the beef strips until you can bend the jerky and it cracks, but does not break into pieces.
Suggested Wood Pellet Flavor: Use cherry pellets.
Serving Suggestion: Serve with chili lime sauce or any other sauce.
Variation Tip: Use pork.
Nutritional Information per Serving: Calories 155| Fat 2.7g |Sodium 513mg | Carbs 29.3g | Fiber 4.6g | Sugar 3.6g | Protein 5.7g

Smoked Juicy BBQ Beef Sandwich

Prep Time: 20 minutes | Cook Time: 6 hours | Serves: 12

Ingredients:

4-pound beef roast
2 tsp salt
½ tsp pepper
1 tsp onion powder
1 tsp garlic powder

3 tbsp all-purpose rub
1 cup hard apple cider
1 cup beef broth
2 cups barbecue sauce

Preparation:

1. Preheat your Pit Boss Wood Pellet Grill to 200 degrees F. 2. Combine all of the ingredients and rub them all over the meat roast. 3. Smoke for 3-4 hours at a temperature of roughly 200 degrees F. 4. In a foil pan or a Dutch oven, place the roast. Cover the pan with a tight-fitting lid and pour in the hard apple cider and beef broth. 5. Preheat the Pit Boss Wood Pellet Grill to 300-325 degrees F and cook the roast until it reaches a temperature of 205 degrees F and is fork-tender and shreddable. 6. Shred the roast, reserving the liquids and removing the excess fat. Get rid of any excess fat or parts of the roast that aren't tender shredded beef. 7. Add more barbecue sauce and part of the leftover juices to the mix. 8. Toast your buns and stuff them full of meat. Serve with coleslaw on the side.
Suggested Wood Pellet Flavor: Hickory / Mesquite / Whiskey.
Serving Suggestion: Serve the BBQ beef sandwiches with salad.
Variation Tip: Use pork or chicken.
Nutritional Information per Serving: Calories 766| Fat 47g |Sodium 813mg | Carbs 39.3g | Fiber 1g | Sugar 10g | Protein 57g

Bacon Wrapped Beef Tenderloin

Prep Time: 10 minutes | Cook Time: 60 minutes | Serves: 4

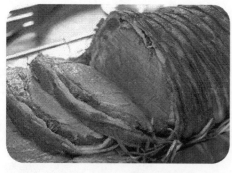

Ingredients:

4 pounds Beef, Loins
4 ounces Pit Boss Prime Beef Rub

8 strips bacon
4 ounces coffee rub

Preparation:

1. When ready to cook, start the Pit Boss Wood Pellet Grill according to grill instructions. Set the temperature to 275°F and preheat, lid closed, for 10 to 15 minutes. 2. Season the tenderloin lightly with the Pit Boss Prime Beef Rub and wrap with bacon. Season again with another layer of coffee rub. 3. Cook the tenderloin for 30 minutes on the grill. Check the inside temperature; 120°F is the ideal temperature. If the required temperature has not been reached, continue to cook, checking every 5 minutes until it is. 4. Remove the tenderloin from the grill and raise the temperature to 450°F. Return tenderloin to grill after 10 minutes and sear for 5 minutes. Check the internal temperature once more; it should be 135°F at this point. 5. If the tenderloin has not reached the desired temperature, flip it and sear for another 5 minutes, or until it reaches 135°F. 6. Remove tenderloin from grill and let rest for 10 minutes before slicing and serving. Enjoy!
Suggested Wood Pellet Flavour: Use Cherry Pellets.
Serving Suggestion: Serve the Roasted Bacon Wrapped Beef Tenderloin with salad.
Variation Tip: Use pork.
Nutritional Information per Serving: Calories 1048 | Fat 44.2g | Sodium 7113mg | Carbs 24.3g | Fiber 0g | Sugar 0g | Protein 151.7g

Delicious Grilled Sirloin Steaks

Prep Time: 05 minutes | Cook Time: 05 minutes | Serves: 2

Ingredients:

2 sirloin steaks
1 teaspoon garlic powder
1 teaspoon onion powder
1 teaspoon paprika

1 teaspoon chile powder
1 teaspoon brown sugar
1 tablespoon Kosher Sea Salt
1 tablespoon ground black pepper

Preparation:

1. Set the Pit Boss Wood Pellet Grill to 500°F and preheat for 15 minutes with the lid covered when you're ready to cook. 2. Take the steaks out of the fridge and pat them dry. 3. Combine garlic, onion, paprika, brown sugar, chile, salt, and pepper in a mixing bowl. Rub the salt and spice combination on both sides of the steak. 4. Place steaks on the outer rim of the grill when it's hot, as this is usually the hottest portion of the grill. Before checking them, close the lid and wait 3 to 4 minutes. 5. Cook the steak until it reaches the appropriate internal temperature on one side only (130°F for medium-rare). 6. Pull the steaks and let rest for 5 to 10 minutes. Serve and enjoy!

Suggested Wood Pellet Flavour: Use Apple Pellets.
Serving Suggestion: Serve the Grilled Sirloin Steaks.
Variation Tip: Use Ribeye or New York strip steaks.
Nutritional Information per Serving: Calories 194 | Fat 5.7g | Sodium 519mg | Carbs 8.3g | Fiber 1.6g | Sugar 2.6g | Protein 26.7g

Juicy Tri Tip Beef Roast

Prep Time:120 minutes | Cook Time:20 minutes | Serves: 2

Ingredients:

4 tablespoons Beef & Brisket Rub
1 stick unsalted softened butter
1 garlic clove, minced
Juice from 1 orange
⅓ cup soy sauce
2 tablespoons Worcestershire sauce

⅓ cup brown sugar
½ teaspoon Cayenne pepper
2 tablespoons olive oil
1 tablespoon paprika, powder
3-4 pounds trimmed tri tip roast

Directions:

1. In a resealable plastic bag, combine the brown sugar, orange juice, Worcestershire sauce, minced garlic, and soy sauce. Place the tri tip in the bag, seal it, and massage it to evenly coat it with the marinade. Place the bag in the refrigerator for 2 hours to marinate the tri tip. 2. Take the bag out of the fridge and drain the marinade. Take the steak out of the bag and pat it dry with paper towels. 3. Combine the softened butter, 2 tablespoons Beef & Brisket Rub, paprika, and Cayenne pepper in a small mixing bowl. Mix in the butter until it is completely incorporated. Place aside. 4. Rub the olive oil into the tri tip and generously season with the remaining Beef & Brisket Rub. 5. Set the temperature on your Pit Boss Wood Pellet Grill to 450°F after preheating. Set your grill to high heat if you're using a gas or charcoal grill. Insert a temperature probe into the thickest part of the steak and grill it. Sear the tri tip for 3-5 minutes on one side, then flip and sear for another 3-5 minutes on the other. 6. Reduce the heat to 250°F and continue to grill the tri tip for 15 minutes, or until the internal temperature reaches 135°F.

Serving suggestion: Serve this with sweet potato wedges.
Variation tip: Add spices you like and some veggies.
Nutritional Value (Amount per Serving): Calories 1628 | Fat 77.68g | Carbs 51.96g | Sugar 45.44g | Protein 171.7g

Cheesy Beef & Beans Stuffed Peppers

Prep Time: 15 minutes | Cook Time: 40 minutes | Serves: 6

Ingredients:

6 large red bell pepper
1 small onion, diced
2 clove garlic, minced
2 tablespoons Cajun seasoning
⅔ cups salsa, or diced tomatoes with chiles
2 cups cooked white rice

1 cup black beans, rinsed and drained
1 cup corn
1½ cup grated Colby and Monterey Jack cheese
Stuffing:
1-pound ground beef

Preparation:

1. Using cold running water, thoroughly rinse each pepper. With a paring knife, cut each in half lengthwise through the stem and remove the seeds and ribs. 2. Make the Stuffing: In a large frying pan, brown the ground beef, breaking it up with a wooden spoon. 3. In the same frying pan, add the onion and garlic. 2–3 minutes of sautéing. Combine the Cajun seasoning, salsa, rice, black beans, and corn in a mixing bowl. Cook for 5 minutes, or until the flavours have melded. Stuff each half of a pepper with the filling. 4. When ready to cook, set Pit Boss Wood Pellet Grill temperature to 350°F and preheat, lid closed for 15 minutes. 5. Arrange the peppers directly on the grill grate, stuffing-side up, balancing them between the rungs. Bake for 40 minutes. 6. Over the peppers, evenly distribute the grated cheese. Cook for another 5 minutes, or until the cheese has melted. Enjoy!

Suggested Wood Pellet Flavour: Use Mesquite Pellets.
Serving Suggestion: Serve the Stuffed pepper with fried rice.
Variation Tip: Use ground turkey.
Nutritional Information per Serving: Calories 574 | Fat 8.5g | Sodium 165mg | Carbs 85.5g | Fiber 8.7g | Sugar 8.8g | Protein 38.5g

rves: 6

Chapter 2 Pork Recipes

Honey Smoked Ham 27

Pumpkin Spice Grilled Pork Ribs 27

Smoked Mustard Pork Loin 27

Bacon Wrapped Cheesy Stuffed Jalapeno Peppers 27

Pulled Pork & Egg Breakfast Burritos 28

Smoked Sausage & Egg Breakfast Skillet 28

Honey Glazed Pork Tenderloin 28

BBQ Pulled Pork Sandwich 29

Smoked Hawaiian Pineapple Pork Butt 29

Smoked Sweet Bacon 29

Grilled Sweet Pork Tenderloin 30

Raspberry Chipotle BBQ Pork Ribs 30

Delicious Grilled Cocoa-Crusted Pork Tenderloin 30

Grilled BBQ Pulled Pork Sliders 30

Smoked BBQ Pork Ribs 31

Grilled Teriyaki Pineapple Pork Sliders 31

Spicy Grilled Pork Tacos 31

Cheese-Stuffed Bacon Slaw Hot Dogs 32

Grilled Sweet Pork Ribs 32

Juicy Grilled Pork Roast 32

Smoked Sweet Pork Belly 33

BBQ Pork Belly & Pickled Slaw Tacos 33

Roasted Rosemary Pork Tenderloin 33

Smoked Garlicky Porchetta 34

Sausage and Pesto Cheese Lasagna 34

Smoked Rosemary Pork Chops 34

Smoked Cumin Pork Chili Verde 35

Delicious Pulled Pork Eggs Benedict 35

Teriyaki BBQ Pork Pineapple Skewers 35

Flavorful Pulled Pork Mac and Cheese 36

Cheesy Pulled Pork Stuffed Avocado 36

Maple BBQ Pork Tenderloin 36

BBQ Sweet and Smoky Pork Ribs 37

Grilled Lemony Pork Tenderloin 37

Smoked Bacon Cheese Log 37

Honey Smoked Ham

Prep Time:10 minutes | Cook Time: 1 hour 5 minutes | Servings: 10

Ingredients:

1 smoked ham, pre-cooked and spiral sliced
Pit Boss Pecan Maple Walnut Rub, to taste
¼ cup honey

4 tbsps. olive oil
¼ cup apple Juice

Preparation:

1. Warm up your Pit Boss Wood Pellet Grill to 250°F. 2. Lightly coat a pre-cooked ham in olive oil, then coat the entire ham in Pecan Maple Walnut Spice. 3. Arrange the ham cut side down on the Pit Boss Wood Pellet Grill and cook until the temperature from inside reaches 130°F, about 15 minutes per pound. 4. Glaze with a mixture of 14 cup apple juice, honey, and 2 tablespoons PB spice mix, and continue to simmer for another 30 minutes before serving.

Serving Suggestions: Serve with mashed potatoes.
Variation Tip: For the glaze, you can use pineapple or orange juice instead.
Nutritional Information per Serving: Calories: 81 | Fat: 5.9g | Sat Fat: 0.9g | Carbohydrates: 7.8g | Fiber: 0.1g | Sugar: 7.6g | Protein: 0.5g

Pumpkin Spice Grilled Pork Ribs

Prep Time:10 minutes | Cook Time: 6 hours | Servings: 6

Ingredients:

4 tbsps. olive oil
2 racks of pork ribs

Pit Boss Pumpkin Spice Rub, to taste
½ cup butter

Preparation:

1. Preheat your Pit Boss Wood Pellet Grill to 225°F. 2. Remove the membrane from the ribs' bone side. Lightly coat the ribs with olive oil, then season generously with Pumpkin Spice Rub. Grill the ribs with the meat side up. 3. Wrap each rack of ribs in foil with a tablespoon of butter and slightly more rub after 3 hours. Return to the Pit Boss Wood Pellet Grill for a total of 1½ hours. 4. Unwrap the ribs after 1½ hours and bring them to the Pit Boss Wood Pellet Grill for 45 minutes to 1 hour. 5. Remove the ribs when they bend 90°F, slice them, and serve.

Serving Suggestions: Serve with mint yogurt dip.
Variation Tip: For a more tender, fall-off-the-bone rib, mix some apple juice into the wrap with the butter and rub it in.
Nutritional Information per Serving: Calories: 987 | Fat: 77.1g | Sat Fat: 27.4g | Carbohydrates: 32.9g | Fiber: 2.7g | Sugar: 14.7g | Protein: 39.5g

Smoked Mustard Pork Loin

Prep Time:10 minutes | Cook Time: 3 hours | Servings: 8

Ingredients:

1 whole pork loin, boneless
Pit Boss Bourbon Apple Rub, to taste

1 cup Dijon Mustard

Preparation:

1. Preheat your Pit Boss Wood Pellet Grill to 225°F. 2. Lightly smear the whole pork loin with Dijon Mustard and cover completely in Bourbon Apple spice. 3. Grill for 2½ to 3 hours, depending on size, until the thickest section of the pork loin reaches the internal temperature of 145°F. 4. Cover and set aside for 10 minutes before slicing thinly and serving.

Serving Suggestions: Serve with stuffing, potatoes, or roasted vegetables.
Variation Tip: You can use Pit Boss Hickory Blend Hardwood Pellets.
Nutritional Information per Serving: Calories: 43 | Fat: 2.3g | Sat Fat: 0.5g | Carbohydrates: 1.7g | Fiber: 1g | Sugar: 0.3g | Protein: 4.4g

Bacon Wrapped Cheesy Stuffed Jalapeno Peppers

Prep Time:20 minutes | Cook Time: 25 minutes | Servings: 24

Ingredients:

1 garlic clove, chopped
12 bacon strips, cut in half
1 cup mozzarella cheese, shredded
8 (oz.) cream cheese, room temperature
½ tsp. smoked paprika

24 toothpicks
12 fresh jalapeno peppers, cut in half lengthwise
Salt, to taste

Preparation:

1. Prepare your Pit Boss Wood Pellet Grill on SMOKE, open the lid, until a fire in the burn pot is started. Then, preheat it to 300°F. 2. Combine the mozzarella cheese, cream cheese, garlic, salt, and paprika in a mixing bowl, then distribute evenly into all 24 jalapeño halves. 3. Fold a half slice of bacon around each packed jalapeno and secure it with a toothpick in the center. 4. Grill each stuffed pepper for about 25 minutes on each side. 5. Eliminate the pan from the Pit Boss Wood Pellet Grill and serve right away.

Serving Suggestions: Serve with grilled vegetables.
Variation Tip: Start the dish on SMOKE mode for 30 minutes before grilling for even more smoky tastes.
Nutritional Information per Serving: Calories: 90 | Fat: 8.1g | Sat Fat: 3.7g | Carbohydrates: 0.9g | Fiber: 0.3g | Sugar: 0.3g | Protein: 3.2g

Pulled Pork & Egg Breakfast Burritos

Prep Time:15 minutes | Cook Time: 10 minutes | Servings: 4

Ingredients:

½ cup cheddar cheese, shredded
½ cup barbecue sauce
1 onion, sliced
1 tbsp. salsa
1 cup scrambled eggs
1 red pepper, strips

2 cups pulled pork, leftover
½ cup black beans, canned, rinsed, and drained
½ tbsp. pit boss pulled pork seasoning
4 extra-large tortillas

Preparation:

1. Preheat your Pit Boss Wood Pellet Grill to 350°F. Grill the peppers and onions until tender, about 5-7 minutes, with Pit Boss Pulled Pork Spice. Allow to cool after removing from the Pit Boss Wood Pellet Grill. 2. To make the morning burritos, mix the pulled pork with the barbecue sauce, then layer a tiny bit of pork, black beans, eggs, pepper, onions and top the tortillas with salsa and shredded cheese. 3. Make a burrito out of the remaining burrito fillings and repeat with the remaining burritos. 4. Cook the burritos per side for 3 minutes, or until the tortillas are golden and crisp. 5. Eliminate the steaks from the Pit Boss Wood Pellet Grill and serve right away.

Serving Suggestions: Serve your burritos alongside a delicious fruity smoothie.
Variation Tip: You can use either wheat or corn tortillas.
Nutritional Information per Serving: Calories: 720 | Fat: 24.8g | Sat Fat: 9.4g | Carbohydrates: 82.8g | Fiber: 7g | Sugar: 19.3g | Protein: 30g

Smoked Sausage & Egg Breakfast Skillet

Prep Time:30 minutes | Cook Time: 20 minutes | Servings: 4

Ingredients:

1 bag frozen hash browns with peppers and onions
½ cup cheddar cheese, shredded
½ tbsp. Pit Boss Sweet Rib Rub

1 package raw breakfast sausage
4 eggs
½ cup green onions, sliced

Preparation:

1. Preheat your Pit Boss Wood Pellet Grill to 350°F and cook the morning sausage for 10 minutes on each side. 2. Let it slightly cool and then chop into small pieces. 3. Merge hash browns, sausage, and sweet rib rub seasoning in a cast iron skillet. 4. Make four small indentations in the hash brown mixture, then crack the eggs into them. 5. Cook for 10 minutes on the Pit Boss Wood Pellet Grill, or until the potatoes are tender and the eggs are the proper consistency.

Serving Suggestions: Top with shredded cheese and green onions.
Variation Tip: You can also use Boursin Cheese instead of Cheddar Cheese for a richer flavor.
Nutritional Information per Serving: Calories: 238 | Fat: 14.9g | Sat Fat: 5.4g | Carbohydrates: 15.1g | Fiber: 1.6g | Sugar: 1.3g | Protein: 11.1g

Honey Glazed Pork Tenderloin

Prep Time:10 minutes | Cook Time: 3 hours | Servings: 4

Ingredients:

⅛ tbsp. cinnamon, ground
1 tbsp. brown sugar
1 tsp. paprika, smoked
1 tbsp. chili powder

1 pork, tenderloin
1 jar salsa
3 tbsps. honey

Preparation:

1. Prepare your Pit Boss Wood Pellet Grill on SMOKE, with the lid open, until a fire in the burn pot is started. Then, preheat it to 225°F. 2. Spoon salsa in the center of the pork tenderloin. To equally distribute salsa, fold in the sides and roll tenderloin carefully. 3. Secure the tenderloin by wrapping butcher's thread around both ends. 4. Mix together the brown sugar, chili powder, ground cinnamon, and smoked paprika in a mixing bowl. Mix thoroughly. 5. Drizzle the hot honey over the pork tenderloin. Brush the tenderloin all over with the rub. Place the meat on the Pit Boss Wood Pellet Grill once it has been completely coated. 6. Smoke the tenderloin for two to three hours, or until the internal temperature of the pork reaches 145°F. Slice and serve right away.

Serving Suggestions: Serve with cooked Basmati Rice.
Variation Tip: For even more tender pork loin, consider soaking it in a brine overnight.
Nutritional Information per Serving: Calories: 102 | Fat: 1.1g | Sat Fat: 0.4g | Carbohydrates: 18.2g | Fiber: 1g | Sugar: 16.2g | Protein: 6.4g

BBQ Pulled Pork Sandwich

Prep Time:20 minutes | Cook Time: 5 hours | Servings: 4

Ingredients:

1 qt. chicken stock
⅓ cup apple cider vinegar
3 tbsps. Pit Boss Home-style Pork Rub, divided

1½ cups BBQ sauce, divided
1 (4 lb.) pork shoulder, bone in
4 pretzel buns
⅓ cup ketchup

Preparation:

1. Preheat your Pit Boss to 400°F. Set the Pit Boss Wood Pellet Grill to MEDIUM-HIGH heat if using a gas or charcoal grill. 2. Combine the chicken stock, apple cider vinegar, ketchup, and 1 tablespoon Pit Boss Home-style Pork Rub in a mixing dish. Set aside after whisking everything together thoroughly. 3. Season the pork shoulder on all sides with the remaining 2 tablespoons Pit Boss Home-style Pork Rub, then place on the Pit Boss Wood Pellet Grill and sear until golden brown on all sides, about 10 minutes. 4. Place the pork shoulder in the disposable aluminum pan after removing it from the Pit Boss Wood Pellet Grill. 5. Trickle the sauce on top of the pork shoulder. It should reach a third to a quarter of the way up the side of the pork shoulder. Cover the aluminum foil tightly over the top of the pan. 6. Lower the temperature of your Pit Boss Wood Pellet Grill to 250°F. Cook on the Pit Boss Wood Pellet Grill for 4 to 5 hours in a foil pan, or until the pork is tender. 7. Take the pork from the Pit Boss Wood Pellet Grill and set it aside for 15 minutes to rest. Drain approximately a cup of the liquid from the pan, then shred the pork and top with the conserved liquid. 8. Set aside 3½ to 4 cups of pulled pork for sandwiches and reserve the rest for later. 9. Heat 1 cup of BBQ sauce in a skillet to simmer while the pork is resting. Toss in the shredded pork that has been set aside. Pork should be divided across four pretzel buns. Serve with ketchup if you like.

Serving Suggestions: Spoon additional BBQ sauce over the top.
Variation Tip: When the internal temperature of the pork shoulder reaches 205°F, it pulls the best. Always keep an eye out for probe tenderness.
Nutritional Information per Serving: Calories: 2456 | Fat: 123.8g | Sat Fat: 43.7g | Carbohydrates: 188.6g | Fiber: 4.1g | Sugar: 102.2g | Protein: 138.2g

Smoked Hawaiian Pineapple Pork Butt

Prep Time:15 minutes | Cook Time:12 hours | Servings: 10

Ingredients:

1 (8-10 lb.) pork butt roast, bone-in
8 pineapple rings

2 cups pineapple juice
¼ cup sweet heat rub

Preparation:

1. Preheat your Pit Boss Smoker to 225°F. Set up the smoker for indirect smoking if you're not using a Pit Boss Wood Pellet Smoker. 2. Drain any surplus liquid from the pork butt by removing it from its package. Dry the pork butt with paper towels before discarding them. 3. Season the pork butt generously with the Sweet Heat Seasoning, ensuring that the roast is well-coated on all sides. 4. Arrange the pineapple rings evenly over the fat side of the pork shoulder and secure using toothpicks. Place the pork butt in a 9x13-inch baking pan and pour the pineapple juice over it. 5. Place the frying pan in the smoker. To ensure consistent cooking, lay the pork butt as close to the center of the rack as feasible. 6. Insert a temperature probe into the thickest portion of the pork butt and smoke the meat until it reaches a temperature of 201°F on the inside. The pork should be well-browned and have a strong porky aroma. 7. Eliminate the pork butt from the Pit Boss Wood Pellet Grill after it has reached its internal temperature and wrap it tightly in foil. Keep aside for about 1 hour before shredding the roast. 8. Shred the pork with your meat claws once the roast has rested for an hour, eliminating any large lumps of fat. Serve right away.

Serving Suggestions: Serve this shredded Hawaiian Pork Butt inside your favorite bread.
Variation Tip: Pit Boss Apple Blend Hardwood Pellets are ideal for this recipe. Fill your hopper to the brim with sweet scents that go great with pork!
Nutritional Information per Serving: Calories: 766 | Fat: 45.2g | Sat Fat: 16.1g | Carbohydrates: 23.8g | Fiber: 1.9g | Sugar: 18g | Protein: 65.1g

Smoked Sweet Bacon

Prep Time:3 hours | Cook Time: 1 hour | Servings: 4

Ingredients:

½ cup maple syrup
1 pack bacon, thick cut

½ cup brown sugar
4 tbsps. Pit Boss Cajun BBQ Rub

Preparation:

1. In a deep dish, place the bacon. Refrigerate for about 12 hours after adding the maple syrup. 2. Start your Pit Boss Wood Pellet Grill on SMOKE, with the lid ajar, until a fire in the burn pot is established. Preheat the Pit Boss Wood Pellet Grill to 225°F. 3. Place the bacon directly on the grilling grids after the Pit Boss Wood Pellet Grill has heated up and sprinkle with Cajun BBQ Rub and brown sugar. 4. Every 15 minutes, double-check. Flip and rotate the bacon after 30 minutes, then baste with syrup. 5. Allow for another 30 minutes of high smoking, or until the bacon is cooked to your preference. 6. Serve after cooling for a while on a wire rack.

Serving Suggestions: Serve with roasted asparagus.
Variation Tip: For a low sugar version, use the low-carb maple syrup and brown sugar substitute.
Nutritional Information per Serving: Calories: 197 | Fat: 2.1g | Sat Fat: 0.7g | Carbohydrates: 44.3g | Fiber: 0g | Sugar: 41g | Protein: 1.8g

Grilled Sweet Pork Tenderloin

Prep Time:1 hour | Cook Time: 20 minutes | Servings: 4

Ingredients:

2 tbsps. Pit Boss Tennessee Apple Butter
Seasoning
2 tbsps. brown sugar

2 tbsps. olive oil
1 pork tenderloin, trimmed with silver skins
removed

Preparation:

1. Whisk together the olive oil, brown sugar, and Tennessee Apple Butter Seasoning in a small bowl until thoroughly blended. 2. Brush the pork tenderloin generously with the mixture. Allow 1 hour for the pork tenderloin to marinate. 3. Set your Pit Boss Wood Pellet Grill to SMOKE mode. Preheat t the temperature to 350°F. 4. Cook the tenderloin on the Pit Boss Wood Pellet Grill for 7 minutes on each side, flipping only once, until the internal temperature reaches 145°F. 5. Take the tenderloin from the Pit Boss Wood Pellet Grill and let it aside for 10 minutes before slicing and serving.

Serving Suggestions: Serve with grilled peaches.

Variation Tip: Marinate the tenderloin in apple juice overnight, covered in the refrigerator, for a wonderfully sweet apple flavor.

Nutritional Information per Serving: Calories: 107 | Fat: 7.8g | Sat Fat: 1.3g | Carbohydrates: 4.4g | Fiber: 0g | Sugar: 4.4g | Protein: 5.6g

Raspberry Chipotle BBQ Pork Ribs

Prep Time:1 hour | Cook Time: 3 hours | Servings: 4

Ingredients:

Baby Back Rib
Pit Boss Raspberry Chipotle Spice Rub, to

taste
Pit Boss Original BBQ Sauce, to taste

Preparation:

1. Start by washing your ribs lightly in cool water. Discard the thin membrane on the underside of the ribs and pat dry to allow the spice to penetrate the meat completely. 2. Season your ribs well with Raspberry Chipotle seasoning and chill for an hour to let the flavors to meld. 3. Preheat your Pit Boss Wood Pellet Grill to 250°F. Cook for 2 hours on the BBQ with your seasoned rack of ribs. 4. Slather the ribs in a thick layer of Original BBQ Sauce, crank up the heat to 300°F, and let them cook for another hour. 5. Remove, cut, and serve for a supper that will undoubtedly become a weekly staple.

Serving Suggestions: Serve with mashed carrots.

Variation Tip: You can also use some tomato sauce for an additional tangy flavor.

Nutritional Information per Serving: Calories: 122 | Fat: 6g | Sat Fat: 2.5g | Carbohydrates: 2.8g | Fiber: 0.1g | Sugar: 2g | Protein: 13g

Delicious Grilled Cocoa–Crusted Pork Tenderloin

Prep Time: 40 minutes | Cook Time: 25 minutes | Serves: 2

Ingredients:

1 pork tenderloin
½ tablespoons ground fennel
2 tablespoons unsweetened cocoa powder
1 tablespoon smoked paprika
½ tablespoons salt

½ tablespoons black pepper
1 tablespoon oil
3 green onions, thinly sliced
Dill for garnishing

Preparation:

1. Remove the connective tissue from the tenderloin. 2. Mix the remaining ingredients in a bowl and rub the tenderloin with the paste. Refrigerate the pork for 30 minutes. 3. Preheat the Pit Boss Wood Pellet Grill to 500 degrees F. 4. Sear the pork on the grill for about 3 minutes on each side. 5. Reduce the grill temperature to 350 degrees F and cook the pork for 15 minutes. 6. Remove the pork tenderloin from the grill and let it stand for 10 minutes before slicing. Garnish the pork with dill and serve.

Serving suggestion: Serve pork tenderloin with grilled squash cubes.

Variation Tip: process fennel seeds in the food processor and grill squash cubes sprinkled with oil alongside the pork.

Nutrition-Per Serving: Calories 382 | Fat 12g |Sodium 2152mg | Carbs 7g | Fiber 5g | Sugar 1g | Protein 61g

Grilled BBQ Pulled Pork Sliders

Prep Time: 15 minutes | Cook Time: 8 hours | Serves: 8

Ingredients:

8–10 lb pork butt
2 tbsps Killer Hogs AP seasoning

2 tbsps Killer Hogs BBQ Rub

Preparation:

1. Season the pork tenderloin with AP and The BBQ Rub on all sides. 2. Let the pork rest on a grill in the refrigerator for at least 2 hours. 3. Prepare a pellet grill for a simmer and simmer at 200 degrees F. 4. Place the roast pork on the grill with the fat side down. 5. Smoke at 200 degrees F for 8 hours, then increase the cooking temperature to 220 degrees F. 6. Continue cooking until the internal temperature reaches 190 degrees F, or a probe thermometer slips in with little or no resistance. 7. Remove the roast pork from the grill and let it sit for 15 minutes before discarding.

Suggested Wood Pellet Flavor: Mesquite pellets.

Serving Suggestion: Serve BBQ pulled pork sliders with fries.

Variation Tip: Use beef or lamb.

Nutritional Information per Serving: Calories 223| Fat 14.7g |Sodium 113mg | Carbs 0.3g | Fiber 0.6g | Sugar 0.6g | Protein 22.7g

Smoked BBQ Pork Ribs

Prep Time: 15 minutes | Cook Time: 4 hours 45 minutes | Serves: 12

Ingredients:

3 racks baby back ribs
¾ cup dry rib rub

¾ cup BBQ sauce

Preparation:

1. Trim excess fat from the backside of the ribs and peel off the membrane. Season the ribs with a dry rub. 2. Preheat the Pit Boss Wood Pellet Grill to 180 degrees F. 3. Place the ribs on the grill grate and smoke them for 4 hours. 4. Remove the ribs from the grill. Then, increase the grill temperature to 350 degrees F. 5. Pour the BBQ sauce on a double-wall aluminium foil and place the ribs on top. Wrap the foil tightly. 6. Grill the wrapped ribs for 45 minutes. Let the ribs rest for 20 minutes then slice. Serve and enjoy.

Serving suggestion: Serve pork ribs with a fresh salad of choice.

Variation Tip: use homemade rub and some apple cider vinegar.

Nutrition-Per Serving: Calories 220 | Fat 12g |Sodium 497mg | Carbs 11g | Fiber 0.5g | Sugar 5g | Protein 3g

Grilled Teriyaki Pineapple Pork Sliders

Prep Time: 20 minutes | Cook Time: 20 minutes | Serves: 6

Ingredients:

1½ tablespoons salt
1 tablespoon onion powder
1 tablespoon paprika
½ tablespoons garlic powder
½ tablespoons cayenne pepper1½ pork

tenderloin
1 can pineapple rings
1 package Hawaiian rolls
8-ounce teriyaki sauce
Lettuce leaves for serving

Preparation:

1. Add all dry ingredients to a mixing bowl and mix well to make a rub. 2. Apply the paprika on the tenderloin until well coated. 3. Preheat your Pit Boss Wood Pellet Grill to 325 degrees F. 4. Place the tenderloin on the grill and cook while the lid is closed while turning occasionally after every 4 minutes until the internal temperature reaches 145 degrees F. 5. While the pork is cooking, place the pineapple rings on the grill. flip the rings once they have brown marks on them. 6. Cut the rolls in halves and place them on the grill alongside tenderloin and pineapple rings. Let them cook until they have grill marks and are toasty brown. 7. Assemble the sliders by putting the bottom roll followed by the lettuce leaf, tenderloin, pineapple ring, teriyaki sauce, and the top roll. 8. Serve and enjoy.

Serving suggestion: Serve the pork sliders alongside potato chips and tomato sauce.

Variation Tip: Use regular buns and some veggies such as onions and lettuce.

Nutrition-Per Serving: Calories 243 | Fat 5g |Sodium 2447mg | Carbs 15g | Fiber 1g | Sugar 10g | Protein 33g

Spicy Grilled Pork Tacos

Prep Time: 15 minutes | Cook Time: 6 hours | Serves: 8

Ingredients:

3 tablespoons brown sugar
1 tablespoon salt
1 tablespoon garlic powder
1 tablespoon paprika

1 tablespoon onion powder
¼ tablespoons cumin
1 tablespoon cayenne pepper
5 pounds pork shoulder roast

Preparation:

1. Add all ingredients to a mixing bowl except pork to make a dry rub. 2. Rub the pork with the rub until well coated. 3. Preheat the Pit Boss Wood Pellet Grill. Place the pork in the Pit Boss Wood Pellet Grill and cook at 250 degrees F for 6 hours or until the internal temperature is 190 degrees F. 4. Let the pork rest for about 10 minutes before shredding and serving in tacos. Enjoy.

Serving suggestion: Serve with taco fixings of choice like peppers, parsley, and onions

Variation Tip: Don't shred and serve it alongside cooked white rice.

Nutrition-Per Serving: Calories 566 | Fat 42g |Sodium 660mg | Carbs 4g | Fiber 0g | Sugar 2g | Protein 44g

Cheese–Stuffed Bacon Slaw Hot Dogs

Prep Time: 10 minutes | Cook Time: 10 minutes | Serves: 8

Ingredients:

8¼ lbs all-pork hot dogs
8 pieces bacon, thick-cut
8 slices Cheddar cheese
2 cups coleslaw, prepared

For topping, Texas Smoky & Spicy BBQ
Sauce
8 toothpicks

Preparation:

1. Preheat the Pit Boss to medium-high heat. 2. Split the hot dogs lengthwise about a third through. Fold each cheese slice in half and then in half again, then insert inside the divided hot dog. 3. Secure one end of a strip of bacon with the toothpick and spiral wrap it securely, slightly overlapping, around the hot dog. When finished, secure the other end with another toothpick. 4. Place hot dogs on the griddle top and regularly toss to ensure that the bacon is cooked evenly on both sides. Remove the hot dogs from the grill once the bacon is cooked, remove the toothpicks, and place each hot dog into a bun. 5. Top each hot dog with a liberal layer of coleslaw, then drizzle with Texas BBQ Sauce.

Suggested Wood Pellet Flavor: Combination of cherry, maple and hickory pellets.
Serving Suggestion: Serve cheese-stuffed bacon slaw dogs with salad.
Variation Tip: Use ham.
Nutritional Information per Serving: Calories 645| Fat 42.7 g |Sodium 1513mg | Carbs 9.3g | Fiber 0.6g | Sugar 0.6g | Protein 42.7g

Grilled Sweet Pork Ribs

Prep Time: 10 minutes | Cook Time: 10 hours | Serves: 4

Ingredients:

2 racks pork ribs
1 cup BBQ rub
24 Ounce hard apple cider

1 cup dark brown sugar
2 batches BBQ sauce

Preparation:

1. Preheat your Pit Boss Wood Pellet Grill to 180 degrees F. 2. Meanwhile, remove the membrane from the ribs and coat with BBQ rub. 3. Smoke the ribs for 5 hours. Transfer the pork ribs to a baking pan and pour apple cider into the pan. 4. Rub the ribs with sugar and cover the pan with foil. 5. Place the pan on the grill and cook for an additional 4 hours. 6. Place the ribs directly on the grill grates and increase the temperature to 300 degrees F. 7. Brush BBQ sauce on the ribs regularly as you cook them for an additional 1 hour. Serve and enjoy.
Serving suggestion: Serve pork ribs with a fresh salad of choice.
Variation Tip: experiment with a different pre-made rub or homemade rub.
Nutrition-Per Serving: Calories 1073 | Fat 42g |Sodium 1663mg | Carbs 111g | Fiber 3g | Sugar 99g | Protein 61g

Juicy Grilled Pork Roast

Prep Time: 5 minutes | Cook Time: 1 hour 30 minutes | Serves: 4

Ingredients:

1 crown roast of pork
¼ cup pork rub

1 cup apple juice
1 cup BBQ sauce

Preparation:

1. Preheat your Pit Boss Wood Pellet Grill to 375 degrees F. 2. Season the pork with pork rub and marinate for 30 minutes. 3. Wrap the tip of the crown roast of pork with aluminium foil and place them on the grill grate. 4. Grill the pork for 1 hour 30 minutes spraying the roast with apple juice after every 30 minutes during cooking. 5. Baste the crown roast of pork with BBQ sauce and allow the glaze to set. 6. Let the crown roast of pork rest for 15 minutes then slice. 7. Serve and enjoy.
Serving suggestion: Serve crown roast of pork ribs with a dipping sauce and some fresh salad.
Variation Tip: use apple cider vinegar in place of apple juice or fresh or dried herbs for seasoning.
Nutrition-Per Serving: Calories 454 | Fat 19g |Sodium 1023mg | Carbs 11g | Fiber 2g | Sugar 1g | Protein 57g

Smoked Sweet Pork Belly

Prep Time: 10 minutes | Cook Time: 370 minutes | Serves: 15

Ingredients:

Peanut oil
Pit Boss Mandarin Habanero Spice
13 lbs. Pork, belly (Skin and Fat)

Salt
Sweet Barbecue Sauce

Preparation:

1. Start your grill on "smoke," with the lid open until a fire is established in the burn pot (3-4 minutes). Preheat to 250 degrees F. 2. Rub the pork with oil and Pit Boss Mandarin Habanero Spice. Place the pork belly, meat side down, on the prepared grill grates. Smoke until the internal temperature reaches 195 degrees F (this usually takes about 6 hours). 3. Open the flame broiler and turn the pork belly over so the meat side is facing up. Brush the BBQ sauce on top (on meat side). Cook for about 5 minutes on the fat side, or until crispy. 4. Remove the pork belly from the grill with your grill gloves and wrap it in aluminium foil for 15 minutes, or until it's cool enough to peel apart. Alternatively, cut into cubes using a knife. 5. Serve immediately.

Suggested Wood Pellet Flavor: Competition Blend Hardwood Pellets.
Serving Suggestion: Serve smoked pork belly with salad.
Variation Tip: Use beef or lamb.
Nutritional Information per Serving: Calories 547| Fat 14.7g |Sodium 272mg | Carbs 1g | Fiber 0g | Sugar 0.6g | Protein 102.7g

BBQ Pork Belly & Pickled Slaw Tacos

Prep Time:30 minutes | Cook Time: 120 minutes | Serves: 6

Ingredients:

Pork Belly
4 tbsp salt
4 tbsp brown sugar
½ tsp black pepper
4 pounds pork belly, skin removed and scored
Pickled Slaw
2 large carrots, peeled and julienned
1 large red onion, thinly sliced

2 large Persian cucumbers, thinly sliced
¼ cup rice wine vinegar
¾ cup water
2 tbsp salt
3 tbsp sugar
1 tsp red pepper flakes
Tortillas, for serving
Fresh chopped cilantro, for serving

Preparation:

1. Combine salt, sugar, and black pepper in a bowl for the pork belly. Coat pork belly evenly with the mixture. Allow to sit in the refrigerator overnight, covered. 2. Set the Pit Boss Grill to 500 degrees F and preheat for 15 minutes with the lid covered when you're ready to cook. 3. Place the pork belly in a baking pan and place the pan on the grill. Cook for 30 minutes until a little bit of color has developed. 4. Reduce the temperature to 250 degrees F and continue cooking for 1 to 2 hours, or until pork belly is tender. 5. Remove from the grill and allow to rest for 30 minutes before slicing. 6. For slaw: In a medium mixing dish, combine the carrots, onion, and cucumber. In a small bowl, whisk together the vinegar, water, salt, sugar, and red pepper flakes until the sugar is dissolved. Pour the carrot mixture over the top and refrigerate until the vegetables are completely submerged. 7. Allow at least 30 minutes in the refrigerator before serving. 8. For the Tacos: After the pork belly has rested, slice into ¼-inch pieces. Fill each tortilla with one slice or two of pork belly and top with pickled slaw. Finish with fresh cilantro leaves. Enjoy!

Suggested Wood Pellet Flavor: Apple pellets.
Serving Suggestion: Serve pork belly tacos with sauce and salad.
Variation Tip: Use lamb.
Nutritional Information per Serving: Calories 117| Fat 4.9g |Sodium 1513mg | Carbs 11.3g | Fiber 0.9g | Sugar 8.6g | Protein 8.7g

Roasted Rosemary Pork Tenderloin

Prep Time: 15 minutes | Cook Time: 25 minutes | Serves: 4

Ingredients:

2 pounds pork tenderloin
Salt and black pepper to taste
2 tablespoons dried rosemary

2 tablespoons oil
1 lemon, sliced
Basil for garnishing

Preparation:

1. Preheat the Pit Boss Wood Pellet Grill to 350 degrees F. 2. Rinse the pork and dry it with a paper towel. Season it with salt, pepper, and rosemary. 3. Heat oil in a skillet and sear the pork for 2 minutes per side. 4. Place the skillet on the grill grate and cook for 20 minutes. 5. Let the pork rest for five minutes then slice. 6. Serve the pork with lemon slices and garnish with basil.

Serving suggestion: Serve pork tenderloin with balsamic strawberry sauce.
Variation Tip: Add strawberries to the skillet and roast them alongside the pork tenderloin.
Nutrition-Per Serving: Calories 360 | Fat 11g |Sodium 130mg | Carbs 1g | Fiber 0.6g | Sugar 0g | Protein 60g

Smoked Garlicky Porchetta

Prep Time: 30 minutes | Cook Time: 180 minutes | Serves: 8

Ingredients:

4 cloves garlic, minced
2 tbsp rosemary, chopped
2 tsp salt
1 tsp black pepper
1 tsp red pepper flakes

6-pound skin-on pork belly
Salt
Black pepper
3-pound center-cut pork loin

Preparation:

1. For the garlic mixture: In a medium bowl, combine the chopped garlic, rosemary, salt, pepper and red pepper flakes. 2. Place the belly skin on a clean work surface and mark the skin with a stripe pattern. Turn the stomach over and season the meat side with salt & pepper and half the garlic mixture. 3. Place the sliced pork tenderloin in the middle of the breast and rub in the remaining garlic mixture, and season with salt and pepper. 4. Roll the pork belly around the loin to form a cylindrical shape. Tie tightly with kitchen twine at 1-inch intervals. Season the skin with salt and pepper and transfer to the refrigerator uncovered, and let it air dry overnight. 5. When ready to cook, set temperature of you Pit Boss Grill to 180 degrees F. Close the lid and preheat for 15 minutes. 6. Place the porchetta seam side down directly on the grill grate and smoke for 1 hour. 7. After an hour, increase the grill temperature to 325 degrees F and broil until the internal temperature reaches 135 degrees F. Cover with foil if the exterior begins to burn before the desired interior temperature is reached. 8. Remove from the grill and let it rest for 30 minutes before slicing. Enjoy!
Suggested Wood Pellet Flavor: Apple pellets.
Serving Suggestion: Serve with salad.
Variation Tip: Use beef and lamb.
Nutritional Information per Serving: Calories 1201| Fat 122.7 g |Sodium 613mg | Carbs 1.3g | Fiber 0.6g | Sugar 0g | Protein 22.7g

Sausage and Pesto Cheese Lasagna

Prep Time: 40 minutes | Cook Time: 60 minutes | Serves: 8

Ingredients:

2 tsp olive oil
1 ½ pound bulk Italian sausage
2 jars (25 oz.) tomato basil pasta sauce or marinara
kosher salt
4 cups shredded mozzarella cheese, divided

15 ounces whole milk ricotta, drained
¾ cup grated Parmesan cheese, divided
Freshly ground black pepper
1 large egg, whisked
1 whole pack lasagna sheets
½ cup prepared pesto

Preparation:

1. Set the Pit Boss Grill to 400 degrees F and preheat for 15 minutes with the lid covered. 2. Heat the olive oil in a large pan over medium heat. Add the sausage to the pan and spread it about the bottom, allowing it to brown before rotating it. Cook, stirring constantly, until the sausage is fully cooked, about 5 to 8 minutes. 3. Add a few tbsps of tomato sauce to coat the bottom of the lasagna pan. Combine the sausage and tomato sauce in a saucepan and cook for 10 to 15 minutes, or until the flavors have melded. If required, season with salt. 4. Make the cheese filling while the sauce is simmering. Combine 3 cups mozzarella, ricotta, and ½ cup grated Parmesan cheese in a medium mixing bowl. 5. To blend, stir everything together. If necessary, season with a bit of salt and freshly ground pepper. Incorporate the egg into the mixture by stirring it in. 6. In a small mixing bowl, add the remaining cup of mozzarella and the remaining ¼ cup of Parmesan. Set aside. 7. Spread the saved tbsps of tomato sauce across the bottom of an 8x12 or 9x13 inch baking dish to start assembling the lasagna. 8. Place four lasagna sheets crosswise on a baking sheet, allowing them to overlap slightly if required. (If the sheets you're using don't span the entire length of the pan, start by layering three sheets lengthwise.). 9. Spoon half of the ricotta cheese mixture across the sheets in spoonfuls. To make an equal coating, spread it out evenly with a spatula or even your hands if necessary. 10. ⅓ of the meat sauce should be poured over the cheese and distributed evenly with a spatula. 11. Repeat with a third of the meat sauce, the remaining ricotta mixture, all of the pesto, and another layer of sheets. Add the final layer of sheets, followed by the remaining sauce, making sure the sheets are completely covered. 12. Over the entire lasagna, sprinkle the remaining mozzarella and Parmesan. 13. A piece of aluminium foil should be carefully wrapped around the pan. Place it on a baking sheet and bake for 45 minutes on the Pit Boss Grill. 14. Lift a corner of the foil and cut into the lasagna with a knife. If the sheets are easily pierced, remove the cover and bake for another 5 to 10 minutes, or until bubbling. Cover it again and simmer for 5–10 minutes more before testing to see if it's done. 15. Allow the lasagna to cool for 10 to 15 minutes before slicing. Serve immediately. Enjoy!
Suggested Wood Pellet Flavor: Classic Blend pellets.
Serving Suggestion: Serve sausage and pesto lasagna with salad.
Variation Tip: Use beef or chicken.
Nutritional Information per Serving: Calories 510| Fat 37.8g |Sodium 1013mg | Carbs 13g | Fiber 1g | Sugar 4.6g | Protein 29.7g

Smoked Rosemary Pork Chops

Prep Time:180 minutes | Cook Time:10 minutes | Serves: 4

Ingredients:

6 tablespoons brown sugar
4 pork chops
2 tablespoons dried rosemary, springs

1 cup soy sauce
½ cup water, warm

Directions:

1. Start your Pit Boss Wood Pellet Grill on Smoke, leaving the lid open, until a fire forms in the burn pot (3-7 minutes). Preheat the grill to 350°F. 2. Lightly oil the grill grate. Remove the pork chops from the marinade, shake off the excess, and discard. 3. Grill the pork chops for about 4-5 minutes on each side, or until no longer pink in the center, brushing occasionally with the reserved marinade. 4. Serve the pork chops hot off the grill. 5. Enjoy!
Serving suggestion: Serve it with asparagus.
Variation tip: Add fried rice with it.
Nutritional Value (Amount per Serving): Calories 514 | Fat 28.9g | Carbs 16.05g | Sugar 12.2g | Protein 44.7g

Smoked Cumin Pork Chili Verde

Prep Time: 30 minutes | Cook Time: 180 minutes | Serves: 2

Ingredients:

3-pound boneless pork shoulder
Pit Boss Home Style Pork Rub
1 jar (16 oz.) Herdez salsa verde
¼ cup water
½ yellow onion, diced
2 cloves garlic, minced

1 tbsp ground cumin
Salt
Black pepper
Corn or flour tortillas, for serving
Rice and beans, for serving

Preparation:

1. Start your Grill on "smoke" and preheat to 250 degrees F. 2. Season the pork shoulder generously with Pit Boss Home Style Pork Rub. 3. Place the pork shoulder directly on the grill grate and smoke for 1 hour. 4. Increase the Pit Boss Grill temperature to 350 degrees F and cook pork until the internal temperature hits 160 degrees F. 5. Remove pork from grill and let it rest on a sheet tray for 15 minutes. 6. After resting, cut the pork shoulder into small cubes and remove any excess fat or gristly tissue. Set aside. 7. In a medium mixing dish, combine the carrots, onion, and cucumber. In a small bowl, whisk together the vinegar, water, salt, sugar, and red pepper flakes until the sugar is dissolved. 8. Pour the carrot mixture over the top and refrigerate until the vegetables are completely submerged. Place pan back on the grill at 350 degrees F for 20 minutes, or until meat is tender. 9. Serve and enjoy.
Suggested Wood Pellet Flavor: Mesquite pellets.
Serving Suggestion: Serve with rice or tortillas.
Variation Tip: Use beef or lamb.
Nutritional Information per Serving: Calories 1071| Fat 25.7g |Sodium 613mg | Carbs 20.3g | Fiber 3.6g | Sugar 4.6g | Protein 182.7g

Delicious Pulled Pork Eggs Benedict

Prep Time: 30 minutes | Cook Time: 300 minutes | Serves: 4

Ingredients:

⅔ cup apple cider vinegar
2 sticks butter
6 cups chicken broth
2 egg yolks
8 eggs
4 English muffins

⅔ cup ketchup
1 tsp lemon juice
1 cup Maple Chipotle Rub Seasoning
4 lbs pork shoulder
To taste, salt & pepper

Preparation:

1. Turn your Pit Boss Pellet Grill on "smoke" and let it run for 10 minutes with the lid open, then preheat to 350 degrees F. 2. Combine the chicken broth, tomato sauce, apple cider vinegar, and 4 tablespoons of maple chipotle spice in a bowl. Beat well to combine and set aside. 3. Generously season all sides of the pork shoulder with the remaining ¾ cup of maple chipotle spice. Place on the grill and fry on all sides for about 10 minutes until it is golden. 4. Remove the pork shoulder from the grill and place it in a foil pan. Pour the chicken broth mixture over the pork shoulder. It should rise ⅓ to ½ on the side of the pork shoulder. Cover the top of the pan tightly with more foil. 5. Reduce the temperature of your Pit Boss Grill to 250 degrees F. Place the aluminum pan on the grill for four to five hours, or until the pork is tender and comes off the bone. 6. Remove the pork from the grill and let cool a bit. Pour the liquid from the pan into a cup, then chop the pork and cover with the liquid. Put aside. 7. Preparing the Hollandaise Sauce. 8. To make the hollandaise sauce, put a saucepan of boiling water and place the two egg yolks in a container that will stand above the boiling water without touching it. 9. Heat the egg yolk over boiling water, constantly stirring, until it thickens into a ribbon-like fillet when lifted with the whisk. 10. Melt the butter in a measuring cup. Place the bowl of egg yolks on a flat surface that will prevent them from sliding or moving. 11. While stirring vigorously, slowly pour the butter over the eggs. The sauce should thicken as more butter is added to the yolks. 12. Season with lemon juice and S&P. 13. Benedict Assembly. 14. Fill a saucepot 4" up the side with water and bring to a boil. Add vinegar and salt if desired and poach the 8 eggs. 15. Toast the English muffins in the toaster and build the benedicts. 16. Top the benedicts with hollandaise and a sprinkle of Maple Chipotle. Enjoy!
Suggested Wood Pellet Flavor: Apple pellets.
Serving Suggestion: Serve pulled pork eggs benedict with salad.
Variation Tip: Use beef or lamb.
Nutritional Information per Serving: Calories 1085| Fat 87g |Sodium 1513mg | Carbs 38g | Fiber 2.6g | Sugar 13.6g | Protein 42.7g

Teriyaki BBQ Pork Pineapple Skewers

Prep Time: 3 hours | Cook Time: 10 minutes | Serves: 2

Ingredients:

1-pound pork sirloin
18 pieces pineapple, fresh
6 scallions

6 wooden skewers
1 cup Carne Asada Marinade, of choice

Preparation:

1. Thread a pork cube, a bit of pineapple, and a piece of green onion through the thin side of a skewer; repeat the cycle, using 3 or 4 pieces of pork per skewer. Rep with the remaining skewers. 2. Pour the marinade over the skewers in a glass pan or pie plate, rotating them to cover both sides. Refrigerate for 1 to 3 hours after wrapping in plastic wrap. 3. When ready to cook, set temperature to High and preheat Pit Boss Wood Pellet Grill, lid closed for 15 minutes. 4. Drain and discard the marinade from the skewers. Place the skewers on the grill grate and cook for 10 minutes, or until the pork is cooked through, flipping once. Transfer the skewers to a platter and serve right away with some steamed rice. Enjoy!
Suggested Wood Pellet Flavour: Use Hickory Pellets.
Serving Suggestion: Serve the Sticky teriyaki BBQ Pork & pineapple skewers.
Variation Tip: Use boneless pork loin roast.
Nutritional Information per Serving: Calories 567 | Fat 21.1g | Sodium 252mg | Carbs 47.6g | Fiber 6.3g | Sugar 34.1g | Protein 49.3g

Flavorful Pulled Pork Mac and Cheese

Prep Time: 20 minutes | Cook Time: 30 minutes | Serves: 6

Ingredients:

1 tablespoon vegetable oil
1-pound Elbow macaroni or Cavatappi noodles
4 cups milk
8 tablespoons butter, divided
½ cup flour
4 cups grated Gruyere cheese
2 cups grated extra-sharp Cheddar cheese

½ tablespoon salt
½ teaspoon freshly ground black pepper
½ teaspoon ground nutmeg
2 cups pulled pork
1½ cup fresh white breadcrumbs
Pit Boss Texas Smoky and Spicy BBQ Sauce, for serving

Preparation:

1. When ready to cook, set Pit Boss Wood Pellet Grill temperature to 375°F and preheat, lid closed for 15 minutes. 2. Pour the oil into a big pot of salted boiling water. Add the noodles and cook according to the package guidelines. Drain thoroughly. 3. In the meantime, heat the milk in a small saucepan, do not boil it. 4. Melt 6 tablespoons butter in a separate big 4 quart pot and add flour. Cook, stirring constantly, for 2 minutes over low heat. Add the heated milk while whisking and cook for another 1-2 minutes, until thickened and smooth. 5. Remove the pot from the heat and stir in the Gruyere, Cheddar, salt, pepper, and nutmeg. Stir in the cooked noodles and any remaining pulled pork. 6. Fill a 3-quart baking dish or a pan halfway with the ingredients. Melt the remaining 2 tablespoons of butter and mix with the new breadcrumbs before sprinkling on top. 7. Bake on the Pit Boss Wood Pellet Grill for 30 to 35 minutes, or until the sauce is bubbly and the breadcrumbs are browned on the top. Serve warm with an extra sprinkle of cheese and barbecue sauce. Enjoy!

Suggested Wood Pellet Flavour: Use Pecan Pellets.
Serving Suggestion: Serve the Pulled Pork Mac & cheese with Roasted Broccoli.
Variation Tip: Use canned or fresh jackfruit.
Nutritional Information per Serving: Calories 1163 | Fat 62.7g | Sodium 1519mg | Carbs 93g | Fiber 4g | Sugar 12.6g | Protein 55.2g

Cheesy Pulled Pork Stuffed Avocado

Prep Time:15 minutes | Cook Time: 30 minutes | Serves: 8

Ingredients:

6 whole avocados
3 cups pulled pork
1½ cup Monterey Jack cheese, shredded

1 cup salsa, tomato
¼ cup cilantro, finely chopped
8 whole eggs

Preparation:

1. When ready to cook, set the Pit Boss Wood Pellet Grill to 375°F and preheat, lid closed, for 10 to 15 minutes. 2. Remove the pits from the avocados, removing some avocado from the center if needed. 3. In a bowl, mix together pork, cheese, salsa and cilantro. Place pork mixture on top of avocados and place in grill. Cook for 25 minutes. 4. Take a spoon and make a divot or nest for the quail egg. Carefully crack the quail egg into the nest and cook for an additional 5 to 8 minutes or until the egg reaches desired doneness. 5. Remove from the grill and serve. Enjoy!

Suggested Wood Pellet Flavour: Use Pecan Pellets.
Serving Suggestion: Serve the Smoked Stuffed Avocado with salad.
Variation Tip: Use Edam Cheese.
Nutritional Information per Serving: Calories 432 | Fat 35.7g | Sodium 487mg | Carbs 14.3g | Fiber 9.6g | Sugar 2.6g | Protein 19.7g

Maple BBQ Pork Tenderloin

Prep Time: 5 minutes | Cook Time: 50 minutes | Serves: 4

Ingredients:

2 pounds pork tenderloin
3 ounces Pit Boss 14.75 Chop House Steak

1 cup Pit Boss Kansas City Maple and Molasses BBQ Sauce

Preparation:

1. Trim the pork tenderloin of any excess fat and silver skin. Allow 30 minutes for the pork tenderloin to rest after being seasoned with Chop House Steak. 2. Preheat the grill. When ready to cook, start the Pit Boss Wood Pellet Grill on Smoke setting. Once it reaches temperature, put the pork tenderloins on the grate and smoke for 45 minutes. 3. Remove the tenderloins from the grill and warm on high for 15 minutes with the lid closed. 4. Once the Pit Boss Wood Pellet Grill reaches High temperature, grill each side of the pork tenderloin for 90 seconds or until it reaches an internal temperature of 145°F. 5. Before pulling off the grill, brush meat with Pit Boss Kansas City Maple and Molasses BBQ Sauce. Let rest in a pan or on a cutting board for 20 minutes before serving. Enjoy!

Suggested Wood Pellet Flavour: Use Cherry Pellets.
Serving Suggestion: Serve the Apricot Pork Tenderloin with salad.
Variation Tip: Use Beef tenderloin.
Nutritional Information per Serving: Calories 194 | Fat 5.7g | Sodium 519mg | Carbs 8.3g | Fiber 1.6g | Sugar 2.6g | Protein 26.7g

BBQ Sweet and Smoky Pork Ribs

Prep Time: 4 hours | Cook Time: 5 hours | Serves: 6

Ingredients:

2 rack pork spare ribs
6 cups apple juice
2 tablespoons Pit Boss 11.5 ounces Homestyle

Pork Rub
2 cups Pit Boss Sweet Heat BBQ Sauce
¼ cup brown sugar

Preparation:

1. Remove the thin papery membrane off the bone-side of the ribs if your butcher hasn't already done so by pushing the tip of a butter knife underneath the membrane over a middle bone. To gain a strong hold, use paper towels, then peel the membrane away. 2. In a baking dish, arrange the ribs. Pour the apple juice over the ribs, using as much as is necessary to completely soak the meaty side. Coat on the other side. 3. Cover and refrigerate ribs for 4 to 6 hours or overnight. Remove the ribs from the apple juice; reserve juice. 4. Sprinkle ribs on all sides with Homestyle Pork Rub. 5. When ready to cook, set the Pit Boss Wood Pellet Grill to 225° F and preheat, lid closed for 15 minutes. 6. Transfer the apple juice to a saucepan and place in a corner of the grill, the juice will keep the cooking environment moist. 7. Arrange the ribs bone side down, directly on the grill grate. Cook for 4 to 5 hours, or until a skewer or paring knife inserted between the bones goes in easily. 8. Check the internal temperature of the ribs, the desired temperature is 202°F. If not at temperature, cook for an additional 30 minutes or until temperature is reached. 9. In a small saucepan, combine the BBQ sauce and brown sugar. During the last hour of cooking, generously coat the ribs on both sides with the BBQ sauce. 10. Cut the slabs into separate ribs with a sharp knife. Serve. Enjoy!

Suggested Wood Pellet Flavour: Use Hickory Pellets.
Serving Suggestion: Serve the BBQ Sweet and Smoky Ribs.
Variation Tip: Use Ribeye or New York strip steaks.
Nutritional Information per Serving: Calories 222 | Fat 5.3g | Sodium 326mg | Carbs 37.3g | Fiber 0.5g | Sugar 31.6g | Protein 6.7g

Grilled Lemony Pork Tenderloin

Prep Time: 20 minutes | Cook Time: 20 minutes | Serves: 4

Ingredients:

2 lemons, zested
1 clove garlic, minced
1 teaspoon freshly minced parsley
1 teaspoon lemon juice

¼ teaspoon black pepper
½ teaspoon Kosher salt
2 tablespoons olive oil
1 (2 pounds) pork tenderloin

Preparation:

1. Everything but the tenderloin should be whisked together in a small basin. 2. Trim the tenderloin of any silver skin or extra fat. 3. Pork should be placed in a big resalable bag. Zip the tenderloin shut after pouring the marinade over it. Refrigerate for at least 2 hours but no more than 8 hours. 4. When ready to cook, set Pit Boss Wood Pellet Grill temperature to 375°F and preheat, lid closed for 15 minutes. 5. Take the tenderloin out of the bag and throw away the marinade. 6. When the grill is hot, set the tenderloin directly on the grate and cook for 15 to 20 minutes, flipping halfway through, until the internal temperature reaches 145°F. 7. Remove from the heat and let rest 5 to 10 minutes before slicing. Enjoy!

Suggested Wood Pellet Flavour: Use Apple Pellets.
Serving Suggestion: Serve the Grilled Lemon Pepper Pork Tenderloin.
Variation Tip: Use lime.
Nutritional Information per Serving: Calories 789 | Fat 30.1g | Sodium 842mg | Carbs 6.2g | Fiber 1.8g | Sugar 1.6g | Protein 119.7g

Smoked Bacon Cheese Log

Prep Time: 10 minutes | Cook Time: 60 minutes | Serves: 8

Ingredients:

16 ounces cream cheese
3 cup shredded Cheddar cheese
1 tablespoon Worcestershire sauce
1 teaspoon hot sauce

8 slices bacon
2 green onions
1 cup coarsely chopped pecans

Preparation:

1. Combine the cream cheese (room temperature) and the Cheddar cheese in a mixing bowl with an electric mixer or a large spoon. 2. Combine the Worcestershire sauce and spicy sauce in a mixing bowl. Recombine the ingredients. 3. Cook the bacon until it's crumbled, then add the chopped green onions. Mix until everything is well blended. 4. Refrigerate for 4 hours, or until the cheese mixture is stiff enough to mould, after covering the bowl with plastic wrap. Form it into a log and sprinkle the toasted pecans on top. 5. Wrap the dish in plastic wrap. To keep the cheese log from becoming too soft while it's smoking, freeze it overnight. 6. The next day set Pit Boss Wood Pellet Grill to 180°F and preheat for 10-15 minutes. 7. Take the cheese log out of the freezer and unwrap. Place on a cooking sheet and smoke for 1 hour. Keep an eye on it to make sure it doesn't get too soft. 8. Move the cheese log to a serving tray and serve with your favourite crackers. (If the cheese is too soft, throw it in the fridge for an hour or two.)

Suggested Wood Pellet Flavour: Use Pecan Pellets.
Serving Suggestion: Serve the Holiday Smoked Cheese Log with salad.
Variation Tip: Use walnut.
Nutritional Information per Serving: Calories 487 | Fat 43g | Sodium 907mg | Carbs 3.2g | Fiber 0.3g | Sugar 0.9g | Protein 22.1g

Chapter 3 Lamb Recipes

Herb–Mustard Grilled Rack of Lamb

Prep Time:25 minutes | Cook Time: 30 minutes | Servings: 8

Ingredients:

2 tbsps. Dijon Mustard
4 tbsps. Pit Boss Chop House Steak Rub
2 racks of lamb, chine bones removed, and

excess fat trimmed
1 tsp. rosemary, finely chopped
1 tbsp. fresh parsley, chopped

Preparation:

1. Arrange the racks of lamb on a level work surface and thoroughly smear them with Dijon Mustard all over. 2. Season the meat with Pit Boss Chop House Steak Spice and parsley and rosemary on all sides. Preheat your Pit Boss Wood Pellet Grill to 400°F. 3. If using a gas or charcoal grill, make sure it's set to HIGH heat. 4. Insert a temperature probe into the thickest portion of the rack of lamb and sear it for about 6 minutes, meaty side down. 5. Remove the lamb from the Pit Boss Wood Pellet Grill and reduce the heat to 300°F. 6. Move the lamb to the Pit Boss Wood Pellet Grill, leaning the two racks against each other to stand upright. Cook for another 20 minutes until the 130°F temperature is internally reached. 7. Take the racks from the Pit Boss Wood Pellet Grill and let rest for 10 minutes before cutting and serving.

Serving Suggestions: Top with fresh coriander leaves.
Variation Tip: Consider using a cast iron skillet on your BBQ for a fantastic sear that will result in the fluids being infused back into the meat's crust.
Nutritional Information per Serving: Calories: 43 | Fat: 1.7g | Sat Fat: 0.6g | Carbohydrates: 0.3g | Fiber: 0.2g | Sugar: 0g | Protein: 6.2g

Citrus Grilled Lamb Chops

Prep Time:1 hour | Cook Time: 15 minutes | Servings: 6

Ingredients:

2-pound rib chops or lamb loin, thick cut
2 tbsps. chophouse steak seasoning
Juice from ½ lime
4 garlic cloves, finely minced

¼ cup olive oil
3 tbsps. orange juice
Juice from ½ lemon
¼ cup red wine vinegar

Preparation:

1. In a big bowl, combine all of the ingredients, including 2 tablespoons Chophouse Steak. In a glass baking pan, place the lamb chops and pour the marinade over them. Toss the chops a few times to ensure proper coating. 2. Cover the glass pan with aluminum foil and marinate the lamb chops for 12 hours. Drain and discard the extra marinade once the meat has finished marinating. 3. Preheat your Pit Boss Wood Pellet Grill to 400°F. Set the Pit Boss Wood Pellet Grill to MEDIUM-HIGH heat if you're using a charcoal or gas grill. Grill the chops for 7 minutes each side on one side, then flip and cook for another 7 minutes on the other side at 350°F or MEDIUM heat. 4. Take the lamb chops from the Pit Boss Wood Pellet Grill, cover with foil, and set aside for 5 minutes before serving.

Serving Suggestions: Serve with the topping of sliced lemons and limes.
Variation Tip: Fill your hopper with Fruitwood Hardwood Pellets for a sweet and tangy flavor.
Nutritional Information per Serving: Calories: 434 | Fat: 26.3g | Sat Fat: 7.7g | Carbohydrates: 5.4g | Fiber: 0.3g | Sugar: 2.8g | Protein: 42.7g

Herbed Chipotle Lamb

Prep Time:30 minutes | Cook Time: 2 hours | Servings: 6

Ingredients:

¾ cup olive oil, extra-virgin
¼ cup Pit Boss Applewood Bacon Rub
Black pepper, to taste
2 tbsps. Italian parsley
2 tbsps. sage, fresh

3 garlic cloves
2 tbsps. rosemary, fresh
1 tbsp. chipotle peppers, crushed
1 rack lamb ribs
2 tbsps. thyme, fresh sprigs

Preparation:

1. For the Dry Rub: Brush olive oil on the lamb ribs and season with black pepper and chipotle powder. Refrigerate the lamb ribs for at least 15 minutes before serving. 2. Preheat your Pit Boss Wood Pellet Grill to 275°F. 3. For the Wet Rub: Blend cilantro, rosemary, Italian parsley, thyme, sage, and oregano in a bowl with Pit Boss Smoke Infused Applewood Bacon, garlic cloves, and ¼ cup olive oil. 4. Brush the moist rub all over the ribs of lamb. 5. Place your bone-in lamb ribs on the Pit Boss Wood Pellet Grill and smoke them until they reach an internal temperature of 120-125°F. 6. Preheat your Pit Boss Wood Pellet Grill to 425°F and sear until the internal temperature reaches 135-145°F. 7. Carve it up after 15 minutes and enjoy it!

Serving Suggestions: Serve with roasted broccoli.
Variation Tip: Set your smoke temp for 225°F for smokier flavor.
Nutritional Information per Serving: Calories: 227 | Fat: 25.6g | Sat Fat: 3.8g | Carbohydrates: 2.3g | Fiber: 1.2g | Sugar: 0.1g | Protein: 0.3g

Herbed Leg of Lamb Roast

Prep Time:1 hour 10 minutes | Cook Time: 4 hours 30 minutes | Servings: 4

Ingredients:

1 tsp. black pepper
1 tsp. coriander, ground
⅓ cup beef stock
2 tsps. brown sugar
1 tbsp. Dijon Mustard
4 garlic cloves, chopped
1 lemon, juice
½ red onion, chopped (for marinade)
¼ cup red wine

1½ tbsps. sage leaves, chopped
2 tsps. salt
2 tsps. Worcestershire sauce
2 tbsps. fresh mint leaves, chopped
2 leg of lamb roasts, bone-in (2 lbs. each)
½ cup olive oil
1 red onion, sliced
1½ tbsps. rosemary leaves
Rosemary sprigs, to taste

Thyme sprigs, to taste

Preparation:

1. Dry the lamb legs with a paper towel before placing them in a resealable plastic bag. 2. Combine beef stock, olive oil, red wine, mint, lemon, rosemary, red onion, sage, Dijon, garlic, brown sugar, Worcestershire sauce, coriander, salt, and pepper in the bowl of a food processor. After 1 minute of processing, pour the marinade over the lamb. Refrigerate for 4 hours after sealing the bag. 3. Eliminate the lamb 30 minutes from the refrigerator before roasting. 4. Preheat your Pit Boss Wood Pellet Grill to 375°F by turning it on SMOKE mode and running it for 10 minutes with the lid open. Set the Pit Boss Wood Pellet Grill to MEDIUM-HIGH heat if using a charcoal or gas grill. 5. In a cast iron skillet, combine the sliced red onion, rosemary, and thyme sprigs, then place the lamb on top. Add 1 cup of water to the skillet. 6. Cook for 55 to 70 minutes on the Pit Boss Wood Pellet Grill, or until an internal temperature of 135°F to 140°F is obtained. 7. Eliminate the lamb from the pan and set it aside to rest for 15 minutes on a cutting board. Slice and serve it warm.

Serving Suggestions: Serve alongside the potato wedges.

Variation Tip: You can also substitute boneless lamb roast.

Nutritional Information per Serving: Calories: 497 | Fat: 34.5g | Sat Fat: 7g | Carbohydrates: 11.8g | Fiber: 4.4g | Sugar: 3.1g | Protein: 35.1g

Korean BBQ Lamb Short Ribs

Prep Time:1 hour | Cook Time: 4 hours | Servings: 4

Ingredients:

2 tbsps. brown sugar
½ cup soy sauce
1 tbsp. beef & brisket rub
1 tbsp. ginger, minced
1 tsp. sesame seeds, toasted

3 garlic cloves, peeled
1 tbsp. Sriracha sauce
1 cup beef broth
4 meaty lamb short ribs

Preparation:

1. If the lamb short ribs haven't been cleaned yet, remove the silvery membrane on the back with a paper towel and discard. 2. Blend soy sauce, beef broth, brown sugar, garlic, sesame, ginger, Sriracha, and Beef & Brisket Rub in a medium mixing bowl. Set aside after thoroughly mixing. 3. Place the lamb short ribs in a baking tray and pour the marinade over them. Cover and store the marinade in the refrigerator for 12 hours. 4. Preheat your Pit Boss Wood Pellet Grill to 250°F. Fire the Pit Boss Wood Pellet Grill to MEDIUM heat if you're using a gas or charcoal grill. Place the short ribs on the Pit Boss Wood Pellet Grill after removing them from the marinade. 5. Grill for 4 hours, brushing residual marinade liquid over the short ribs every now and then, until the flesh starts to pull away from the bone. 6. Remove the Pit Boss Wood Pellet Grill from the heat and set aside for 15 minutes.

Serving Suggestions: Serve with rice and kimchi.

Variation Tip: Open the Flame Broiler Plate and finish them at 450°F for 3 minutes for a well seared crust.

Nutritional Information per Serving: Calories: 53 | Fat: 0.8g | Sat Fat: 0.2g | Carbohydrates: 8.2g | Fiber: 0.5g | Sugar: 5.1g | Protein: 3.5g

Grilled Lemony Lamb Skirt Steak

Prep Time:45 minutes | Cook Time: 5 minutes | Servings: 2

Ingredients:

2 tbsps. mustard, grainy
2 garlic cloves, chopped
2 tbsps. Pit Boss Java Chophouse Seasoning
1 lemon, juice

2-pound lamb skirt steak, trimmed
1 tbsp. Worcestershire Sauce
¼ cup olive oil

Preparation:

1. Blend the Pit Boss Java Chophouse Seasoning, garlic, olive oil, Worcestershire, and lemon juice in a small bowl. Allow the skirt steak to marinade for 45 minutes after rubbing the mixture all over it. 2. Set your Pit Boss Wood Pellet Grill to SMOKE mode. Set the temperature to 400°F once it's started. 3. Grill the skirt steaks for 3-5 minutes per side or until the desired degree of doneness is reached. 4. Eliminate the steaks from the Pit Boss Wood Pellet Grill and set aside for 5 minutes to rest before cutting and serving.

Serving Suggestions: Serve with delicious tomato sauce.

Variation Tip: You can also use flank steaks.

Nutritional Information per Serving: Calories: 1133 | Fat: 61.8g | Sat Fat: 15.7g | Carbohydrates: 9.1g | Fiber: 2.5g | Sugar: 3g | Protein: 130.7g

Cowboy Beans with Lamb Brisket

Prep Time:10 minutes | Cook Time: 3 hours | Servings: 8

Ingredients:

1 (10 oz.) can diced tomatoes with green chilies
1 lb. pinto beans, dried
1 cup BBQ sauce
2 jalapeno peppers, chopped
Water

2 cups lamb brisket, chopped
1 tsp. kosher salt
1 tbsp. Worcestershire sauce
1 yellow onion, chopped
6 garlic cloves, minced
2 tbsps. Pit Boss Home-style Pork Rub

Preparation:

1. Preheat your Pit Boss Wood Pellet Grill to 400°F. Set the Pit Boss Wood Pellet Grill to MEDIUM-HIGH heat if using a charcoal or gas grill. 2. Pour pinto beans into cast iron Dutch oven after carefully rinsing them in a mesh sieve. 3. In a Dutch oven, combine the chopped lamb brisket, water, diced tomatoes, garlic, onion, jalapenos, Pit Boss Home-style Pork Rub, and Worcestershire sauce. Place the saucepan on the preheated Pit Boss Wood Pellet Grill and bring to a boil. 4. Cover the pot and lower the Pit Boss Wood Pellet Grill temperature to 300°F. Cook for 1 hour, stirring regularly, before seasoning with salt. 5. Simmer the beans for another 1½ to 2 hours, or until they are tender. Serve and have fun!
Serving Suggestions: Serve alongside the nachos.
Variation Tip: If you don't have any brisket on hand, then use Pulled Pork or Chuck Roast in this recipe.
Nutritional Information per Serving: Calories: 261 | Fat: 0.9g | Sat Fat: 0.1g | Carbohydrates: 50.7g | Fiber: 9.5g | Sugar: 10.4g | Protein: 12.7g

Bacon Wrapped Lamb Chops with Potatoes & Asparagus

Prep Time:5 minutes | Cook Time: 1 hour | Servings: 2

Ingredients:

1 bunch asparagus
1 bag baby potatoes
2 tbsps. olive oil

4 bacon strips
2 lamb chops

Preparation:

1. Preheat your Pit Boss Wood Pellet Grill on SMOKE, with the lid open, until a fire in the burn pot is started. Preheat the oven to 250°F. 2. Wrap two pieces of bacon around each lamb chop. Place on the grates of your preheated Pit Boss Wood Pellet Grill. Cook the chops for 45 minutes. 3. In a cast iron pan drizzled with olive oil, grill the lamb chops with the baby potatoes. 4. Remove the lamb chops from the Pit Boss Wood Pellet Grill and set aside for 15 minutes to rest. 5. Meanwhile, keep your potatoes on the Pit Boss Wood Pellet Grill by opening your Flame Broiler Plate and turning the burner to HIGH. 6. Position the asparagus on top of the potatoes and boil until tender. Sear each side of the steak for roughly 1 minute each when the Pit Boss Wood Pellet Grill is preheated to HIGH.
Serving Suggestions: Serve with BBQ Sauce.
Variation Tip: For a crispier char, substitute oil with butter.
Nutritional Information per Serving: Calories: 503 | Fat: 38.3g | Sat Fat: 10.3g | Carbohydrates: 5g | Fiber: 1.9g | Sugar: 1.3g | Protein: 33.8g

Sweet Mustard Lamb Ribs

Prep Time:30 minutes | Cook Time: 3 hours 30 minutes | Servings: 4

Ingredients:

2 cups brown sugar
1 cup apple juice
4 tbsps. Pit Boss Sweet Rib Rub

24 oz. Dijon mustard
2 racks lamb rib

Preparation:

1. Preheat your Pit Boss Wood Pellet Grill for 10 minutes at 275°F. 2. Arrange the ribs on the Pit Boss Wood Pellet Grill, back side down.
Every 30 minutes, give the ribs a good spray with apple juice. 3. Ribs are done when the meat begins to break away from the bone and the rib folds over and becomes limp. 4. Place ribs in a pan after removing them from the Pit Boss Wood Pellet Grill. 5. In a mixing dish, pour Dijon Mustard. Brown sugar should be added gradually until the mustard flavor fades and a sweet flavor emerges. 6.Paint a light coat of the sassy glaze on both sides of the ribs. 7. Wrap the ribs in foil and place them in the refrigerator for 15 minutes.
Serving Suggestions: Cut ribs and serve as single bones.
Variation Tip: If you are doing multiple slabs, you can use a rib rack.
Nutritional Information per Serving: Calories: 698 | Fat: 22.7g | Sat Fat: 8.1g | Carbohydrates: 78.1g | Fiber: 0.1g | Sugar: 76.3g | Protein: 44.6g

Garlic–Mustard Crusted Leg of Lamb

Prep Time:15 minutes | Cook Time: 3 hours | Servings: 8

Ingredients:

3 tbsps. Pit Boss Smoked Salt & Pepper Rub
4 leg of lamb roasts, bone-in

2 tbsps. garlic, crushed
1 cup mustard, whole grain

Preparation:

1. Preheat your Pit Boss Wood Pellet Grill to 450°F. 2. In a mixing dish, blend the mustard, garlic, and Smoked Salt & Pepper. Rub the seasoning all over the roast, evenly coating the entire surface. 3. After the Pit Boss Wood Pellet Grill has been prepared, lay the roast on the grates, ribs facing the back of the Pit Boss Wood Pellet Grill. Close the Pit Boss Wood Pellet Grill lid after you've placed the roast on it. 4. Reduce the Pit Boss Wood Pellet Grill temperature to 325°F after 45 minutes. Cook for another 2.5 hours, or until the inner temperature has reached 125°F. 5. Eliminate the roast from the oven and let it rest for about 15 minutes.

Serving Suggestions: Serve with mint sauce.
Variation Tip: You can also make it with prime rib roast.
Nutritional Information per Serving: Calories: 310 | Fat: 13.6g | Sat Fat: 3.1g | Carbohydrates: 7.6g | Fiber: 3g | Sugar: 1.4g | Protein: 38.6g

Grilled Lamb & Apricots Kabobs

Prep Time: 15 minutes | Cook Time: 10 minutes | Serves: 4

Ingredients:

½ cup olive oil
½ tbsp salt
2 tsp black pepper
2 tbsp fresh mint
½ tbsp cilantro, finely chopped
3-pound boneless Leg of Lamb, cut into 2-inch

cubes
1 tsp cumin
½ cup lemon juice
1 tbsp lemon zest
15 whole apricots, dried
2 whole red onions, cut into eighths

Preparation:

1. In a medium bowl, combine olive oil, salt, pepper, lemon juice, zest, cumin, mint and cilantro and mix well. Add the shoulder of lamb and throw it in the coat. 2. Put in the refrigerator and let marinate overnight. 3. Remove the lamb from the marinade and thread the lamb, apricot and red onion alternately until the skewer is full. 4. When ready to cook, set the temperature to 375 degrees F and preheat, lid closed for 10-15 minutes. 5. Place the skewers directly on the grill and cook for 8 to 10 minutes or until the onions are lightly browned and the lamb is cooked to the desired temperature. 6. Remove from the grill and serve.

Suggested Wood Pellet Flavor: Mesquite pellets.
Serving Suggestion: Serve grilled lamb kabobs with coconut rice.
Variation Tip: Use chicken.
Nutritional Information per Serving: Calories 405| Fat 32.7g |Sodium 913mg | Carbs 6.3g | Fiber 1.6g | Sugar 3.6g | Protein 23.7g

Smoked Mustard Rack of Lamb

Prep Time: 15 minutes | Cook Time: 20 minutes | Serves: 4

Ingredients:

1 rack (1½ lb) lamb, frenched
½ cup yellow mustard
1 tbsp salt
1 tsp ground black pepper

1 cup panko breadcrumbs
1 tbsp minced Italian parsley
1 tsp minced sage
1 tsp minced rosemary

Preparation:

1. If your butcher hasn't already done so, cut and trim the lamb. 2. Rub the outside with mustard and season generously with salt and pepper. 3. Combine breadcrumbs and herbs in an ovenproof dish. Drain the lamb in the breadcrumb mixture. 4. Fire up the Pit Boss Pellet Grill on "smoke" mode and let it run with the lid open for 10 minutes, then preheat to 375°F. 5. Place the rack of lamb directly on the grill, bone side down, and cook for 20 minutes or until the internal temperature reaches 120°F. 6. Remove from the grill and let it stand for 5 to 10 minutes before slicing. Enjoy!

Suggested Wood Pellet Flavor: Hickory pellets.
Serving Suggestion: Serve roasted rack of lamb with fried rice.
Variation Tip: Use pork.
Nutritional Information per Serving: Calories 285| Fat 11.7g |Sodium 1113mg | Carbs 19.3g | Fiber 3.6g | Sugar 0.6g | Protein 26.7g

Grilled Garlic–Rosemary Rack of Lamb

Prep Time: 10 minutes | Cook Time: 30 minutes | Serves: 6

Ingredients:

2 racks of lamb, drenched
1 tablespoon minced garlic cloves

1 tablespoon finely chopped rosemary
½ cup oil

Preparation:

1. Rinse the rack of lamb with cold water and dry them with a paper towel. 2. Make a ¼-inch cut down between each bone. 3. Mix the remaining ingredients in a bowl and brush the lamb with the paste. 4. Bend each rack of lamb into a semicircle then put them together to form a circle. 5. Tie the rack of lamb tightly with a butcher's twine to form a crown shape. 6. Preheat your Pit Boss Wood Pellet Grill to 450°F. 7. Place the crown rack of lamb on a baking sheet and cook for ten minutes. 8. Reduce the grill temperature to 300°F and cook for 20 minutes. 9. Remove the rack of lamb from the grill and let it rest for 15 minutes. 10. Serve the lamb while hot.

Serving suggestion: Serve the crown rack of lamb with roasted potatoes or veggies

Variation Tip: Use coriander, vinegar, Dijon mustard, and thyme
Nutrition-Per Serving: Calories 645 | Fat 44g |Sodium 1511mg | Carbs 1g | Fiber 0.5g | Sugar 0g | Protein 63g

Smoked Herbed Rack of Lamb

Prep Time: 10 minutes | Cook Time: 50 minutes | Serves: 4

Ingredients:

1 rack of lamb
¼ cup oil
2 tablespoons freshly ground rosemary
2 tablespoons freshly ground sage
2 tablespoons shallots, roughly chopped
1 tablespoon freshly ground thyme

2 minced garlic cloves
½ tablespoons salt
½ tablespoons black pepper
1 tablespoon honey
Basil for garnishing

Preparation:

1. Remove the silver skin from the rack of lamb and trim off excess fat. 2. Mix the remaining ingredients in a bowl and apply the paste to the lamb. 3. Place the lamb in a plastic wrapper and refrigerate for 24 hours. 4. Remove the lamb from the refrigerator 1 hour before cooking. 5. Preheat your Pit Boss Wood Pellet Grill to 180°F. 6. Place the lamb on the grill and smoke for 1 hour. 7. Remove the lamb from the grill grate and increase the grill temperature to 500°F. Sear the lamb for 2 minutes on each side. 8. Let the rack of lamb rest for 10 minutes then slice into chops. 9. Garnish the lamb with basil and serve.

Serving suggestion: Serve lamb chops with root vegetable puree.
Variation Tip: use the combination of your favourite herbs.
Nutrition-Per Serving: Calories 613 | Fat 56g |Sodium 362mg | Carbs 7g | Fiber 1g | Sugar 5g | Protein 19g

Smoked Garlicky Leg of Lamb

Prep Time: 15 minutes | Cook Time: 4 hours | Serves: 6

Ingredients:

2 pounds leg of lamb
4 minced garlic cloves
2 tablespoons salt
1 tablespoon black pepper

2 tablespoons oregano
1 tablespoon thyme
2 tablespoons oil
Rosemary

Preparation:

1. Clean the leg of the lamb. 2. Trim off excess fat from the leg of lamb. 3. Mix the remaining ingredients in a bowl and rub the paste over the lamb. 4. Wrap the lamb with a plastic wrapper and marinate for 1 hour. 5. Preheat your Pit Boss Wood Pellet Grill to 250°F. 6. Place the lamb on the grill and cook it for 4 hours. 7. Remove the leg from the grill and slice. 8. Garnish the lamb with rosemary and serve.

Serving suggestion: serve the leg of lamb with sautéed zucchini and squash.
Variation Tip: Use fresh herbs and lemon juice.
Nutrition-Per Serving: Calories 356 | Fat 16g |Sodium 2474mg | Carbs 3g | Fiber 1g | Sugar 1g | Protein 49g

Red Wine–Marinated Lamb Roast

Ingredients:

⅓ cup beef stock
1 tsp black pepper
2 tsp brown sugar
1 tsp coriander, ground
1 tbsp Dijon mustard
2 tbsp fresh mint leaves, chopped
4 garlic cloves, chopped
2 legs of lamb roasts, bone-in (2 lbs. each)
1 lemon, juice

½ cup olive oil
½ red onion, chopped (for marinade)
1 red onion, sliced
¼ cup red wine
1½ tbsp rosemary leaves
1½ tbsp sage leaves, chopped
To taste, rosemary sprigs
2 tsp salt
To taste, thyme sprigs

2 tsp Worcestershire sauce

Preparation:

1. Pat the legs of the lamb dry with a paper towel, then place them in a resalable plastic bag. 2. In the bowl of a food processor, combine the olive oil, beef broth, red wine, lemon, mint, rosemary, sage, red onion, garlic, Dijon, Worcestershire sauce, brown sugar, salt, pepper and cilantro. 3. Mix for 1 minute, then pour the marinade over the lamb. Close the bag and refrigerate for 4 hours. 4. Take the lamb out of the refrigerator 30 minutes before grilling it. 5. Put your Pit Boss Pellet Grill on "smoke" mode and let it run for 10 minutes with the lid open, then preheat it to 375°F. 6. Put the red onion sprigs, rosemary and sliced thyme in a cast iron pan [preferably rectangular], then place the lamb on top. Add 1 cup of water to the pot. 7. Grill for 55 to 70 minutes until an internal temperature of 135 to 140°F is reached. 8. Remove the lamb and let it sit on a cutting board for 15 minutes, then cut the lamb into slices and serve hot.

Suggested Wood Pellet Flavor: Fruitwood Blend Hardwood Pellets.
Serving Suggestion: Serve lamb roast with potato salad.
Variation Tip: Use pork.
Nutritional Information per Serving: Calories 475| Fat 33.7g |Sodium 1313mg | Carbs 9.3g | Fiber 2.6g | Sugar 3.6g | Protein 34.7g

Lamb Chops with Rosemary Sauce

Ingredients:

½ cup extra-virgin olive oil
¼ cup coarsely chopped onion or shallot
2 cloves garlic, coarsely chopped
2 tbsp soy sauce
2 tbsp balsamic or sherry vinegar
1 tbsp fresh rosemary

2 tsp Dijon mustard
1 tsp Worcestershire sauce
Freshly ground black pepper
4 (8 oz.) lamb chops
Salt and pepper

Preparation:

1. In a small saucepan, sauté the onion and garlic in 1 tablespoon of olive oil over medium heat until softened and translucent. Do not let brown. 2. Transfer to a blender. Add the soy sauce, vinegar, rosemary, mustard and Worcestershire sauce, blend. 3. Season to taste with black pepper. Slowly drizzle in the remaining olive oil while the machine is running until the sauce is emulsified. 4. Add one tablespoon of water if the sauce is too thick. Set aside. 5. When ready to cook, set the Pit Boss temperature to 500°F and preheat, lid closed for 15 minutes. 6. Brush the lamb chops on both sides with olive oil and season generously with salt and pepper. 7. Grill until lamb chops reach an internal temperature of 135°F for medium-rare, about 4 to 6 minutes per side. 8. Serve with the rosemary sauce for dipping. Enjoy!

Suggested Wood Pellet Flavor: Apple pellets.
Serving Suggestion: Serve with fried rice.
Variation Tip: Use chicken.
Nutritional Information per Serving: Calories 445| Fat 28.7g |Sodium 443mg | Carbs 3.3g | Fiber 0.4g | Sugar 0.6g | Protein 43g

Grilled Lamb Meatballs

Ingredients:

1-pound lamb shoulder, ground
¼ cup panko breadcrumbs
3 tablespoons diced shallot
3 garlic cloves, finely diced
1 egg
1 tablespoon salt

½ tablespoons black pepper
½ tablespoons cumin
½ tablespoons smoked paprika
¼ tablespoons red pepper flakes
¼ tablespoons ground cinnamon

Preparation:

1. Preheat your Pit Boss Wood Pellet Grill to 250°F. 2. In a bowl mix all the ingredients until well combined. 3. Scoop 1 spoonful of the lamb mixture and knead into the form of balls. Place the meatballs on a baking sheet. 4. Place the baking sheet on the grill and cook for 1 hour. 5. Remove the meatballs from the grill and serve immediately.

Serving suggestion: Serve the meatballs with lettuce and sauce in pita bread or alongside pasta.
Variation Tip: use the combination of your favourite coriander.
Nutrition-Per Serving: Calories 385 | Fat 20g |Sodium 1660mg | Carbs 4g | Fiber 1g | Sugar 1g | Protein 37g

Grilled Citrus Lamb Chops

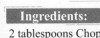

Prep Time:45 minutes | Cook Time:60 minutes | Serves: 6

Ingredients:

2 tablespoons Chophouse Steak Seasoning
2 pounds thick cut rib chops or lamb loin
Juice from ½ lime
3 tablespoons orange juice

4 finely garlic clove, minced
Juice from ½ lemon
¼ cup olive oil
¼ cup red wine vinegar

Directions:

1. In a mixing bowl, combine all of the ingredients, including 2 tablespoons Chophouse Steak. Then, place the lamb chops in a glass baking dish and drizzle with the marinade. To ensure that the chops are completely coated, flip them over a few times. 2. Cover the glass pan with aluminum foil and marinate the lamb chops for 4-12 hours. Drain and discard the excess marinade once the meat has finished marinating. 3. Preheat your Pit Boss Wood Pellet Grill to 400°F and start cooking. Set your grill to medium high heat if you're using a gas or charcoal grill. Grill the chops for 5-7 minutes per side, then reduce to 350°F or medium heat and flip for another 5-7 minutes. 4. Remove the lamb chops from the grill and cover with foil for 5 minutes before serving.

Serving suggestion: Serve it with fries and garlic bread.
Variation tip: Add cauliflower with roasted tomatoes and parsley to it.
Nutritional Value (Amount per Serving): Calories 347 | Fat 22.7g | Carbs 3.8g | Sugar 1.14g | Protein 31.5g

Garlicky Lamb Skewers

Prep Time:15 minutes | Cook Time:10 minutes | Serves: 4

Ingredients:

⅓ cup olive oil
1½ tablespoons red wine vinegar
1½ tablespoons freshly squeezed lemon juice
1½ tablespoons chopped fresh oregano
½ teaspoon salt

¼ teaspoon ground black pepper
2 cloves garlic, minced
1½ pounds boneless leg of lamb, trimmed of all fat and cut into 1-inch cubes

Directions:

1. In a mixing bowl, combine the olive oil, lemon juice, red wine vinegar, oregano, garlic, salt, and pepper. Stir in the cubed lamb until it is completely coated with the marinade. Refrigerate for 3 hours, or overnight. 2. Preheat an outdoor Pit Boss Wood Pellet Grill to medium-high heat and brush the grate lightly with oil. 3. Thread the marinated lamb onto skewers, reserving any marinade that remains. Grill the skewers for 10 to 12 minutes, basting with the reserved marinade and turning occasionally to ensure even cooking.

Serving suggestion: Serve it with coconut rice.
Variation tip: Add cucumber and potatoes to it.
Nutritional Value (Amount per Serving): Calories 346 | Fat 29.3g | Carbs 1.4g | Sugar 0.1g | Protein 18.8g

Lemony Butterflied Leg of Lamb

Prep Time: 08 minutes | Cook Time: 40 minutes | Serves: 4

Ingredients:

1 whole lemon, juiced and rinds reserved
¼ cup red wine vinegar
4 cloves garlic, minced
2 ½ tsp rosemary, minced
1 tsp thyme

1 tsp salt
1 tsp ground black pepper
1 cup olive oil
5-pound leg of lamb, butterflied and boneless
1 whole onion, sliced into rings

Preparation:

1. For the marinade: Cut the lemon into quarters and remove the pits. Squeeze the lemon juice into a bowl and save the lemon zest. Add the red wine vinegar, garlic, rosemary, thyme, salt and pepper and stir until the salt crystals are dissolved. Stir in olive oil. 2. Remove all fillets from the lamb and place it in a large resealable plastic bag. Pour the marinade into the bag and add the reserved onion and lemon zest. Massage the bag to distribute the marinade and herbs. Refrigerate for several hours or overnight. 3. Remove the lamb from the marinade and pat it dry with paper towels. Discard the marinade. 4. When ready to cook, arrange the lamb on the grill grate, fat-side down. Grill for 30-40 minutes per side or until the internal temperature reaches 135°F for medium-rare. Let the lamb leg rest for 5 minutes before slicing. 5. To serve, slice thinly across the grain. Enjoy!

Suggested Wood Pellet Flavor: Hickory pellets.
Serving Suggestion: Serve grilled butterflied leg of lamb with salad.
Variation Tip: Use pork or beef.
Nutritional Information per Serving: Calories 745| Fat 42.7g |Sodium 503mg | Carbs 1.3g | Fiber 0.3g | Sugar 0.6g | Protein 79.8g

Roasted Leg of Lamb with Red Wine Jus

Prep Time: 4 hrs | Cook Time: 2 hrs | Serves: 8

Ingredients:

1 (6-8 lb) bone-in leg of lamb
10 cloves garlic, peeled and thinly sliced
3 tbsp chopped rosemary
2 tsp chopped thyme leaves
2 tbsp olive oil
1 tbsp kosher salt

½ tsp freshly ground black pepper
Red Wine Jus
1 cup red wine
1 cup chicken or beef stock
3 tbsp unsalted butter
Salt and pepper

Preparation:

1. Rinse the leg of lamb with water and dry it. Use a sharp kitchen knife to make 20 1-inch slits around the 1-inch-deep leg of lamb. Place a slice of garlic in each slit. 2. Combine the chopped thyme and rosemary with olive oil, salt and pepper. Brush the lamb evenly with the herb oil with your hands. 3. Gently wrap the lamb in plastic wrap, place on a platter and refrigerate for at least 4 hours or overnight. 4. Take the lamb out of the refrigerator an hour before grilling it. Remove the plastic wrap and place the lamb on a roasting pan on a large frying pan. 5. Pour the red wine and broth to the bottom of the pot, being careful not to let the liquid touch the meat. If it is close, use only half the wine and broth. 6. Fire up your Pit Boss Grill on SMOKE mode and let it run with the lid open for 10 minutes, then preheat to 375°F. 7. Place the lamb in its roasting pan directly on the grill grate and roast for 20 minutes. Reduce heat to 350°F and roast for an hour or more, or until the temperature reaches 130°F in the thickest part of the leg. 8. Remove the meat from the grill and loosely tent with foil on a cutting board. Allow it to rest for 15 to 20 minutes. 9. Meanwhile, strain the juices from the pan into a medium saucepan removing any excess fat that has dropped into the pan. 10. Bring the juices to a boil, reduce to a simmer and cook until it can coat the back of a spoon, about 10 minutes. 11. Whisk in the butter and taste, adding more salt and pepper as needed. 12. Carve the lamb and serve with the red wine jus. Enjoy!

Suggested Wood Pellet Flavor: Apple pellets.
Serving Suggestion: Serve roasted leg of lamb with roasted potatoes.
Variation Tip: Use pork.
Nutritional Information per Serving: Calories 345| Fat 22.7g |Sodium 913mg | Carbs 2.3g | Fiber 0.6g | Sugar 0.6g | Protein 24.7g

Grilled Lamb with Ginger–Sugar Glaze

Prep Time: 1hour 15 minutes | Cook Time: 10 minutes | Serves: 4

Ingredients:

¼ cup brown sugar
2 tablespoons ginger, ground
2 tablespoons tarragon, dried
1 tablespoon cinnamon, ground

1 tablespoon garlic powder
½ tablespoons salt
1 tablespoon black pepper
4 lamb chops

Preparation:

1. In a mixing bowl, mix sugar, ginger, tarragon, cinnamon, garlic powder, salt, and pepper to make a rub. 2. Rub the seasoning on the lamb chops then place on a plate, cover, and refrigerate for 1 hour. 3. Preheat the grill to high heat and brush the grill grate with oil. 4. Grill for 5 minutes on each side. Remove the chops from the grill and let cool before serving.

Serving suggestion: Serve the lamb with cooked green peas and potato wedges.
Variation Tip: Use an herb blend of parsley, chives, and tarragon in place of dried tarragon.
Nutrition-Per Serving: Calories 241 | Fat 13g |Sodium 339mg | Carbs 16g | Fiber 1g | Sugar 14g | Protein 15g

Grilled Lemon Leg of Lamb

Prep Time: 30 minutes | Cook Time: 60 minutes | Serves: 8

Ingredients:

1 (7-8 pounds) bone-in leg of lamb
2 teaspoons extra-virgin olive oil
1 tablespoon crushed garlic
4 clove garlic, sliced lengthwise

4 sprig rosemary, cut into 1 inch pieces
2 lemons
Salt
Black pepper

Preparation:

1. Combine olive oil and crushed garlic in a mixing bowl. Rub the lamb leg with the mixture.
2. Make about 2 dozen small, ¾-inch deep perforations in the lamb with a paring knife. Fill the perforations with slivered garlic and rosemary sprigs. 3. Lemons should be zested and juiced, and the zest and juice should be uniformly distributed over the lamb. Season the lamb with salt and pepper before serving. 4. When ready to cook, set Pit Boss Wood Pellet Grill temperature to 500°F and preheat, lid closed for 15 minutes. Place the leg of lamb on the grill and cook for 30 minutes. 5. Reduce the Pit Boss Wood Pellet Grill temperature to 350°F and cook for 60 to 90 minutes, or until the internal temperature reaches 130°F for medium-rare. 6. Allow 15 minutes for the lamb to rest before cutting. Enjoy!

Suggested Wood Pellet Flavour: Use Cherry Pellets.
Serving Suggestion: Serve Roasted Leg of Lamb with salad.
Variation Tip: Use lime.
Nutritional Information per Serving: Calories 940 | Fat 68g | Sodium 249mg | Carbs 3.6g | Fiber 0.7g | Sugar 0.4g | Protein 71.2g

Lamb Burgers with Pickled Onions & Herbed Yoghurt Sauce

Prep Time: 10 minutes | Cook Time: 10 minutes | Serves: 4

Ingredients:

½ red onion, thinly sliced
6 tablespoons lime juice
2 teaspoon Kosher salt
½ teaspoon raw cane sugar
1 cup Greek yogurt
2 tablespoons lemon juice
5 cloves garlic, minced
2 tablespoons finely chopped herbs, such as mint, dill, parsley
1 tablespoon olive oil
½ red onion, finely diced
1-pound ground lamb
8 ounces ground pork

3 tablespoons fresh mint
2 tablespoons package fresh dill, roughly chopped including stems
3 tablespoons parsley, minced
1 ½ teaspoon ground cumin
1 teaspoon ground coriander
½ teaspoon freshly ground black pepper
6 buns
1 tomato, sliced
Seedless cucumber, peeled and cut into ½" Pieces
Butter lettuce

Preparation:

1. Pickle the onions in a small basin with the onion, lime juice, salt, and sugar. Stir to mix, cover, and let aside to soften for about 2 hours at room temperature. Keep it refrigerated until you're ready to use it. 2. To make the yoghurt sauce, combine the yoghurt, lemon juice, garlic, herbs, and ½ teaspoon salt in a small bowl. Season with salt to taste. Cover and chill for up to 2 days, or until ready to serve. 3. To create the lamb burgers, follow these steps: Warm the olive oil in a small skillet over medium heat. Cook, turning regularly, until the onion is softened, about 7 minutes. Allow to cool on a small plate. 4. Combine the lamb, pork, mint, dill, parsley, garlic, cumin, coriander, salt, pepper, and cooled onions in a large mixing bowl. Using your hands, gently combine the ingredients. Make sure the meat isn't overworked. 5. Make 6 equal balls out of the mixture. Form into patties and place on a baking pan lined with parchment paper. If not using right away, cover and chill for up to 8 hours. 6. Set the temperature to High and preheat for 15 minutes with the lid covered when ready to cook. 7. Place the burgers on the Pit Boss Wood Pellet Grill and cook for 2 to 3 minutes on each side for medium-rare, or 5 minutes per side for well done. 8. Before serving, place the burgers on a plate to rest for 5 minutes. 9. Top burgers with a big dollop of herbed yoghurt sauce and some pickled onions on buns. 10. If desired, garnish with lettuce, sliced tomatoes, or cucumbers. Serve right away. Enjoy!

Suggested Wood Pellet Flavour: Use Hickory Pellets.
Serving Suggestion: Serve Grilled Lamb Burger with Pickled Onion with sauce.
Variation Tip: Use ground beef.
Nutritional Information per Serving: Calories 392 | Fat 12.1g | Sodium 1095mg | Carbs 30.2g | Fiber 2.3g | Sugar 6.7g | Protein 39.8g

BBQ Lamb Shoulder with Yogurt Sauce

Prep Time: 20 minutes | Cook Time: 300 minutes | Serves: 4

Ingredients:

¼ tsp caraway seeds
¼ tsp coriander seeds
¼ tsp cumin seeds
2 ounces dried ancho chiles, stemmed and seeded
2 tbsp water
Main
3-pound bone-in lamb shoulder
Yogurt Sauce
½ cup Greek yogurt
¼ cup chopped cilantro

1 tbsp smoked paprika
1 tbsp lemon juice
2 cloves garlic
2 tbsp extra-virgin olive oil
1 tbsp kosher salt
1 tsp dried mint leaves

Naan bread, for serving

1 clove garlic, mashed to a paste
2 tbsp olive oil

Preparation:

1. In a spice grinder, finely grind the caraway, coriander and cumin seeds. 2. In a microwave-safe bowl, cover the ancho chiles with water and microwave on high for 2 minutes. Let it cool slightly, then transfer soft chiles and 2 tbsps of water to a blender. 3. Add the ground spices, paprika, lemon juice, garlic cloves, olive oil, salt and dried mint leaves. Puree the harissa sauce until smooth. 4. Set lamb in a medium roast pan and rub ½ cup of the harissa sauce all over the meat. Let stand at room temperature for at least 2 hours. 5. When ready to cook, set Pit Boss Grill temperature to 325°F and preheat, lid closed for 15 minutes. 6. Add ½ cup of water to the roasting pan and cover the pan loosely with foil. Cook the lamb for 2-½ hours, adding water to the pan a few times. 7. Remove foil and cook for about 2½ hours longer, until the lamb is brown and tender, occasionally spooning pan juices on top. Let it stand for 20 minutes after removing from the Pit Boss. 8. Meanwhile, combine the yogurt with cilantro, mashed garlic clove, and olive oil in a small bowl. 9. Using a fork, pull the lamb off the bone in large chunks. Using your fingers, pull the lamb into smaller shreds and serve with the yogurt sauce, naan bread and the remaining harissa sauce. Enjoy!

Suggested Wood Pellet Flavor: Cherry pellets.
Serving Suggestion: Serve lamb shoulder with salad and bread.
Variation Tip: Use chicken thighs.
Nutritional Information per Serving: Calories 345| Fat 15.7g |Sodium 1003mg | Carbs 1.3g | Fiber 0.6g | Sugar 0.6g | Protein 47g

Pistachio Crusted Roasted Lamb with Carrot & Potatoes

Prep Time: 20 minutes | Cook Time: 40 minutes | Serves: 6

Ingredients:

2 tbsp vegetable oil
2 lamb racks
1 tsp herbs de Provence
Salt
Black pepper
1 bunch tri color carrots, peeled & chopped
1-pound fingerling potatoes
1 tbsp olive oil

½ tsp kosher salt
½ tsp ground black pepper
1 clove garlic, minced
2 tsp thyme, minced
⅔ cup pistachios, chopped
2 tbsp breadcrumbs
1 tbsp butter, melted
3 tbsp Dijon mustard

Preparation:

1. Fire up your grill on "smoke" mode and let it run with the lid open for 10 minutes, then preheat to 375°F. 2. Place a large cast-iron skillet on the grill and add 1 tbsp of vegetable oil. Close the lid and let preheat for 20 minutes. 3. Pat the lamb dry with paper towels and generously season each rack of lamb with Provence herbs, salt and black pepper. 4. Peel the carrots cut them into 1"pieces, and add them to a large mixing bowl. Add the potatoes, olive oil, salt, pepper, garlic and thyme. Stir to combine. 5. Place the lamb in the pan and cook, browning all sides, 6 to 8 minutes. Transfer the lamb to an ovenproof dish, leaving the pan on the grill and set aside. 6. Combine pistachios, breadcrumbs, butter, olive oil and a pinch of salt and black pepper in a bowl. 7. Spread mustard on the fat side of each rack of lamb. Pour the pistachio mixture over the mustard. 8. Place the racks directly on the grill next to the pan. Add the potatoes and seasoned carrots to the pan. Close the lid and cook for 15 minutes. 9. After 15 minutes, open the grill and stir the potatoes and carrots. Loosely cover the rack of lamb with aluminium foil. 10. Continue cooking for another 5 to 10 minutes or until a thermometer inserted diagonally into the thickest part of the meat registers an internal temperature of 125°F. 11. Remove the lamb from the grill with the foil still intact and let it rest for 10 minutes. 12. Check the potatoes with a fork to see if they are tender. Otherwise, let the potatoes and carrots cook for another 5 minutes or until tender. 13. Cut each rack of lamb into 4 double chops and serve with carrots and roasted potatoes. Enjoy!

Suggested Wood Pellet Flavor: Cherry pellets.
Serving Suggestion: Serve pistachio crusted roasted lamb with salad and bread.
Variation Tip: Use turkey.
Nutritional Information per Serving: Calories 365| Fat 18.7g |Sodium 263mg | Carbs 16.3g | Fiber 2.6g | Sugar 1.6g | Protein 34.7g

Garlic–Rosemary Lamb Steaks

Prep Time: 10 minutes | Cook Time: 10 minutes | Serves: 4

Ingredients:

4 lamb steaks
¼ cup oil
4 cloves garlic, minced

1 tablespoon rosemary, freshly chopped
Salt and pepper to taste

Preparation:

1. Place lamb steaks in a shallow dish then cover with oil, garlic, rosemary, salt, and pepper. 2. Coat the steak on all sides with the rub then let sit for 30 minutes. 3. Preheat the Pit Boss Wood Pellet Grill to high heat then lightly oil the grill grates. 4. Cook the steak for 5 minutes on each side or until it has an internal temperature of 140°F

Serving suggestion: Serve the leg of lamb with sautéed broccoli and carrots
Variation Tip: Use roasted garlic powder in place of minced garlic
Nutrition-Per Serving: Calories 327 | Fat 22g |Sodium 112mg | Carbs 2g | Fiber 0.2g | Sugar 0.2g | Protein 30g

Simple Smoked Lamb

Prep Time:10 minutes | Cook Time:480 minutes | Serves: 8

Ingredients:

12-15 pounds lamb

Pit Boss Lamb Rub

Directions:

1. Set your Pit Boss Wood Pellet Grill to Smoke mode, allow the fire to catch, and then preheat your grill to 225°F. 2. While your grill is heating up, season lamb with your favorite rub - whatever floats your boat! Place your lamb on the grill grates, fat side up. Allow it to smoke for 8 to 10 hours, or until the internal temperature reaches 190°F. 3. Wrap in pink butcher paper, followed by a towel. Allow it to sit in the cooler for up to an hour to allow the juices to settle. 4. Serve by slicing against the grain. 5. Enjoy!

Serving suggestion: Serve it with bread.
Variation tip: Add chopped basil or sage to it.
Nutritional Value (Amount per Serving): Calories 1891 | Fat 124g | Carbs 0g | Sugar 0g | Protein 181g

Chapter 4 Chicken & Poultry Recipes

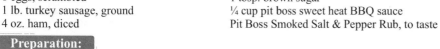

Pulled Chicken with Smoked Queso Dip
Prep Time:1 hour | Cook Time: 10 minutes | Servings: 6

Ingredients:

1 lb. chicken breasts, boneless
1 tsp. cumin, ground
Ale House Beer Can Chicken Seasoning, to taste
1 tbsp. cilantro, chopped

2 jalapeños, chopped
1 bag tortilla chips
1 cup milk
2 tsps. olive oil
1 lb. white American cheese, cubed

Preparation:

1. Preheat your Pit Boss to SMOKE mode and then set to 350°F. Set the Pit Boss Wood Pellet Grill to MEDIUM-HIGH heat if using a charcoal or gas grill. 2. Carve the chicken, then coat it with olive oil and Ale House Beer Can Chicken seasoning. 3. Place the chicken on the Pit Boss Wood Pellet Grill for 8 to 10 minutes, flipping once or twice. 4. Eliminate the chicken from the Pit Boss Wood Pellet Grill and lower the heat to 225°F. Allow 10 minutes for the chicken to rest before pulling apart with two forks. Remove from the equation. 5. Warm up a cast iron skillet on the Pit Boss Wood Pellet Grill while the chicken is resting. Partially open the sear slide, then add the cubed cheese, jalapeno, milk, and cumin to the skillet. 5 minutes, stirring periodically until the cheese melts Close the cover and smoke the dip for up to 45 minutes after folding in the pulled chicken. 6. Eliminate from the heat and set aside to thicken for 10 minutes.
Serving Suggestions: Serve warm with fresh cilantro and tortilla chips.
Variation Tip: You can also use chicken thighs instead of chicken breasts.
Nutritional Information per Serving: Calories: 175 | Fat: 6.7g | Sat Fat: 2.1g | Carbohydrates: 4.2g | Fiber: 0.4g | Sugar: 2g | Protein: 23.6g

BBQ Turkey Bacon Wrapped Breakfast Sausage
Prep Time:20 minutes | Cook Time: 35 minutes | Servings: 6

Ingredients:

10 oz. turkey bacon
6 eggs, scrambled
1 lb. turkey sausage, ground
4 oz. ham, diced

4 oz. cheddar cheese, cut into sticks
1 tbsp. brown sugar
¼ cup pit boss sweet heat BBQ sauce
Pit Boss Smoked Salt & Pepper Rub, to taste

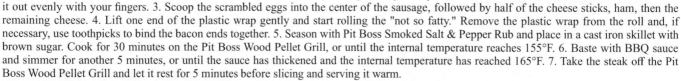

Preparation:

1. Preheat your Pit Boss to SMOKE mode and then set to 375°F. Set the Pit Boss Wood Pellet Grill to MEDIUM-HIGH heat if using a charcoal or gas grill. 2. Lay down a piece of plastic wrap and weave your favorite turkey bacon into it. Smooth the turkey sausage on top and spread it out evenly with your fingers. 3. Scoop the scrambled eggs into the center of the sausage, followed by half of the cheese sticks, ham, then the remaining cheese. 4. Lift one end of the plastic wrap gently and start rolling the "not so fatty." Remove the plastic wrap from the roll and, if necessary, use toothpicks to bind the bacon ends together. 5. Season with Pit Boss Smoked Salt & Pepper Rub and place in a cast iron skillet with brown sugar. Cook for 30 minutes on the Pit Boss Wood Pellet Grill, or until the internal temperature reaches 155°F. 6. Baste with BBQ sauce and simmer for another 5 minutes, or until the sauce has thickened and the internal temperature has reached 165°F. 7. Take the steak off the Pit Boss Wood Pellet Grill and let it rest for 5 minutes before slicing and serving it warm.
Serving Suggestions: Serve alongside stir fried vegetables.
Variation Tip: To make wrapping up the fatty easier, apply the plastic wrap with non-stick spray.
Nutritional Information per Serving: Calories: 494 | Fat: 35.2g | Sat Fat: 12.8g | Carbohydrates: 2.9g | Fiber: 0.3g | Sugar: 2g | Protein: 37.3g

Smoked Chicken with Lime BBQ Sauce
Prep Time:25 minutes | Cook Time: 25 minutes | Servings: 4

Ingredients:

¼ cup beer, any brand
1-pound chicken breasts, boneless and skinless
½ cup barbecue sauce
1 tbsp. butter
2 garlic cloves, minced
1 tsp. hot sauce

1 tbsp. olive oil
2 tbsps. Sweet Heat Rub
¼ tsp. ground thyme
Juice of 1 lime
½ tsp. oregano
1 tbsp. Worcestershire sauce

Preparation:

1. Blend the Sweet Heat Rub, oregano, and ground thyme in a small mixing dish. 2. Brush the chicken breasts with olive oil all over, making sure the meat is well covered. Season the chicken breasts with the Sweet Heat mixture on all sides. 3. Preheat your Pit Boss to SMOKE mode and then set to 350°F. Set the Pit Boss Wood Pellet Grill to MEDIUM-HIGH heat if using a charcoal or gas grill. 4. Insert a food thermometer into the thickest section of one of the chicken breasts and then move the chicken on the Pit Boss Wood Pellet Grill. 3. Cook the chicken breasts per side for 12 minutes, then flip and grill for another 7 minutes, or until golden brown and juicy and internal temperature reaches 165°F. 4. Take the chicken from the Pit Boss Wood Pellet Grill and set it aside for 10 minutes. 5. For Sauce: In a heatproof saucepan, mingle the barbecue sauce, butter, beer, lime juice, Worcestershire sauce, and garlic. Place on the Pit Boss Wood Pellet Grill. 6. Toss in the sauce and bring to a boil. Eliminate it from the stove once it has reached a boil, mix it together, and serve with the chicken.
Serving Suggestions: Serve alongside roasted veggies.
Variation Tip: Fill your hopper with Fruity Hardwood Pellets to offer fruitier flavors to balance out the Cajun Sauce's heat.
Nutritional Information per Serving: Calories: 334 | Fat: 14.9g | Sat Fat: 4.6g | Carbohydrates: 14.2g | Fiber: 0.4g | Sugar: 9.1g | Protein: 33.1g

Crispy Chicken Quarters with Alabama White Sauce

Prep Time:1 hour | Cook Time: 55 minutes | Servings: 4

Ingredients:

1 tbsp. champion chicken
4 chicken leg quarters
2 cups Alabama White Sauce
1 tbsp. olive oil
For Alabama White Sauce:
½ cup sour cream
1 cup mayonnaise
¼ cup apple cider vinegar

1 tbsp. spicy brown mustard
2 tsps. lemon juice
¼ tsp. cayenne pepper
2 tbsps. brown sugar
1 tbsp. horseradish
¼ tsp. sea salt
⅛ tsp. white pepper, ground

Preparation:

1. Blend the sour cream, mayonnaise, apple cider vinegar, spicy brown mustard, brown sugar, lemon juice, horseradish, white pepper, salt, and cayenne in a big bowl. Set aside after mixing until thoroughly incorporated. 2. Arrange the chicken leg quarters on an aluminum foil-lined sheet tray. Pull the skin away from the chicken leg quarters gently, then sprinkle with olive oil both inside and out. Champion Chicken season the chicken leg quarters all over and under the skin. 3. Preheat your Pit Boss Wood Pellet Grill to 450°F. Set the Pit Boss Wood Pellet Grill for MEDIUM-HIGH heat and direct heat if you're using a charcoal or gas grill. 4. Crisp up the leg quarters on all sides over direct heat until golden brown and crispy. Close the sear slide and place it on indirect heat. Turn down the heat to 350°F and grill the chicken for 45 minutes, rotating twice, until the internal temperature acquires 165°F. 5. Eliminate the chicken from the Pit Boss Wood Pellet Grill and set it aside for 10 minutes to rest. 6. With a heavy sprinkling of Alabama white sauce, serve the chicken hot.

Serving Suggestions: Serve alongside simmering hot tea.

Variation Tip: The homemade sauce can be stored in the refrigerator for up to two weeks. Everything from fish to potatoes should be tried with it.

Nutritional Information per Serving: Calories: 1083 | Fat: 69.3g | Sat Fat: 20.2g | Carbohydrates: 76.8g | Fiber: 4.4g | Sugar: 18.3g | Protein: 44.8g

Grilled Hand Pulled Chicken & White BBQ Sauce

Prep Time:30 minutes | Cook Time: 1 hour 30 minutes | Servings: 4

Ingredients:

½ lemon, juiced
2 tbsps. sugar
2 tbsps. apple cider vinegar
1 tbsp. olive oil
4 tbsps. champion chicken

1 cup mayo
1 (3-4 pound) chicken, giblets removed and patted dry
1 clove garlic, minced
½ tsp. paprika, powder

Preparation:

1. Preheat your Pit Boss Wood Pellet Grill. Adjust the temperature to 350°F once it's preheated. 2. Combine all of the ingredients in a large mixing basin. Set aside the sauce in two separate bowls. 3. Arrange your chicken breast side down on a clean, level surface. Remove the spine with kitchen shears and discard. Flip the chicken breast side up by opening it up and flipping it over. Flatten the chicken by pressing the breastbone down with the heel of your hand. 4. Brush the olive oil and Champion Chicken all over the chicken. Place the skin-side up on the Pit Boss Wood Pellet Grill Grates. Grill for 1½ hours, basting every 20 minutes with half of the leftover sauce, until the internal temperature reaches 175°F. 5. Eliminate the chicken from the Pit Boss Wood Pellet Grill and set aside for 10 minutes, loosely covered. 6. Discard the skin and bones from the chicken and shred it with forks. 7. Serve the chicken with the rest of the white BBQ sauce on the side.

Serving Suggestions: Serve with grilled vegetables.

Variation Tip: Pit Boss All-Natural Fruit Premium Barbecue Hardwood Pellets are mild with fruity undertones and add flavor to pork, chicken, fish, and baking.

Nutritional Information per Serving: Calories: 2264 | Fat: 88.5g | Sat Fat: 30.3g | Carbohydrates: 201.2g| Fiber: 16.3g | Sugar: 27g | Protein: 177.3g

BBQ Cheese Chicken Stuffed Bell Peppers

Prep Time:20 minutes | Cook Time: 15 minutes | Servings: 4

Ingredients:

½ cup cheddar cheese, shredded
½ cup BBQ sauce
2 tbsps. champion chicken rub

2 cups leftover chicken, chopped
4 bell peppers, cut in half lengthwise and deseeded

Preparation:

1. Get your Pit Boss ready to go. Preheat the temperature to 350°F once it's started. 2. Merge the chicken, cheese, Champion Chicken Rub, and barbecue sauce in a big bowl, then stuff into the pepper halves. 3. Grill the peppers for 10 minutes. Eliminate the skewers from the Pit Boss Wood Pellet Grill and place them on a serving platter.

Serving Suggestions: Top with extra shredded cheese.

Variation Tip: You can also use Boursin Cheese instead of Cheddar Cheese for a richer flavor.

Nutritional Information per Serving: Calories: 248 | Fat: 7.2g | Sat Fat: 3.6g | Carbohydrates: 20.5g | Fiber: 1.8g | Sugar: 14.2g | Protein: 25g

Sweet Lime Chicken Wings

Prep Time:5 minutes | Cook Time: 40 minutes | Servings: 4

Ingredients:

16 chicken wings
3 tbsps. lime juice

Pit Boss Sweet Heat Rub, to taste

Preparation:

1. Spread the wings in a baking dish lengthwise. Splash lime juice over the wings in an equal layer. 2. Add the Sweet Heat Rub to a shaker and give it a good shake. Season the wings on the Pit Boss Wood Pellet Grill, flipping them to coat them evenly. 3. Preheat your Pit Boss Wood Pellet Grill to 350°F. 4. Place the wings on the grate immediately. Grill until crispy, about 25 minutes per side, over indirect heat. 5. Dish out the wings on a serving plate.

Serving Suggestions: Serve the chicken wings with your favorite dipping sauce.

Variation Tip: You can also use lemon instead of lime.

Nutritional Information per Serving: Calories: 1072 | Fat: 41.5g | Sat Fat: 11.4g | Carbohydrates: 2.8g | Fiber: 0.2g | Sugar: 0.6g | Protein: 162.1g

Smoked Sweet & Sour Chicken Drumsticks

Prep Time:30 minutes | Cook Time: 2 hours 30 minutes | Servings: 4

Ingredients:

8 chicken drumsticks
3 tbsps. brown sugar
1 tbsp. garlic, minced
2 tbsps. honey
½ lemon, juice
½ lime, juiced

¼ cup soy sauce
1 tbsp. ginger, minced
1 cup ketchup
2 tbsps. rice wine vinegar
1 tbsp. sweet heat rub

Preparation:

1. Mingle the soy sauce, ketchup, rice wine vinegar, honey, ginger, brown sugar, garlic, lime, lemon, and Sweet Heat Rub together in a mixing dish. 2. Set aside half of the mixture for the dipping sauce. Fill a big resalable plastic bag halfway with the remaining half. 3. Place the drumsticks in the bag and close it. Refrigerate for a minimum of 10 hours before serving. Eliminate the chicken from the bag and toss out the marinade. 4. Preheat your Pit Boss to SMOKE mode and then set to 225°F. Set the Pit Boss Wood Pellet Grill to MEDIUM-HIGH heat if using a charcoal or gas grill. 5. Cook the chicken for 3 hours over indirect heat with the Pit Boss Wood Pellet Grill lid covered, flipping once or twice, until it reaches 180°F. Feel free to add extra glaze during the last half hour. 6. Eliminate the pan from the Pit Boss Wood Pellet Grill and set aside for 10 minutes.

Serving Suggestions: Spoon additional sauce over the top.

Variation Tip: This recipe goes great with chicken wings as well!

Nutritional Information per Serving: Calories: 297 | Fat: 5.6g | Sat Fat: 1.5g | Carbohydrates: 34.8g | Fiber: 1g | Sugar: 29.5g | Protein: 27.8g

Maple Smoked Turkey

Prep Time:20 minutes | Cook Time:6 hours 5 minutes | Servings: 8

Ingredients:

½ cup maple syrup
1 cup butter, room temperature

2 tbsps. Pit Boss Chicken & Poultry Rub
1 turkey, whole (pre-brined)

Preparation:

Maple Turkey Marinade:
1. Melt half cup of butter and add half cup of maple syrup to it in a saucepan. 2. Eliminate the saucepan from the heat and let it aside to cool for a few moments. Inject the solution into the thickest parts of the breast, thighs, and wings using a marinade injector.

Smoking the Turkey:
1. Start your grill on SMOKE, keeping the lid open until a fire in the burn pot is started. 2. Preheat the Pit Boss Wood Pellet Grill to 250°F. 3. In a mixing dish, whisk together the melted butter and maple syrup. Fill the marinade injector with the butter and syrup combination and use the needle to pierce the meat while pulling on the plunger to inject the taste. The thickest region of the breast, thigh, and wings should be injected with the marinade. 4. Spread the room temperature butter and Pit Boss Chicken & Poultry Rub all over the turkey, making sure to get beneath the skin as well. 5. Place the turkey on the Pit Boss Wood Pellet Grill in an aluminum pan to catch all the drippings. 6. Eliminate the turkey from the Pit Boss Wood Pellet Grill when the breast and thigh meat reaches 165°F to 170°F and set aside to rest for 15 minutes before carving.

Serving Suggestions: Serve this with mashed potatoes.

Variation Tip: When the turkey reaches 155°F internal temperature, turn the Pit Boss Wood Pellet Grill to HIGH and cook it until the skin is crispy.

Nutritional Information per Serving: Calories: 285 | Fat: 23.9g | Sat Fat: 14.9g | Carbohydrates: 13.2g | Fiber: 0g | Sugar: 11.7g | Protein: 5.4g

Juicy Bourbon Glazed Smoked Turkey Breast

Prep Time:10 minutes | Cook Time: 4 hours | Servings: 6

Ingredients:

½ cup bourbon
½ tbsp. black pepper
½ tbsp. garlic powder
¼ cup maple syrup
½ tbsp. onion powder
¼ cup orange juice
1 sweet potato, halved

½ tbsp. thyme, dried
1 yellow onion, halved
1½ tbsps. kosher salt
2 tbsps. olive oil
9 lbs. turkey breast, whole, bone-in
2 tbsps. tamari
1 stick butter

Preparation:

1. Using paper towels, wipe dry the turkey after rinsing it completely under cold water. 2. Brush the turkey with olive oil, then spice with garlic powder, salt, black pepper, dried thyme, and onion powder on the inside and outside of the cavity. 3. Place in a skillet and prop up with onion and potato on either side. Remove from the equation. 4. Preheat your Pit Boss Wood Pellet Grill to SMOKE mode and then set to 250°F. Set the Pit Boss Wood Pellet Grill to MEDIUM-HIGH heat if using a charcoal or gas grill. 5. Place the turkey on the Pit Boss Wood Pellet Grill and cook for 3 to 3½ hours, until an internal temperature acquires 165°F, turning after 1½ hours. 6. Meantime, melt the butter in a small saucepan over medium heat to make the glaze. 7. Blend the maple syrup, bourbon, orange juice, and soy sauce in a mixing bowl. Bring it to the boiling point, then lower to a low heat. Simmer for about 10 minutes and keep aside. 8. After flipping the turkey, baste it with the glaze every 30 minutes. 9. Eliminate the turkey from the Pit Boss Wood Pellet Grill and set it aside for 20 minutes. Slice and serve.

Serving Suggestions: Serve with roasted asparagus.
Variation Tip: Allow 3 days in the refrigerator to properly defrost the turkey, then set aside for 1 hour at room temperature before smoking.
Nutritional Information per Serving: Calories: 111 | Fat: 4.9g | Sat Fat: 0.4g | Carbohydrates: 14.8g | Fiber: 2.9g | Sugar: 7.9g | Protein: 2.6g

Butter Grilled Turkey

Prep Time:15 minutes | Cook Time: 4 hours | Servings: 6

Ingredients:

1 lb. butter
½ cup coarse black pepper

½ cup salt, kosher
1 brined turkey

Preparation:

1. Preheat the Pit Boss Wood Pellet Grill to 300°F. 2. Season the turkey liberally with kosher salt and coarse black pepper. 3. Grill until the internal temperature reaches 145°F or the skin has darkened to your preference. 4. Position the turkey in a roasting pan and cover it with a pound of minced butter. 5. Return the thigh and breast to the Pit Boss Wood Pellet Grill until the internal temperature reaches 165°F. 6. Carve and serve after 30 minutes of resting.

Serving Suggestions: Serve with grilled peaches.
Variation Tip: For a faster cooking time, try to spatchcocking the turkey.
Nutritional Information per Serving: Calories: 550 | Fat: 61.4g | Sat Fat: 38.9g | Carbohydrates: 2.1g | Fiber: 0.9g | Sugar: 0.1g | Protein: 1g

Sweet Heat Cajun Turkey

Prep Time:3 hours | Cook Time: 30 minutes | Servings: 7

Ingredients:

Pit Boss Sweet Heat Rub, to taste
16 oz. Cajun Butter

1 turkey, brined

Preparation:

1. Preheat the Pit Boss Wood Pellet Grill to 300°F. 2. Trickle Cajun butter over the turkey and liberally season with Pit Boss Sweet Heat Rub. 3.Cook until the thighs and breasts reach 165°F on the Pit Boss Wood Pellet Grill. 4. Set aside for 30 minutes before serving.

Serving Suggestions: Serve with mashed carrots.
Variation Tip: Don't forget to thaw your turkey a few days ahead of time. Each 4–5 pound of turkey can take up to 24 hours to defrost thoroughly.
Nutritional Information per Serving: Calories: 921 | Fat: 14.7g | Sat Fat: 10.6g | Carbohydrates: 167.2g | Fiber: 3.4g | Sugar: 3.4g | Protein: 29.7g

Grilled Mini Buffalo Chicken Flatbread

Prep Time: 5 minutes | Cook Time: 30 minutes | Serves: 6

Ingredients:

6 pita bread, mini
1½ cups buffalo sauce
4 cups chicken breasts, cooked and cubed

3 cups mozzarella cheese
Blue cheese for drizzling

Preparation:

1. Preheat your Pit Boss Wood Pellet Grill to 400°F. 2. Meanwhile, place the pita breads on a working surface and spread buffalo sauce on each. 3. Toss the chicken breast cubes in buffalo sauce then divide them among the 6 breads. 4. Top each bread with cheese then place them on the grill grates and over indirect heat. 5. Close the lid and cook for 7 minutes or until the cheese has melted. 6. Remove the mini pizzas from the grill and drizzle with blue cheese. Serve.

Serving suggestion: serve with blue cheese and ranch.
Variation Tip: use Cholula buffalo sauce.
Nutrition-Per Serving: Calories 311 | Fat 25g |Sodium 235mg | Carbs 7g | Fiber 1g | Sugar 1g | Protein 29g

Smoked Whole Turkey

Prep Time: 30 minutes | Cook Time: 1 hour 15 minutes | Serves: 8

Ingredients:

1 whole turkey
½ cup oil
¼ cup chicken rub
1 tablespoon onion powder
1 tablespoon garlic powder

1 tablespoon rubbed sage
For Garnishing:
Parsley
1 orange, sliced
1 lemon sliced

Preparation:

1. Preheat your Pit Boss Wood Pellet Grill to 500°F. 2. Place the turkey on a flat surface with the breast side down. 3. Cut up both sides of the backbone through the ribs and remove the spine. 4. Rub both sides of the turkey with oil and season it with chicken rub, onion powder, garlic powder, and sage. 5. Place the turkey on the grill with the skin side up. Grill the turkey for 30 minutes. 6. Reduce the grill temperature to 325°F and grill for an additional 45 minutes. 7. Remove the turkey from the grill and let it rest for 20 minutes. 8. Garnish the turkey with parsley, orange slices, and lemon slices. 9. Serve and enjoy.

Serving suggestion: serve the spatchcock turkey with mashed potatoes.

Variation Tip: preferred seasoning can be used.

Nutrition-Per Serving: Calories 724| Fat 38g |Sodium 165mg | Carbs 2g | Fiber 0 g | Sugar 0 g | Protein 89g

Grilled Pineapple–Flavored Chicken wings

Prep Time: 20 minutes | Cook Time: 45 minutes | Serves: 6

Ingredients:

¾ cup soy
½ cup pineapple juice
1 tablespoon sriracha
⅛ cup miso
⅛ cup gochujang

½ cup water
½ cup oil
2 Pounds chicken wings
Togarashi

Preparation:

1. Combine all ingredients in a mixing bowl. Toss the chicken wings with the marinade until well coated. 2. Let marinate in the fridge for 12 hours. 3. Preheat your Pit Boss Wood Pellet Grill to 375°F. 4. Place the chicken wings on the grill grates and close the lid. Cook for 45 minutes or until the internal temperature reaches 165°F. 5. Remove the chicken wings from the grill and sprinkle with togarashi. Serve.

Serving suggestion: Serve the chicken wings with grilled vegetable pasta salad.

Variation Tip: add dark brown sugar and sake.

Nutrition-Per Serving: Calories 703 | Fat 56g |Sodium 1156mg | Carbs 24g | Fiber 1g | Sugar 6g | Protein 27g

Smoked Crispy Chicken

Prep Time: 15 minutes | Cook Time: 180 minutes | Serves: 8

Ingredients:

2 (3 to 3½ lb) whole fryer chickens
Vegetable oil
Kosher salt and black pepper
1-quart buttermilk
2 tbsp Crystal Hot Sauce
1 tbsp brown sugar
2½ cups all-purpose flour

2 tbsp garlic powder
2 tbsp onion powder
1 tbsp Pit Boss Chicken & Poultry Rub
2 tbsp kosher salt (use only 1 tbsp if substituting table salt)
Freshly ground black pepper
Peanut or grapeseed oil, for frying

Preparation:

1. When ready to cook, set Pit Boss temperature to 200°F and preheat, lid closed for 15 minutes. 2. Rinse the chicken under the cold running water. Place on a rimmed baking sheet. 3. Rub the outside with vegetable oil and season with salt and pepper. 4. Place chicken directly on the grill and smoke for 2½ hours, or until the internal temperature at the thickest part of the thigh reads 150°F. 5. Transfer the smoked chickens to a clean baking sheet and allow them to cool. 6. Cut the chicken into 20 parts: 4 thighs, 4 thighs, 4 wings and 8 breast quarters (remove the 4 breast halves, then cut them in half). 7. Divide the chicken into 2 Ziploc bags. 8. Meanwhile, beat buttermilk with hot sauce and brown sugar in a large bowl until the sugar crystals dissolve. 9. Pour half into each bag of chicken. Close, then refrigerate for 1 hour. 10. In a separate bowl, whisk together the flour, garlic powder, onion powder, poultry seasoning and 2 tbsps of kosher salt and black pepper. Put aside. 11. On the stovetop, peanut or grapeseed oil (a true roast chicken connoisseur would use melted lard) over medium-high heat to 375°F in a Dutch oven, deep cast-iron skillet, or pan. 12. Drain the chicken pieces. Dredge a few at a time into the flour mixture. 13. Sauté the chicken in portions (do not overcrowd the pan), turning with tongs as needed, until browned, about 6 minutes for the breasts and 8 minutes for the thighs, wings and sides. 14. Drain on paper towels before serving. Enjoy!

Suggested Wood Pellet Flavor: Mesquite pellets.

Serving Suggestion: Serve with sauce of your preference.

Variation Tip: Use turkey.

Nutritional Information per Serving: Calories 342| Fat 10.7g |Sodium 2513mg | Carbs 32.3g | Fiber 1.6g | Sugar 7.6g | Protein 22.7g

BBQ Chicken Wings

Prep Time: 10 minutes | Cook Time: 30 minutes | Serves: 4

Ingredients:

1½ pounds chicken wings
Salt and pepper to taste
Garlic powder
Onion powder

Cayenne
Paprika
Seasoning salt
BBQ sauce

Preparation:

1. Preheat your Pit Boss Wood Pellet Grill to low heat. 2. Mix all the seasoning in a mixing bowl to make a rub then generously season the chicken wings with it. 3. Grill the chicken wings for 20 minutes while turning them occasionally. 4. Remove the wings from the grill and let them cool for 5 minutes. 5. Toss them with BBQ sauce and serve with a salad of choice.

Serving suggestion: Serve the BBQ Chicken wings cheesy orzo.
Variation Tip: Use homemade BBQ sauce.
Nutrition-Per Serving: Calories 311 | Fat 15g |Sodium 1400mg | Carbs 22g | Fiber 3g | Sugar 12g | Protein 22g

BBQ Buffalo Chicken Breast

Prep Time: 10 minutes | Cook Time: 25 minutes | Serves: 6

Ingredients:

5 chicken breasts, boneless
2 tablespoons BBQ rub

1 cup buffalo sauce

Preparation:

1. Preheat your Pit Boss Wood Pellet Grill to 400°F. 2. Meanwhile, slice the chicken breasts into long strips then rub the BBQ rub. 3. Place the chicken breast strips in your gill then paint both sides with BBQ sauce. 4. Grill for 4 minutes, flip, and paint with BBQ sauce. Continues with the princess until the internal temperature reaches 165°F. 5. Remove from the grill, let cool, and serve.

Serving suggestion: Serve Buffalo chicken breast with pan-fried potato wedges or salad.
Variation Tip: Use homemade Cholula sauce or green jalapeno sauce in place of buffalo sauce.
Nutrition-Per Serving: Calories 176 | Fat 4g |Sodium 631mg | Carbs 1g | Fiber 0g | Sugar 1g | Protein 32g

Sweet & Spicy Chicken Drumsticks

Prep Time: 20 minutes | Cook Time: 30 minutes | Serves: 4

Ingredients:

½ cup apple cider vinegar
12 chicken drumsticks
2 tbsp Dijon mustard
¼ cup honey

¼ cup ketchup
1 tbsp Pit Boss Sweet Heat Rub
½ cup soy sauce

Preparation:

1. In a bowl, add apple cider vinegar, Dijon mustard, honey, ketchup and pit boss sweet heat rub mix well and add chicken drumsticks on it. 2. Preheat the grill. Light the grill on SMOKE. Once lit, set the temperature to 225°F. Remove the wings from the marinade and place the drumsticks on the rack. 3. Smoke for 60 minutes or until a thermometer inserted into the thickest part indicates a temperature of 170°F. 4. Increase the heat to 350°F and cook for 5 to 10 minutes so that the skin becomes crisp. 5. Serve immediately and enjoy!

Suggested Wood Pellet Flavor: Mesquite Blend Hardwood Pellets.
Serving Suggestion: Serve with cauliflower rice.
Variation Tip: Use turkey.
Nutritional Information per Serving: Calories 351 | Fat 8.7g |Sodium 2313mg | Carbs 26.3g | Fiber 0.6g | Sugar 21.6g | Protein 40.7g

Beer Grilled Whole Chicken

Prep Time: 10 minutes | Cook Time: 75 minutes | Serves: 4

Ingredients:

1 can of beer (any brand you like)
2 tbsps olive oil
4-6 tbsps of Pit Boss Chicken & Poultry

Seasoning
1 whole chicken

Preparation:

1. Season chicken generously with pit boss Chicken & poultry seasoning. including inside the cavity. 2. Preheat your Pit Boss Grill to 350°F, lid closed for 15 minutes. 3. Open the can of beer and set the chicken on top of the beer. Make sure all but the bottom 1½ inch of the beer can is in the chicken cavity. Tip: you can also place the beer can directly on the grill grates, then place the chicken on top. 4. Place the entire chicken and beer can directly on the grill grate. Cook for 60 to 75 minutes, or until the internal temperature registers 165°F in the thickest part of the breast. 5. Remove the chicken from the grill, let it stand for 15 minutes and serve.

Suggested Wood Pellet Flavor: Hickory Hardwood Pellets.
Serving Suggestion: Serve with salad and gravy.
Variation Tip: Use turkey.
Nutritional Information per Serving: Calories 197| Fat 12.7g |Sodium 1213mg | Carbs 5.3g | Fiber 0.1g | Sugar 2.6g | Protein 8.7g

Lemony Whole Chicken with Potatoes

Prep Time: 15 minutes | Cook Time: 60 minutes | Serves: 8

Ingredients:

2 whole chickens
6 cloves garlic, minced
2 tbsp salt
3 tbsp pimentón (Spanish smoked paprika)
6 tbsp extra-virgin olive oil
2 bunches fresh thyme

3 pound Yukon gold potatoes
Salt
Ground black pepper
2 lemons, halved
½ cup chopped flat-leaf parsley

Preparation:

1. Remove giblets, if any, and rinse the chickens, inside and out, under cold running water. Dry thoroughly with paper towels. Tie the legs together with butcher's string and tuck the wings behind the backs. 2. Prepare the spice paste: In a small bowl, combine the garlic, salt and paprika and mix well. Add 3 tbsps of olive oil. Distribute the mixture all over the outside of the chickens. Put a bunch of thyme in each bird's main den. Place on a rimmed baking sheet. Then place it in a cool place without a lid for at least 6 hours or overnight. 3. Place the washed potatoes in a large bowl and season with salt and pepper. Drizzle with the remaining 3 tbsps of oil and flip to coat. Divide the potatoes in a large baking dish or large rimmed baking sheet. 4. Place the chickens side by side on top of the potatoes. Squeeze the lemons over the chickens and add the zest to the potatoes. 5. When you're ready to cook, fire up the Pit Boss Grill. Set the temperature to 400-450°F. Preheat 10 to 15 minutes with the lid closed. 6. Brown the chicken, potatoes and lemons for 30 minutes. Stir the potatoes. 7. Reduce temperature to 350°F and continue frying until an instant-read meat thermometer inserted into the thickest part of the thigh reads 75°F about 40 minutes more. 8. Place the potatoes and lemons in a large bowl. Sprinkle with paprika and garnish with parsley. Put the chickens on it. Enjoy!

Suggested Wood Pellet Flavor: Pecan pellets.
Serving Suggestion: Serve roast chicken & Pimenton potatoes with salad.
Variation Tip: Use turkey.
Nutritional Information per Serving: Calories 275| Fat 12.7g |Sodium 1213mg | Carbs 12.3g | Fiber 1.6g | Sugar 0.6g | Protein 12.7g

Buffalo Chicken legs

Prep Time: 5 minutes | Cook Time: 50 minutes | Serves: 6

Ingredients:

12 chicken legs
1 tablespoon Buffalo seasoning

½ tablespoons salt
1 cup Buffalo sauce

Preparation:

1. Preheat your Pit Boss Wood Pellet Grill 325°F. 2. Toss the chicken legs with seasoning and salt then place them in the grill. 3. Grill for 40 minutes while turning occasionally during the cooking period. 4. Brush the legs chicken with buffalo sauce and cook for an additional 10 minutes or until the internal temperature reaches 165°F. 5. Remove the chicken wings from the grill, brush with more sauce and serve.
Serving suggestion: serve chicken leg with celery stalks and ranch.
Variation Tip: add mayo, garlic, and spicy chorizo.
Nutrition-Per Serving: Calories 956 | Fat 47g |Sodium 1750mg | Carbs 1g | Fiber 0g | Sugar 0g | Protein 124g

Korean–Style Chicken Wings with Hot Pepper Butter Sauce

Prep Time: 180 minutes | Cook Time: 60 minutes | Serves: 4

Ingredients:

Brine
1-gallon water
1 cup sea salt
½ cup sugar
1 large lemon, halved
Main
3 pounds chicken wings
2 tbsp olive oil
½ cup green onions, sliced
¼ cup crushed peanuts
Sauce
½ cup Gochujang Hot Pepper Paste
¼ cup soy sauce
⅓ cup honey

1 head garlic, halved
4 sprigs thyme
10 whole peppercorns

2 tbsp toasted sesame seeds
Fresh cilantro, for serving
Lime wedges, for serving

2 tbsp rice wine vinegar
2 tbsp fresh squeezed lime juice
2 tbsp toasted sesame oil

¼ cup butter, melted
4 cloves garlic, minced
1 tbsp ginger, peeled and grated

Preparation:

1. For the brine: Put 1 gallon of water, salt and sugar in a saucepan and stir well. Bring to a boil, then remove from heat and add lemon, garlic, thyme and peppercorns. Let cool to room temperature. 2. Soak the wings, cover and refrigerate for 2 to 4 hours. 3. After the cooking time, set the grill to 375°F and preheat for 15 minutes with the lid closed. 4. Remove the wings from the brine and dry them completely with paper towels. Discard the brine. 5. Swirl the wings in olive oil and cover completely. 6. Place the chicken wings directly on the grill grate and cook for about 45 to 60 minutes at an internal temperature of 165°F. 7. For the sauce: Combine all the ingredients for the sauce in a bowl and stir until smooth. Heat over medium heat until the sauce is simmering, then remove from heat and set aside. 8. Remove the cooked wings with ⅔ of the sauce, then the spring onions, peanuts and sesame seeds. Serve the wings with fresh cilantro, lemon wedges and additional sauce for dipping. Enjoy!
Suggested Wood Pellet Flavor: Cherry pellets.
Serving Suggestion: Serve s wings with salad.
Variation Tip: Use turkey.
Nutritional Information per Serving: Calories 675| Fat 36.7g |Sodium 2213mg | Carbs 52.3g | Fiber 2.6g | Sugar 49.6g | Protein 33.7g

Cola Grilled Chicken Wings

Prep Time: 25 minutes | Cook Time: 120 minutes | Serves: 8

Ingredients:

16 chicken wings, trimmed and patted dry
2 tsp Carolina BBQ Rub
1 cup Memphis Hickory & Vinegar BBQ Sauce
1 (12oz.) Coca Cola
3 tsp dried chili flakes
1 tsp garlic powder
1 (18.5 oz.) Gold Peak sweet tea
½ cup green onion, chopped

2 tbsp light soy sauce
½ cup noion, minced
2 tbsp peanut oil
1 tsp powdered ginger
1 tbsp red wine vinegar
1 tsp salt
1 scallion, chopped
2 tbsp white wine

Preparation:

1. In a large bowl, add the oil, chili flakes, ginger, garlic, ½ bottle of cola and mix well. Add the chicken wings, brush evenly and refrigerate for 2 to 24 hours. 2. Preheat the Pit Boss Grill to 250°F. Place the wings on the grill and cook for 75 minutes, turning if necessary. 3. In a deep cast-iron saucepan with a lid, combine the remaining ½ bottle of Coke, 1 bottle of Gold Peak Sweet Tea, wine, vinegar, salt, onion, Carolina Rub and Memphis barbecue sauce. 4. Put the grill wings in the pan and brush them well with the liquid. Cover the pan and leave it on the grill. 5. Increase the heat to 350 on the Pit Boss Grill and cook the wings, covered, for 1 to 1.5 hours. 6. When you're done, place the wings on a platter and garnish with any cilantro or spring onions of your choice and enjoy.

Suggested Wood Pellet Flavor: Competition Blend Hardwood Pellets.
Serving Suggestion: Serve braised chicken wings with salad.
Variation Tip: Use turkey.
Nutritional Information per Serving: Calories 355| Fat 12.7g |Sodium 2013mg | Carbs 12.3g | Fiber 0.6g | Sugar 6.6g | Protein 42.7g

Smoked Buffalo Chicken Wings

Prep Time: 10 minutes | Cook Time: 2 hours | Serves: 6

Ingredients:

3 lb chicken wings
1 tbsp all-purpose seasoning

Buffalo sauce

Preparation:

1. Preheat your Pit Boss Wood Pellet Grill to 180°F. 2. Coat the chicken wings with the all-purpose seasoning and place them on the grill. 3. Smoke the wings for 2 hours turning them halfway through the smoking process. 4. Remove the chicken wings from the grill and raise the grill temperature to 375°F. 5. Place the wings back on the grill and cook for about 6 minutes. 6. Drain excess grease from the wings then toss them in buffalo sauce. 7. Serve and enjoy.

Serving suggestion: Serve the chicken wings with roasted broccoli.
Variation Tip: buffalo sauce can be replaced with a sauce of choice.
Nutrition-Per Serving:
Calories 755| Fat 55g |Sodium 1747mg | Carbs 24g | Fiber 1g | Sugar 2g | Protein 39g

Grilled Bourbon BBQ Chicken Kabobs

Prep Time: 15 minutes | Cook Time: 10 minutes | Serves: 4

Ingredients:

3 pounds chicken breasts, cut into 1 inch cubes
½ cup Pit Boss Texas Smoky and Spicy BBQ Sauce
½ cup Pit Boss Sweet Heat BBQ Sauce

¼ cup bourbon
2 tablespoons honey
1 teaspoon garlic
1 teaspoon onion powder

Preparation:

1. In a 2 quart resalable bag, combine all ingredients and marinate in the refrigerator overnight. 2. Using skewers, thread the marinated chicken portions. 3. When ready to cook, set Pit Boss Wood Pellet Grill temperature to 450°F and preheat, lid closed for 15 minutes. 4. Place the skewers on the front of the grill for a nice char. Then move them to the center of the grill and finish grilling, about 8 to 10 minutes more, or until chicken reaches an internal temp of 165°F. Enjoy!

Suggested Wood Pellet Flavour: Use Mesquite Pellets.
Serving Suggestion: Serve Bourbon BBQ Chicken Kabobs with sauce.
Variation Tip: Use tofu.
Nutritional Information per Serving: Calories 763 | Fat 25.2g | Sodium 626mg | Carbs 21.4g | Fiber 0.1g | Sugar 20.7g | Protein 98.7g

BBQ Garlic Chicken Breasts

Prep Time: 20 minutes | Cook Time: 30 minutes | Serves: 4

Ingredients:

4 whole chicken breasts
¼ cup olive oil
1 tsp freshly pressed garlic

1 tbsp Worcestershire sauce
Pit Boss Chicken and Poultry Rub
½ cup Pit Boss Sweet & Heat BBQ Sauce

Preparation:

1. In a small bowl, beat together the olive oil, garlic, Worcestershire sauce, and Pit boss chicken and poultry rub. Cover chicken breasts with mixture. 2. In a separate bowl, combine equal parts Pit Boss Sweet & Heat and BBQ sauce. 3. When ready to cook, set Pit Boss Grill temperature to 500°F and preheat, lid closed for 15 minutes. 4. Place chicken directly on the grill grate and grill for 20 to 30 minutes, or until the internal temperature reaches 160°F in the thickest part of the breast. 5. Five minutes before the chicken is done, glaze the chicken with BBQ sauce mixture. 6. Remove from the grill and let rest 5 minutes before slicing. Enjoy.

Suggested Wood Pellet Flavor: Oak pellets.
Serving Suggestion: Serve with grilled veggies.
Variation Tip: Use turkey.
Nutritional Information per Serving: Calories 885| Fat 62.7g |Sodium 213mg | Carbs 2.3g | Fiber 0.6g | Sugar 0.6g | Protein 60.7g

Smoked Chicken Wings with Hot butter Sauce

Prep Time: 05 minutes | Cook Time: 60 minutes | Serves: 6

Ingredients:

1 tbsp baking powder
1 tsp paprika
½ tsp garlic powder
½ tsp onion powder
½ tsp dried thyme
¼ tsp dried oregano
¼ tsp cumin
¼ tsp kosher salt

¼ tsp freshly ground black pepper
⅛ tsp cayenne pepper
3 pounds chicken wings, flats and drumettes separated
¼ cup butter
¼ cup Louisiana-style hot sauce
1 tbsp Worcestershire sauce

Preparation:

1. **Rub:** In a small bowl, mix together baking powder, paprika, garlic powder, onion powder, thyme, oregano, cumin, salt, pepper and cayenne. 2. Rinse chicken wings and pat dry with paper towels. Place wings in a large bowl and sprinkle on rub, tossing to coat evenly. 3. Set a wire rack inside an aluminium foil-lined baking sheet. Arrange the chicken wings in a single layer leaving a little space between each wing. 4. Place baking sheet with wings in the refrigerator for 8 hours to overnight. 5. When ready to cook, set temperature to 180°F and preheat, lid closed for 15 minutes. 6. Smoke wings for 30 minutes. 7. After 30 minutes, increase the grill temperature to 350°F and roast for 45 to 50 minutes. 8. While the wings are on the grill, combine butter, hot sauce and Worcestershire sauce in a small saucepan. Bring to a simmer over medium heat and cook until combined. 9. Reduce the heat to low and keep warm until the wings are ready to eat. 10. Transfer the wings to a large bowl. Add the sauce and stir to cover the wings completely. 11. Transfer to a platter and serve immediately with carrot sticks, celery sticks, blue cheese, ranch or any sauce you like. Enjoy!

Suggested Wood Pellet Flavor: Apple pellets.
Serving Suggestion: Serve smoked Cajun chicken wings with cauliflower rice or salad.
Variation Tip: Use turkey.
Nutritional Information per Serving: Calories 507| Fat 24.7g |Sodium 613mg | Carbs 2.3g | Fiber 0.3g | Sugar 0.6g | Protein 65.7g

Delicious Smoked Cornish Hen

Prep Time: 10 minutes | Cook Time: 1 hour | Serves: 6

Ingredients:

6 Cornish hens
2 tablespoons oil

6 tablespoons chicken rub

Preparation:

1. Preheat your Pit Boss Wood Pellet Grill to 275°F. 2. Brush the hens with oil then coat them with chicken rub. 3. Place the hens on the grill with the breast side down and smoke for 30 minutes. 4. Remove the hens from the grill and raise the grill temperature to 400°F. 5. Return the hens on the grill with the breast side up and cook for about 30 minutes until the internal temperature is 165°F. 6. Let the hens rest for 10 minutes then serve.

Serving suggestion: serve the Cornish hen with creamy noodles.
Variation Tip: seasoning of your choice can be used.
Nutrition-Per Serving:
Calories 696| Fat 50g |Sodium 165mg | Carbs 1g | Fiber 0 g | Sugar 0 g | Protein 57g
| Fiber 0.3g | Sugar 2.6g | Protein 50.7g

Chapter 5 Vegan and Vegetarian Recipes

Grilled Cheese Garlic Potatoes

Prep Time:5 minutes | Cook Time: 30 minutes | Servings: 6

Ingredients:

1 large onion, sliced
3 tbsps. butter
2 lbs. baby red potatoes

1 tsp. parsley leaves, chopped
3 garlic cloves, sliced
1 cup cheddar cheese, shredded

Preparation:

1. Preheat the Pit Boss Wood Pellet Grill to 350°F, then increase to 400°F. 2. Cut and layer potato pieces on a big piece of aluminum foil, separated by onion and butter slices. 3. Add garlic to the potatoes and season with parsley, salt, and pepper. Arrange the potatoes on aluminum foil. 4. Move the potatoes on the hot Pit Boss Wood Pellet Grill and cook for 40 minutes, or until cooked. Serve immediately.

Serving Suggestions: You can sprinkle potatoes with some parsley.

Variation Tip: Use some more garlic if you desire.

Nutritional Information per Serving: Calories: 713 | Fat: 27.7g | Sat Fat: 12.8g | Carbohydrates: 112.6g | Fiber: 11g | Sugar: 11.6g | Protein: 15.6g

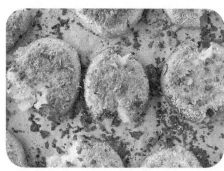

Parmesan Cheese Crusted Smashed Potatoes

Prep Time:20 minutes | Cook Time: 10 minutes | Servings: 4

Ingredients:

¼ tsp. garlic, granulated
3 tbsps. butter, melted
1 tbsp. parsley, leaves
⅓ cup parmesan cheese

2 tbsps. vegetable oil
Salt and black pepper, to taste
2 lbs. Yukon gold potatoes

Preparation:

1. Preheat the griddle on MEDIUM-LOW heat in your Pit Boss Wood Pellet Grill. Preheat a big cast iron pan over MEDIUM-LOW heat if using a gas or charcoal grill. 2. Evenly place the cooled potatoes on a metal sheet pan, drizzle with olive oil, and gently smash each potato to a height of about half an inch with a potato masher or small metal bowl. 3. Merge the butter and garlic in a mixing bowl. Spice with salt and pepper after brushing the mixture over each potato. 4. Spray the griddle with vegetable oil, then add the flattened potatoes. Cook for 3 minutes before flipping and topping with half of the Parmesan cheese. 5. Cook for 4 minutes, flipping once in between with the remaining Parmesan. 6. Transfer to a serving pan and serve immediately.

Serving Suggestions: Serve sprinkled with parsley.

Variation Tip: After boiling the potatoes, drain the water in a metal strainer and place to the Pit Boss Wood Pellet Grill to add smoky flavor.

Nutritional Information per Serving: Calories: 209 | Fat: 16.1g | Sat Fat: 7.2g | Carbohydrates: 15.4g | Fiber: 1.2g | Sugar: 0.6g | Protein: 2.6g

Gluten Free Celery & Carrot Stuffing

Prep Time:20 minutes | Cook Time: 55 minutes | Servings: 9

Ingredients:

5 tbsps. butter
1 baguette, gluten free
4 celery sticks, chopped
⅔ cup feta cheese, crumbled
⅛ cup chicken broth
½ tsp. cinnamon, ground

1 white onion, chopped
⅔ cup craisins
½ tsp. paprika powder
14 mini carrots, peeled and chopped
1 egg
3 tbsps. Pit Boss Chicken & Poultry Rub

Preparation:

1. Preheat your Pit Boss Wood Pellet Grill to 350°F and turn it to SMOKE once the fire pot catches. 2. In a large mixing basin, tear the gluten-free baguette into crouton-sized pieces. 3. Heat butter in a saucepan and add celery, onions, and carrots to the pan. 4. Cook for about 10 minutes, or until the onions are transparent. 5. Toss the torn bread pieces with the pan mixture. Mix. 6. Crack one egg into the mixing basin. Mix. 7. Toss in the craisins and feta crumbles. Mix. 8. Season with Pit Boss Chicken & Poultry Rub, cinnamon, and paprika. 9. Add bone broth and stir until all of the ingredients are properly coated and dispersed. 9. Merge all of the ingredients in a baking dish and cover with foil. 10. Cook for 55 minutes on the Pit Boss Wood Pellet Grill. Every 15 minutes, rotate the dish. 11. Bake for another 10 minutes after taking out the tin foil. 12. Take the stuffing off the Pit Boss Wood Pellet Grill and set it aside to cool for about 10 minutes.

Serving Suggestions: Serve topped with shredded cheese.

Variation Tip: Fill your hopper with Fruity Hardwood Pellets to help balance out the spice of the Cajun sauce.

Nutritional Information per Serving: Calories: 181 | Fat: 9.4g | Sat Fat: 5.9g | Carbohydrates: 19.8g | Fiber: 4g | Sugar: 10.6g | Protein: 4.6g

Grilled Sweet Potato & Marshmallows Casserole

Prep Time:1 hour 30 minutes | Cook Time: 10 minutes | Servings: 4

Ingredients:

¼ cup brown sugar
½ cup butter, softened
4 oz. pecans, chopped
4 sweet potatoes

2 tsps. Pit Boss Sweet Rib Rub
6 oz. mini marshmallows
½ tsp. cinnamon

Preparation:

1. Preheat your Pit Boss to 400°F. Set the Pit Boss Wood Pellet Grill to MEDIUM-HIGH heat if using a gas or charcoal grill. 2. Scrub and wash the potatoes, then wipe them dry with a paper towel. 3. Using softened butter, generously coat the outsides of the potatoes, then set butter aside. Place the sweet potatoes on the Pit Boss Wood Pellet Grill Grate and SMOKE until tender, from 1 to 12 hours depending on their size. 4. When the sweet potatoes are tender, eliminate them from the Pit Boss Wood Pellet Grill. More butter is applied, then brown sugar and Sweet Rib Rub are sprinkled on top. 5. To make an aperture in the sweet potato, slice the middle and press on the sides. Layer butter, brown sugar, cinnamon, chopped pecans, and marshmallows in each sweet potato. 6. Return to the Pit Boss Wood Pellet Grill and cook, covered, for 5 minutes, or until the marshmallows are lightly browned. Remove from Pit Boss Wood Pellet Grill and serve warm.

Serving Suggestions: Serve alongside simmering hot tea.
Variation Tip: Other squashes, such as Butternut and Yams, pair well with these toppings.
Nutritional Information per Serving: Calories: 756 | Fat: 43.7g | Sat Fat: 16.7g | Carbohydrates: 90g | Fiber: 9.6g | Sugar: 31.5g | Protein: 5.9g

Smoked Cheese Potatoes

Prep Time:1 hour | Cook Time: 30 minutes | Servings: 6

Ingredients:

½ cup Colby Jack Cheese, shredded
1 stick of butter
1 medium yellow onion
8 potatoes, slice into ¼ round slices

3 tsps. Pit Boss Smoked Salt & Pepper Rub
¼ cup smoked gouda cheese, sliced
A drizzle of sweet condensed milk

Preparation:

1. Preheat the Pit Boss Wood Pellet Grill to 350°F. 2. Fill the kettle halfway with water and bring to a boil; cook for 2-3 minutes. 3. Begin layering the potatoes and cheese in the cast iron skillet. To begin, take the potatoes from the water with a slotted spoon. 4. Add a layer of sliced onion, a drizzle of sweet condensed milk, Pit Boss Smoked Salt & Pepper, half a stick of butter cut into pats, and a layer of sliced smoked gouda cheese on top of the potatoes. 5. Continue with the second layer. Grated Cheddar Jack or Colby Jack Cheese can be sprinkled on top. 6. Cook for about 1 hour at 325°F-350°F, or until the potatoes are cooked. 7. Enhance the temperature of the Pit Boss Wood Pellet Grill to 425°F for the last 10 to 15 minutes of cooking, or until the cheese is golden brown.

Serving Suggestions: Serve topped with green onions and chives.
Variation Tip: Try cold smoking the cheese with a smoker tube a few days ahead of time for next level smoke tastes!
Nutritional Information per Serving: Calories: 394 | Fat: 19.9g | Sat Fat: 12.6g | Carbohydrates: 47.5g | Fiber: 7.5g | Sugar: 4.2g | Protein: 8.4g

BBQ Quinoa Stuffed Bell Peppers

Prep Time:20 minutes | Cook Time: 15 minutes | Servings: 4

Ingredients:

½ cup Cheddar cheese, shredded
½ cup BBQ sauce
Salt and black pepper, to taste
2 cups quinoa, boiled

½ cup corns
4 bell peppers, cut in half lengthwise and deseeded

Preparation:

1. Prepare your Pit Boss Wood Pellet Grill for action. Once it's started, preheat the grill to 350°F. 2. In a big mixing bowl, combine the quinoa, corns, cheese, salt, black pepper, and barbecue sauce, then pack into the pepper halves. 3. Cook the peppers for 10 minutes on the Pit Boss Wood Pellet Grill. Place the skewers on a serving plate after removing them from the Pit Boss Wood Pellet Grill.

Serving Suggestions: Top with extra shredded cheese.
Variation Tip: You can also use Boursin cheese instead of Cheddar Cheese for a richer flavor.
Nutritional Information per Serving: Calories: 471 | Fat: 10.5g | Sat Fat: 3.6g | Carbohydrates: 78.7g | Fiber: 8.3g | Sugar: 14.8g | Protein: 17.4g

Cheese Bacon Loaded Portobello Mushrooms

Prep Time:5 minutes | Cook Time: 20 minutes | Servings: 4

Ingredients:

1 cup Cheddar cheese, shredded
8 bacon strips
3 garlic cloves, minced

4 large Portobello mushrooms, gills removed and cored
¼ cup green onions

Preparation:

1. Preheat the Pit Boss Wood Pellet Grill to 350°F. 2. Sprinkle garlic, bacon, ¼ cup cheese, additional bacon, and green onions over each mushroom. 3. Place on your grill's grates and cook for around 20 minutes. 4. Serve immediately.
Serving Suggestions: Serve with your desired dipping sauce.
Variation Tip: You can also use some mozzarella cheese.
Nutritional Information per Serving: Calories: 339 | Fat: 27.4g | Sat Fat: 12g | Carbohydrates: 4.6g | Fiber: 1.2g | Sugar: 0.3g | Protein: 18.3g

Buttered Corn on the Cob

Prep Time:5 minutes | Cook Time: 20 minutes | Servings: 6

Ingredients:

6 corn, cob
½ cup butter, melted

Salt and pepper, to taste

Preparation:

1. Preheat the Pit Boss Wood Pellet Grill to 400°F. 2. Remove the silk from the corn and husk it. 3. Brush with melted butter and dust with salt and pepper. 4. Place the corn on the grill grates and rotate every 5 minutes until it reaches your desired level of golden brown. Halfway through, brush with butter.
Serving Suggestions: Serve alongside your favorite tea.
Variation Tip: You can also rub some lemon juice on the corn.
Nutritional Information per Serving: Calories: 268 | Fat: 17.2g | Sat Fat: 10g | Carbohydrates: 29g | Fiber: 4.2g | Sugar: 5g | Protein: 5.2g

Braised Garlicky Collard Greens

Prep Time:3 hours | Cook Time:45 minutes | Servings: 4

Ingredients:

3 lbs. collard greens, stems removed and cut into thick ribbons
2 quarts chicken broth
4 garlic cloves, peeled

Salt and black pepper, to taste
3 ham hock, smoked
2 whole yellow onion, sliced
2 tbsps. sweet BBQ rub

Preparation:

1. Preheat the Pit Boss Wood Pellet Grill to 400°F Merge the chicken broth, Sweet BBQ Rub, chopped onions, garlic, and ham hocks in a large stock pot. Cook for 2-3 hours, or until the ham hocks are soft, covered. Allow time for cooling. 2. Remove and cut the flesh from the ham hocks. Simmer for 45 minutes, or until the collard greens are soft, with the collard greens thoroughly submerged in the broth. 3. Season to taste, and if required, add vinegar.
Serving Suggestions: Serve this with chicken wings.
Variation Tip: You can also use spinach instead of collard greens.
Nutritional Information per Serving: Calories: 358 | Fat: 14.3g | Sat Fat: 4.1g | Carbohydrates: 26.7g | Fiber: 12.5g | Sugar: 3.8g | Protein: 36.4g

Vegan Bacon & Green Beans

Prep Time:15 minutes | Cook Time: 1 hour | Servings: 6

Ingredients:

4 slices vegan bacon
2 lbs. green beans, ends removed
Smoked salt and pepper rub, to taste

1 tbsp. butter, unsalted
2 cups chicken broth
2 cups water

Preparation:

1. Preheat your Pit Boss Wood Pellet Grill to 350°F. Set the Pit Boss Wood Pellet Grill to MEDIUM heat if using a charcoal or gas grill. 2. Preheat the Pit Boss Wood Pellet Grill with a cast iron pan. Place the 4 pieces of bacon in the pan once it has finished preheating and fry for 15 minutes, or until the bacon has rendered and is crispy. 3. Take the bacon out of the pan and set it aside for later. Add the green beans, chicken broth, water, and smoked salt and pepper rub to taste to the pan and drippings on the Pit Boss Wood Pellet Grill. Cook for one hour, or until the beans are cooked, with the lid closed in the Pit Boss Wood Pellet Grill. 4. On a cutting board, chop the bacon and toss it with the butter into the beans. 5. Continue to cook the beans for another minute before removing them from the heat and serving.
Serving Suggestions: Serve with cooked rice and curry.
Variation Tip: Add red potatoes to this recipe for a distinguished flavor!
Nutritional Information per Serving: Calories: 257 | Fat: 7.9g | Sat Fat: 2.1g | Carbohydrates: 35.8g | Fiber: 6.5g | Sugar: 3g | Protein: 12.4g

Grilled Garlicky Broccoli

Prep Time: 5 minutes | Cook Time: 30 minutes | Servings: 6

Ingredients:

1 large onion, sliced
1 broccoli, cut into florets
3 garlic cloves, sliced

3 tbsps. butter
1 tsp. parsley leaves, chopped
1 cup cheddar cheese, shredded

Preparation:

1. Preheat the Pit Boss Wood Pellet Grill to 350°F, then increase to 400°F. 2. Cut and arrange broccoli florets on a big piece of commercial grade aluminum foil, divided by onion and butter slices. If commercial aluminum foil isn't available, layer aluminum foil until it's sturdy enough, or use a baking sheet. 3. Drizzle garlic over broccoli and season with parsley, salt, and pepper. Arrange the broccoli on aluminum foil. 4. Cook for 40 minutes, or until broccoli is cooked, on a prepared Pit Boss Wood Pellet Grill. Serve immediately.
Serving Suggestions: Sprinkle broccoli with shredded mozzarella cheese.
Variation Tip: Use some more garlic if you desire.
Nutritional Information per Serving: Calories: 147 | Fat: 12.1g | Sat Fat: 7.6g | Carbohydrates: 4.6g | Fiber: 1.2g | Sugar: 1.6g | Protein: 5.8g

Roasted Cauliflower with Garlic Parmesan Butter

Prep Time: 15 minutes | Cook Time: 45 minutes | Serves: 4

Ingredients:

1 whole head cauliflower
¼ cup olive oil
Salt and pepper
½ cup butter, melted

¼ cup shredded Parmesan cheese
2 cloves garlic, minced
½ tbsp chopped parsley

Preparation:

1. Preheat your Pit Boss Grill and set the temperature to 450°F. 2. Brush the cauliflower with olive oil and season generously with salt and pepper. 3. Put the cauliflower in a cast-iron skillet, place it directly on the grill grate and cook for 45 minutes until golden brown and the center is tender. 4. Meanwhile, combine the melted butter, garlic Parmesan, and parsley in a small bowl. 5. During the last 20 minutes of cooking, drizzle the cauliflower with the melted butter mixture. 6. Remove the cauliflower from the grill. Garnish with additional Parmesan and parsley if desired. Enjoy!
Suggested Wood Pellet Flavor: Apple pellets.
Serving Suggestion: Serve with sandwiches.
Variation Tip: Use broccoli.
Nutritional Information per Serving: Calories 248| Fat 24.2g |Sodium 161mg | Carbs 7.3g | Fiber 3.3g | Sugar 3.6g | Protein 3.7g

Smoked Devilled Eggs

Prep Time: 15 minutes | Cook Time: 30 minutes | Serves: 4

Ingredients:

7 hard-boiled eggs, peeled
3 tablespoons mayonnaise
3 tablespoons diced chives
1 tablespoon brown mustard
1 tablespoon apple cider vinegar

1 tablespoon hot sauce
Salt and pepper to taste
¼ tablespoons paprika
Parsley leaves

Preparation:

1. Preheat the grill to 180°F. 2. Place the eggs on the grill and smoke for 30 minutes. 3. Remove the eggs from the grill and allow them to cool. 4. Add the egg yolks, mayonnaise, chives, mustard, vinegar, hot sauce, salt, and pepper in a gallon zip bag. 5. Knead the ingredients in the bag until they are smooth. 6. Make a small cut at the corner of the bag and squeeze the egg yolk into egg white. 7. Top the devilled eggs with paprika and parsley. 8. Serve and enjoy.
Serving suggestion: serve these devilled eggs with a cup of coffee.
Variation Tip: Use old bay instead of salt and pepper.
Nutrition-Per Serving: Calories 288| Fat 22g |Sodium 342mg | Carbs 4g | Fiber 0.7 g | Sugar 2 g | Protein 17g

Tasty Smoked Cheddar Cheese

Prep Time: 5 minutes | Cook Time: 2 hours | Serves: 8

Ingredients:

2 pounds cheddar cheese block

Preparation:

1. Preheat your Pit Boss Wood Pellet Grill to 180°F. 2. Fill a deep oven tray with ice and place a wire rack on top. 3. Place the cheese on the wire rack. 4. Place the tray on the grill grate and smoke the cheese for 1 hour. 5. Flip the cheese and add more ice then smoke for an additional 1 hour. 6. Remove the cheese from the grill and wrap it with parchment paper. Refrigerate for 2 days. 7. Serve the cheese on its own or in sandwiches.
Serving suggestion: serve smoked cheddar cheese with favourite cracker and pickled vegetables.
Variation Tip: use frozen cheddar cheese.
Nutrition-Per Serving: Calories 200| Fat 10g |Sodium 1250mg | Carbs 12g | Fiber 0 g | Sugar 8 g | Protein 15g

Baked Cinnamon Sweet Potatoes

Prep Time: 10 minutes | Cook Time: 35 minutes | Serves: 4

Ingredients:

2 pounds sweet potatoes
1 red onion, chopped
2 tablespoons oil
2 tablespoons orange juice

1 tablespoon roasted cinnamon
1 tablespoon salt
¼ tablespoons chipotle chili pepper

Preparation:

1. Preheat your Pit Boss Wood Pellet Grill to 425°F. 2. Meanwhile, toss the sweet potatoes and onions in oil and orange juice. 3. In a separate bowl, mix salt, cinnamon and chili pepper then sprinkle the mixture over the potatoes. Toss until well coated. 4. Spread the sweet potatoes in a lined baking pan then place the pan in the grill. 5. Bake for 35 minutes or until the sweet potatoes are tender and golden brown. 6. Serve and enjoy.
Serving suggestion: serve roasted sweet potato with roasted pork.
Variation Tip: use yellow onion instead of red onion.
Nutrition-Per Serving: Calories 145| Fat 5g |Sodium 428mg | Carbs 23g | Fiber 4g | Sugar 16g | Protein 2g

Smoked Asparagus

Prep Time: 10 minutes | Cook Time: 1hour | Serves: 4

Ingredients:

1 bunch asparagus
2 tablespoons oil

Salt and pepper to taste

Preparation:

1. Preheat the grill then set your Pit Boss Wood Pellet Grill to smoke. 2. Meanwhile, trim the asparagus ends and put them in a mixing bowl. 3. Drizzle oil then season them with salt and pepper. 4. Transfer them to tinfoil and fold the sides to create a basket. 5. Place the basket in the grill and smoke the asparagus for 1 hour or until they are soft. 6. Serve.
Serving suggestion: Serve smoked asparagus with smoked turkey breast.
Variation Tip: Use sliced garlic cloves and onions
Nutrition-Per Serving: Calories 43| Fat 2g |Sodium 148mg | Carbs 4g | Fiber 2g | Sugar 2g | Protein 3g

Smoked Cheese Stuffed mushrooms

Prep Time: 10 minutes | Cook Time: 1 hour 20 minutes | Serves: 12

Ingredients:

12 white mushrooms
½ cup bread crumbs
½ cup parmesan cheese
2 garlic cloves, minced

2 tablespoons fresh parsley
⅓ cup oil
Salt and pepper to taste

Preparation:

1. Preheat your Pit Boss Wood Pellet Grill to 180°F. 2. Remove the stems from the mushrooms. Wash the stems and dice them into small pieces. 3. Mix the mushroom stems, bread crumbs, cheese, garlic, parsley, 3 tablespoons oil, salt, and pepper. 4. Arrange the mushrooms in a pan then fill them with the cheese mixture until they are heaping. Drizzle more oil. 5. Place the pan in the grill and smoke for 1 hour 20 minutes or until the mushrooms are tender. 6. Remove from the grill and serve.
Serving suggestion: serve the stuffed mushrooms with your favourite simple salad.
Variation Tip: Use mozzarella cheese in place of parmesan cheese.
Nutrition-Per Serving:
Calories 319| Fat 8g |Sodium 840mg | Carbs 26g | Fiber 3g | Sugar 14g | Protein 17g

Herbed Mashed Potatoes with Cream

Prep Time: 20 minutes | Cook Time: 60 minutes | Serves: 6

Ingredients:

4½ pounds russet potatoes
1½ cups water
1-pint heavy cream
2 sprigs fresh rosemary
3 sprig fresh thyme, plus more for garnish
6 sage leaves

6 whole black peppercorns
2 clove garlic, peeled and chopped
2 stick unsalted butter, softened
Kosher salt
Ground black pepper

Preparation:

1. Preheatyour Pit Boss Grill and set the temperature to 350°F, lid closed for 15 minutes. 2. For the mashed potatoes: Wash, peel and cut the potatoes into 1-inch cubes. Place the potatoes in an ovenproof bowl with 1½ cups of water, cover and cook for 1 hour or until tender. 3. While the potatoes are boiling, combine the cream with the herbs, peppercorns and garlic cloves in a small saucepan. Place on the grill, cover and let it stand 15 minutes. 4. Pass the cream through a sieve to remove the herbs and garlic, then return to a saucepan and keep warm on the heat. 5. Drain, then using a potato ricer or food mill, rice the potatoes back into the large stockpot. Slowly pour in ⅔ of the cream, then stir in 1 stick of the butter and a tablespoon of salt. Continue to add more cream, butter and salt to reach desired consistency. 6. Serve right away or keep warm in a double boiler or slow cooker set to minimum. Enjoy!
Suggested Wood Pellet Flavor: Cherry pellets.
Serving Suggestion: Serve rosemary and thyme-infused mashed potatoes and cream with cauliflower rice.
Variation Tip: Use sweet potatoes.
Nutritional Information per Serving: Calories 748| Fat 54.7g |Sodium 213mg | Carbs 42.3g | Fiber 7.3g | Sugar 3.6g | Protein 7g

Roasted Crispy Lemony Potatoes

Prep Time: 10 minutes | Cook Time: 30 minutes | Serves: 6

Ingredients:

2 pounds potatoes, scrubbed
Peanut oil, for deep frying
½ lemon, zested
1 tbsp sea salt

1 tbsp minced red onion
Kosher salt and freshly ground black pepper
1 tbsp minced Aleppo pepper

Preparation:

1. Set the Pit Boss temperature to 350°F and preheat for 15 minutes with the lid closed. 2. Place the whole potatoes on a rimmed baking sheet lined with parchment paper. Bake on Pit Boss until they offer little resistance when pierced with a sharp, thin-bladed knife, about 30 to 45 minutes, depending on their size. 3. Let them stand at room temperature until cool. Lightly press the potatoes with your hand and open the skin a little. 4. Meanwhile, pour the oil 3-4 inches deep into a large heavy-bottomed saucepan or other deep saucepan and heat over medium heat until the oil reaches 400°F. 5. While the oil is heating, combine the lemon zest and sea salt in a small bowl. Put aside. 6. Fry the potatoes, in batches, if necessary, until evenly brown all over, about 3 minutes. Remove and place them directly into a large bowl. 7. Adjust the heat between batches as needed to bring the temperature of the oil down to 400°F. 8. While the potatoes are still hot, add the red onion and season with the lemon zest and sea salt mixture, Aleppo pepper, kosher salt and black pepper. Toss gently to coat. 9. Garnish with fresh parsley and serve hot. Enjoy!

Suggested Wood Pellet Flavor: Mesquite pellets.
Serving Suggestion: Serve smoked roasted crispy potatoes with sauce or salad.
Variation Tip: Use sweet potatoes.
Nutritional Information per Serving: Calories 117| Fat 2.4g |Sodium 13mg | Carbs 12.3g | Fiber 3g | Sugar 0.2g | Protein 4g

Grilled Cheese Stuffed Zucchini

Prep Time: 10 minutes | Cook Time: 11 minutes | Serves: 4

Ingredients:

4 zucchinis
5 tablespoons oil
2 tablespoons red onion
¼ garlic cloves, minced
½ cup bread crumbs

½ cup mozzarella cheese, shredded
1 tablespoon fresh mint
½ tablespoons salt
3 tablespoons parmesan cheese

Preparation:

1. Cut the zucchini lengthwise and scoop out the pulp. 2. Brush the shells with 2 tablespoons oil. 3. Sauté pulp and onions in the remaining oil in a pan. Add garlic and cook for an additional 1 minute. Add crumbs and cook for 2 minutes or until golden brown. 4. Remove from heat and stir in cheese, mint, and salt. Spoon the mixture into the zucchini halves. Preheat the Pit Boss temperature to 350°F. 5. Sprinkle cheese and grill with the lid covered at medium heat for 10 minutes or until the zucchini are tender. Serve.

Serving suggestion: Serve the stuffed zucchini with charred pork chops.
Variation Tip: Use another cheese of choice.
Nutrition-Per Serving:
Calories 186| Fat 10g |Sodium 553mg | Carbs 7g | Fiber 3g | Sugar 4g | Protein 9g

Baked Supreme Cheese Pepperoni Pizza

Prep Time: 15 minutes | Cook Time: 30 minutes | Serves: 4

Ingredients:

Extra-virgin olive oil
Ounce pizza dough
½ cup pizza sauce
2 cup mozzarella cheese
Parmesan cheese
1 tsp fresh oregano
1 tsp fresh basil

Pound mild Italian Sausage
1 half green bell pepper
2 tbsp onion, diced
1 half red bell pepper
Mushrooms
Pepperoni, sliced
Black olives

Preparation:

1. Set the Pit Boss Grill on high and preheat with the lid on for 15 minutes. 2. Coat a 10 to 12 inch cast iron skillet with extra virgin olive oil. Add the dough into the pan and press the sides down and up. 3. To assemble the pizza, spread the sauce over the dough and add all the ingredients. Pour the mozzarella and freshly grated Parmesan cheese on top and sprinkle with oregano and basil. 4. Bake for 25-30 minutes or until the crust is golden brown and cheese and sauce are bubbling. 5. Let it stand 5 to 10 minutes before cutting. Enjoy!

Suggested Wood Pellet Flavor: Apple pellets
Serving Suggestion: Serve with salad
Variation Tip: Use salami and veggies of your choice
Nutritional Information per Serving: Calories 547| Fat 42.7g |Sodium 1113mg | Carbs 9.3g | Fiber 1.3g | Sugar 2g | Protein 30g

Roasted Cinnamon Root Vegetables

Prep Time: 15 minutes | Cook Time: 45 minutes | Serves: 6

Ingredients:

1 bunch red beets, scrubbed and trimmed
1 bunch golden beets, scrubbed and trimmed
1 butternut squash, peeled and seeded
1 large yam, peeled
1 large carrot, peeled
1 large red onion, peeled
4 cloves garlic, peeled

3 tbsp fresh thyme leaves
1 cinnamon stick
3 tbsp extra-virgin olive oil
Salt
Black pepper
2 tbsp honey

Preparation:

1. Preheat your Pit Boss Grill and set the temperature to 350°F. 2. Cut the vegetables into ½-inch pieces. In a big bowl, combine the vegetables with the garlic cloves, thyme leaves, olive oil and cinnamon stick. 3. Cover a baking sheet with foil. Distribute the vegetables evenly in a single layer on the baking sheet. Sprinkle generously with salt and pepper. 4. Sauté vegetables on the grill for 45 minutes until tender. When tender, place it on a dish and drizzle with honey. Serve hot. Enjoy!

Suggested Wood Pellet Flavor: Apple pellets.
Serving Suggestion: Serve roasted root vegetables with soup.
Variation Tip: Use your choice of vegetables.
Nutritional Information per Serving: Calories 220 | Fat 12.7g |Sodium 101mg | Carbs 27.3g | Fiber 4.3g | Sugar 13.6g | Protein 2.7g

Smoked Macaroni Carrot Salad

Prep Time: 15 minutes | Cook Time: 20 minutes | Serves: 4

Ingredients:

1-pound elbow macaroni
½ red onion, diced small
1 green bell pepper, diced
½ cup shredded carrots
1 cup mayonnaise

3 tbsp white wine vinegar
2 tbsp sugar
Salt
Black pepper

Preparation:

1. Bring a large pot of salted water to a boil over medium heat and cook the pasta according to the package directions. Make sure to cook al dente, drain and rinse with cold water. 2. Set the Pit Boss Grill to 180°F and preheat with the lid on for 15 minutes when you're ready to cook 3. Place the cooked pasta on a platter and place the platter directly on the grill grate. Smoke for 20 minutes, remove from heat and place in the refrigerator to cool. 4. While the pasta is cooling, stir in the dressing. In a bowl, add mayonnaise, white wine vinegar and sugar and mix. Season to taste with salt and pepper. 5. When the pasta has cooled, combine the chopped vegetables, smoked pasta and dressing in a large bowl. 6. Cover with cling film and refrigerate 20 minutes before serving. Enjoy!

Suggested Wood Pellet Flavor: Hickory pellets.
Serving Suggestion: Serve with cauliflower rice.
Variation Tip: Use apple cider vinegar instead of white wine vinegar.
Nutritional Information per Serving: Calories 697| Fat 21.7g |Sodium 413mg | Carbs 102.3g | Fiber 4.3g | Sugar 15.6g | Protein 15.7g

Crispy Asparagus Fries with Balsamic Mayo Sauce

Prep Time: 15 minutes | Cook Time: 30 minutes | Serves: 4

Ingredients:

1 cup panko breadcrumbs
½ cup shredded Parmesan cheese
1 tsp dried oregano
½ tsp salt
¼ tsp onion powder
¼ tsp garlic powder
¼ tsp freshly ground black pepper
2 large eggs

2 tbsp water
½ cup all-purpose flour
1 bunch asparagus, ends trimmed
Balsamic Mayo
½ cup high-quality balsamic vinegar
1 cup mayonnaise
1 pinch salt
¼ tsp freshly cracked black pepper

Preparation:

1. Set Pit Boss temperature to 500°F and preheat, lid closed for 15 minutes. 2. Spread the panko breadcrumbs on a baking sheet lined with parchment paper and roast in the Pit Boss Grill for about 5 minutes until golden brown. 3. Let the panko cool, then toss it in a shallow bowl or plate with the Parmesan, onion powder, garlic powder, oregano, salt and pepper. 4. Whisk the eggs and 2 tbsps of water in a shallow bowl. 5. Put the flour in a separate shallow bowl and place the flour, egg and panko bowls on the work surface to prepare the asparagus. 6. Roll each asparagus stick in the flour, then in the egg mixture and finally in the panko and breadcrumb mixture. Cover the entire spear on all sides. 7. Lay breaded spears onto a large baking sheet covered with parchment paper. Place the baking pan on the Pit Boss and cook the asparagus for 15 to 20 minutes, or until the asparagus is golden brown and cooked to a tender crispness. Turn the asparagus spears over halfway through the cooking time to brown the other side. 8. Balsamic Mayo: In a pot on the stovetop, reduce the balsamic mayonnaise over medium heat until the vinegar becomes thick and syrupy, about 10 to 15 minutes. 9. In a small bowl, combine the reduced vinegar, mayonnaise, black pepper and, to taste, a pinch of salt or more. Serve the balsamic mayonnaise with the hot fried asparagus. Enjoy!

Suggested Wood Pellet Flavor: Mesquite pellets.
Serving Suggestion: Serve asparagus fries with mayo.
Variation Tip: Use green beans.
Nutritional Information per Serving: Calories 204| Fat 5.7g |Sodium 513mg | Carbs 32.3g | Fiber 3.3g | Sugar 1.6g | Protein 8.7g

Spiced Pumpkin Soup
Prep Time: 15 minutes | Cook Time:120 minutes | Serves: 6

Ingredients:
5-pound pumpkin, whole
3 tbsp butter
1 onion, diced
2 cloves garlic, minced
1 tbsp brown sugar
1 tsp paprika
¼ tsp ground cinnamon

⅛ tsp ground nutmeg
⅛ tsp ground allspice
½ cup apple cider
5 cup vegetable broth
½ cup whipped cream
Fresh parsley

Preparation:
1. Cut the pumpkin into quarters with a knife. Scrape off the seeds and fibers. Separate the seeds from the fibers and save them for roasting if desired. 2. Preheat the Pit Boss Grill and set the temperature to 165°F with the lid closed. 3. Place the pumpkin quarters, skin side down, directly on the grill grate. Smoke for 1 hour. 4. Increase the heat to 300°F and grill the pumpkin until tender and easy to pierce with a fork, about 90 minutes. Let it cool, then separate the pumpkin flesh from the skin. 5. Meanwhile, melt the butter in a 4-liter saucepan over medium heat. 6. Sauté onion and garlic for about 5 minutes, until tender and translucent. 7. Stir in the brown sugar, smoked paprika, cinnamon, nutmeg, and allspice. Immediately add the apple cider, and cook for several minutes until the mixture is reduced and syrupy. 8. Add the pumpkin and vegetable broth. Simmer the soup for 20 to 30 minutes. 9. Using a blender, blend the soup until smooth. 10. Season to taste with salt and pepper. If it is too thick, add more vegetable broth. 11. Divide the soup between bowls and drizzle with cream. Sprinkle with a sprig of parsley if desired.
Suggested Wood Pellet Flavor: Alder pellets.
Serving Suggestion: Serve smoked pumpkin soup with cauliflower rice.
Variation Tip: Use a squash.
Nutritional Information per Serving: Calories 270| Fat 11.7g |Sodium 713mg | Carbs 32.3g | Fiber 11.3g | Sugar 17.6g | Protein 9.7g

Grilled Asparagus with Honey–Glazed Carrots
Prep Time: 15 minutes | Cook Time: 35 minutes | Serves: 4

Ingredients:
1 bunch asparagus, trimmed
2 tablespoons oil
Salt to taste

1 pound carrots cut into halves lengthwise
2 tablespoons honey

Preparation:
1. In a bowl add asparagus, oil, and salt and toss to coat. 2. In a separate bowl add carrots, honey, and salt then toss to coat. 3. Preheat your Pit Boss Wood Pellet Grill to 350°F. 4. Place the carrots on the grill and cook for 15 minutes. 5. Add the asparagus to the grill and cook for 15 minutes. 6. Serve and enjoy.
Serving suggestion: Serve grilled asparagus with honey glazed carrots with goat cheese.
Variation Tip: Add garlic powder and onion powder.
Nutrition-Per Serving: Calories 161| Fat 7g |Sodium 81mg | Carbs 24g | Fiber 6g | Sugar 16g | Protein 4g

Delicious Smoked Ratatouille
Prep Time: 20 minutes | Cook Time: 60 minutes | Serves: 4

Ingredients:
2 tbsp olive oil
1 medium onion, diced
6 cloves garlic, minced
2 red or green bell peppers, diced
Kosher salt
Pepper
1 can (28 oz.) crushed tomatoes
4 tbsp fresh chopped basil

2 eggplants, sliced into ¼" rounds
6 Roma tomatoes, sliced into ¼" rounds
2 yellow squashes, sliced into ¼" rounds
2 zucchinis, sliced into ¼" rounds
1 tsp garlic, minced
2 tbsp parsley, chopped
2 tsp chopped thyme
Parmesan cheese, grated

Preparation:
1. Heat 2 tbsps of olive oil in a 12-inch cast iron skillet. Sauté onions, garlic and peppers until tender. Season with salt and pepper, then add the tomato puree. Stir until the ingredients are completely incorporated. 2. Turn off the heat, then add the basil. Stir again, then use your spatula or spoon to smooth the surface of the sauce. 3. Arrange the cut vegetables alternately on the sauce from the outer edge to the inside of the pan. Season with salt and pepper and sprinkle with herbs. 4. When ready to cook, set the Pit Boss grill to 180°F and preheat for 15 minutes. 5. Place on grill and smoke for 10 minutes. 6. After 10 minutes, cover the pan with foil and increase the temperature to 375°F and cook for 40 minutes. 7. After 40 minutes, remove the foil, grate a generous amount of fresh parmesan cheese on top and continue to cook for an additional 20 minutes or vegetables are soft. 8. Remove from the grill and grate more fresh parmesan cheese over the top and sprinkle with fresh parsley. Serve immediately. Enjoy!
Suggested Wood Pellet Flavor: Alder pellets.
Serving Suggestion: Serve Smoked Ratatouille with bread and salad.
Variation Tip: Use sweet potatoes.
Nutritional Information per Serving: Calories 347| Fat 20.7g |Sodium 1613mg | Carbs 32.3g | Fiber 6.3g | Sugar 6g | Protein 6.5g

Chapter 6 Fish and Seafood Recipes

Blackened Cajun Catfish

Ingredients:

1 tsp. garlic, granulated
½ cup Cajun Seasoning
1 tsp. onion powder
1 tbsp. smoked paprika
1 tsp. ground thyme

4 (5-oz.) catfish fillets, skinless
1 tsp. pepper
¼ tsp. cayenne pepper
1 tsp. ground oregano
1 stick butter, unsalted

Preparation:

1. In a small bowl, mix together the Cajun Spice, smoked paprika, onion powder, granulated garlic, ground oregano, ground thyme, pepper, and cayenne pepper. 2. Sprinkle the fish with salt and set aside for 20 minutes to rest. 3. Preheat your Pit Boss to 450°F. Set the Pit Boss Wood Pellet Grill to MEDIUM-HIGH heat if you're using a gas or charcoal grill. Preheat the Pit Boss Wood Pellet Grill by placing a cast iron skillet on it. 4. While the Pit Boss Wood Pellet Grill is heating up, lightly coat the catfish fillets with the spice mixture. Swirl half of the butter into the preheated cast iron skillet to coat it; add additional butter if necessary. Cook the fillets in a heated skillet for 5 minutes, or until a brown crust forms. Cook for another 5 minutes. 5. Eliminate the fish from the Pit Boss Wood Pellet Grill and top with fresh parsley.

Serving Suggestions: Serve with lemon wedges.

Variation Tip: Before you cook your catfish, add a dash of smoke to it. Set your Pit Boss Wood Pellet Grill to SMOKE mode and season the catfish for 20 minutes on the Pit Boss Wood Pellet Grill before seasoning it.

Nutritional Information per Serving: Calories: 406 | Fat: 34g | Sat Fat: 16.6g | Carbohydrates: 2.5g | Fiber: 1.1g | Sugar: 0.5g | Protein: 23g

Grilled Salmon with Honey–Soy Glaze

Ingredients:

¼ cup chives, chopped
2 tbsps. fresh ginger, minced
1 tsp. chili paste
2 garlic cloves, grated
1 tsp. honey

4 salmon, fillets (skin removed)
2 tbsps. soy sauce, low sodium
2 tbsps. lemon, juice
1 tsp. sesame oil

Preparation:

1. Preheat your Pit Boss Wood Pellet Grill on SMOKE with the lid open until a fire in the burn pot is started (3-7 minutes). Preheat the grill to 400°F. 2. Place the salmon in a resalable bag, along with the remaining ingredients (excluding the chives). 3. Seal the plastic bag and toss the salmon evenly to coat it. Refrigerate the marinade for 20 minutes. 4. After the salmon has marinated for 20 minutes, place it on the Pit Boss Wood Pellet Grill Grates and cook for about 6 minutes, turning once in between. 5. Eliminate the pan from the Pit Boss Wood Pellet Grill, turn off the grill, plate, and top with chives.

Serving Suggestions: Serve alongside stir fried broccoli.

Variation Tip: You can also use cod.

Nutritional Information per Serving: Calories: 274 | Fat: 12.5g | Sat Fat: 1.8g | Carbohydrates: 5.7g | Fiber: 0.7g | Sugar: 2.3g | Protein: 35.6g

Lemon Buttered Shrimp Scampi

Ingredients:

½ tsp. chili pepper flakes
2 tsps. blackened Sriracha rub seasoning
Lemon wedges, to taste
½ cup butter, cubed, divided

1 lemon, juice & zest
1½ lbs. shrimp, peeled & deveined
3 garlic cloves, minced
3 tbsps. parsley, chopped

Preparation:

1. Preheat your Pit Boss Wood Pellet Griddle to a MEDIUM-HIGH setting. Set the Pit Boss Wood Pellet Grill to MEDIUM-HIGH heat if using a gas or charcoal grill. 2. Melt half of the butter on the griddle, then cook the garlic, Sriracha, and chili flakes for 1 minute, or until fragrant. 3. Stir in the shrimp, mix well, and cook for 2 minutes, stirring periodically. 4. Merge the remaining butter, parsley, lemon zest, and juice in a mixing bowl. Retrieve the shrimp from the griddle and transfer to a serving bowl after tossing them in the lemon butter. 5. Serve immediately with toasted bread and fresh lemon wedges.

Serving Suggestions: Serve over linguine, spaghetti or zucchini noodles.

Variation Tip: You might use any kind of shrimp for this shrimp scampi.

Nutritional Information per Serving: Calories: 551 | Fat: 34.6g | Sat Fat: 20.6g | Carbohydrates: 5.6g | Fiber: 0.4g | Sugar: 0.8g | Protein: 52.3g

Grilled Lobster Tails with Herb Butter

Prep Time:1 hour | Cook Time: 55 minutes | Servings: 4

Ingredients:

1 lemon, sliced
2 tbsps. chives, chopped
Salt and black pepper, to taste

1 garlic clove, minced
¾ stick butter, room temp
3 (7-ounce) lobster tail

Preparation:

1. Preheat your Pit Boss Wood Pellet Grill on SMOKE, with the lid open, until a fire in the burn pot is established (about 7 minutes). 2. Preheat the Pit Boss Wood Pellet Grill to 350°F. 3. In a small bowl, merge the butter, chives, minced garlic, and black pepper. Wrap the dish in plastic wrap and set it aside. 4. Flow the tails down the middle of the softer bottom of the shell in a butterfly pattern. Brush the tails with olive oil and dust with salt and pepper. 5. Grill lobsters cut side down for 5 minutes, or until shells are bright red. Toss the tails with a large spoonful of herb butter and serve. 4 minutes more on the Pit Boss Wood Pellet Grill, or until the lobster meat is opaque white. 6. Take the burgers from the Pit Boss Wood Pellet Grill and serve.

Serving Suggestions: Serve with more herb butter and lemon wedges.
Variation Tip: Pair with a nicely charred steak for a delicious dinner.
Nutritional Information per Serving: Calories: 291 | Fat: 18.5g | Sat Fat: 11.2g | Carbohydrates: 1.7g | Fiber: 0.5g | Sugar: 0.4g | Protein: 28.7g

Lemony Cheese Crab Stuffed Mushrooms

Prep Time:15 minutes | Cook Time: 5 minutes | Servings: 6

Ingredients:

1 tbsp. lemon, juice
1 package cream cheese, softened
¾ cup Panko Japanese bread crumbs
12 porcini mushroom caps, cleaned and destemmed

2 tsps. lemon, zest
1 tsp. Pit Boss Chop House Steak Rub
2 tbsps. parsley, fresh
½ (2 oz.) package imitation crab, chopped
½ cup divided parmesan cheese, shredded

Preparation:

1. Get your Pit Boss up and running. Once the temperature has been adjusted to 350°F, eliminate the pan from the grill. 2. Mix the imitation crab, cream cheese, breadcrumbs, 14 cup parmesan cheese, lemon juice, lemon zest, parsley, and Pit Boss Chophouse Steak Seasoning in a large mixing basin. Mix until everything is well blended. 3. Stuff a large rounded tablespoon of the filling into each mushroom cap with a spoon and gently pack it in. 4. Top with the remaining parmesan cheese once all of the mushrooms have been packed. 5. Preheat your Pit Boss Wood Pellet Grill to 350°F. Grill the mushrooms for 5 minutes, or until the cheese is bubbling and golden and the mushrooms are soft. 6. Enjoy while it's still hot.

Serving Suggestions: Serve topped with extra shredded cheese.
Variation Tip: You can use any variety of crab.
Nutritional Information per Serving: Calories: 253 | Fat: 7.3g | Sat Fat: 4.3g | Carbohydrates: 40g | Fiber: 1.4g | Sugar: 2.3g | Protein: 27.1g

Smoked Spicy Lime Shrimp

Prep Time:30 minutes | Cook Time: 10 minutes | Servings: 4

Ingredients:

2 lbs. shrimp
2 garlic cloves, minced
2 tsps. chili paste
¼ tsp. paprika, powder
½ tsp. salt

¼ tsp. red flakes pepper
½ tsp. cumin
1 large lime, juiced
1 tsp olive oil

Preparation:

1. Merge the lime juice, olive oil, chili powder, paprika, cumin, garlic, salt, pepper, and red pepper flakes in a mixing bowl. 2. Decant the mixture into a resealable bag, add the shrimp, toss to coat well, and set aside for 30 minutes to marinate. 3. Preheat your Pit Boss Wood Pellet Grill on SMOKE, with the lid open, until a fire in the burn pot is started (3-7 minutes). Preheat the grill to 400°F. 4. Thread the shrimp onto skewers, lay them on the Pit Boss Wood Pellet Grill, and cook for about 2 minutes per side, or until done. 5. Eliminate the shrimp from the Pit Boss Wood Pellet Grill once they are done and serve.

Serving Suggestions: Top with fresh coriander and serve with your favorite dip.
Variation Tip: You can increase the spices for a spicier version.
Nutritional Information per Serving: Calories: 287 | Fat: 4.4g | Sat Fat: 1.2g | Carbohydrates: 7g | Fiber: 0.6g | Sugar: 1.1g | Protein: 52.1g

Smoked Sweet Salmon

Prep Time:20 minutes | Cook Time: 20 minutes | Servings: 4

Ingredients:

¼ cup brown sugar
½ tbsp. olive oil
2 tbsps. Pit Boss Competition Smoked

Seasoning
4 salmon fillets, skin off

Preparation:

1. Before grilling, soak the untreated cedar board in water for 24 hours. Eliminate the pan and clean it down when you're ready to be grilled. 2. Light your Pit Boss Wood Pellet Grill. Preheat the grill to 350°F. 3. Merge the brown sugar, oil, and pit boss competition smoked seasoning. Rub the salmon fillets generously with the mixture. 4. Place the plank over indirect heat and grill the salmon for 20 minutes, or until it is cooked through and flakes readily with a fork. 5. Eliminate the pan from the heat and serve right away.

Serving Suggestions: Serve with lemon wedges on top.

Variation Tip: Set your Pit Boss Wood Pellet Grill to 225°F and smoke for 60–75 minutes for smoked salmon.

Nutritional Information per Serving: Calories: 291 | Fat: 12.9g | Sat Fat: 1.9g | Carbohydrates: 10.1g | Fiber: 0.2g | Sugar: 8.9g | Protein: 34.7g

Lemon Smoked Salmon with Dill

Prep Time:5 minutes | Cook Time: 1 hour | Servings: 4

Ingredients:

1 lemon, sliced
½ cup fresh dill

2 lbs. salmon, fresh

Preparation:

1. Preheat your Pit Boss Wood Pellet Grill to 225°F. 2. Arrange the salmon on a plank of cedar. Place the lemons on top of the fish. Smoke for around 1 hour on your Pit Boss Wood Pellet Grill. 3. Garnish with fresh dill before serving.

Serving Suggestions: Serve with mint dip.

Variation Tip: Salmon absorbs sweet flavors really well, so feel free to add a drizzle of maple syrup or sprinkle brown sugar prior to smoking.

Nutritional Information per Serving: Calories: 319 | Fat: 14.3g | Sat Fat: 2g | Carbohydrates: 4.7g | Fiber: 1.2g | Sugar: 0.4g | Protein: 45.4g

Shrimp Cabbage Tacos with Lime Crema

Prep Time:10 minutes | Cook Time:10 minutes | Servings: 4

Ingredients:

2 tsps. cilantro, chopped
¼ head cabbage, shredded
8 corn tortillas
¼ cup mayonnaise
¼ red bell pepper, chopped
¼ cup sour cream

½ white onion, chopped
½ lime, cut into wedges
Pit Boss Blackened Sriracha Rub, to taste
1 lb. shrimp, peeled and deveined
2 tsps. vegetable oil

Preparation:

Lime Crema:
1. Merge mayonnaise, sour cream, and fresh lime juice in a small mixing dish. 2. Season with Blackened Sriracha to taste.

Shrimp Tacos:
1. In a medium dish, place the shrimp. Drizzle with vegetable oil after seasoning with Pit Boss Blackened Sriracha Rub. Set aside after tossing by hand to coat well. 2. Merge the onion, red bell pepper, and cilantro in a small mixing dish. Remove from the equation. 3. Preheat your Pit Boss Portable Griddle over MEDIUM-HIGH heat. 4. Warm each side of the tortillas on the griddle, then turn off the burner underneath. 5. Place the shrimp on the heated griddle and cook for 4 to 6 minutes, or until opaque, stirring regularly. Season with more Blackened Sriracha for a hotter shrimp. 6. Assemble tacos with shredded cabbage, shrimp, pepper mixture, and sauce drizzled on top.

Serving Suggestions: Serve warm with fresh lime wedges.

Variation Tip: To prevent the shrimp from sticking to the griddle, make sure it is thoroughly seasoned.

Nutritional Information per Serving: Calories: 370 | Fat: 13.6g | Sat Fat: 3.9g | Carbohydrates: 32.8g | Fiber: 4.8g | Sugar: 4.2g | Protein: 30g

Grilled Blackened Salmon

Prep Time:10 minutes | Cook Time: 15 minutes | Servings: 4

Ingredients:

4 tbsps. Sweet Rib Rub
2 lbs. salmon filet
2 tbsps. olive oil

1 tbsp. cayenne pepper
2 garlic cloves, minced

Preparation:

1. Preheat the Pit Boss Wood Pellet Grill. Set the temperature to 350°F once it's started. 2. Eliminate the salmon's skin and discard it. 3. Rub olive oil thoroughly on both sides of the salmon fillet, then season with cayenne pepper, minced garlic, and Sweet Rib Rub. 4. Cook the salmon for 5 minutes on one side on the Pit Boss Wood Pellet Grill. Cook for another 5 minutes on the other side, or until the salmon reaches an internal temperature of 145°F. 5. Take the burgers off the Pit Boss Wood Pellet Grill and serve.

Serving Suggestions: Serve with roasted asparagus.

Variation Tip: To prevent the shrimp from sticking to the griddle, make sure it is thoroughly seasoned.

Nutritional Information per Serving: Calories: 285 | Fat: 9.2g | Sat Fat: 1g | Carbohydrates: 11.4g | Fiber: 0.5g | Sugar: 0.6g | Protein: 0.3g

Cedar Smoked Salmon Fillets

Prep Time:15 minutes | Cook Time: 1 hour | Servings: 6

Ingredients:

3 cedar plank, untreated
1 tsp. black pepper
1 tsp. garlic, minced
1 tsp. onion salt
2 tbsps. rice vinegar

1 tsp. sesame oil
⅓ cup olive oil
1 tsp. fresh parsley, minced
2 salmon filet, skin removed
⅓ cup soy sauce

Preparation:

1. Soak the cedar planks for an hour or more in warm water. 2. Merge the olive oil, rice vinegar, soy sauce, sesame oil, and minced garlic in a bowl. 3. Toss in the salmon and let aside for 30 minutes to marinate. 4. Preheat your Pit Boss Wood Pellet Grill on SMOKE with the lid open until a fire in the burn pot is started (about 7 minutes). 5. Preheat the Pit Boss Wood Pellet Grill to 225°F. 6. Place the planks on top of the grate and secure them in place. After the boards start to smoke and crackle a little, it's ready for the fish. 7. Drain the marinade and season the fish with onion powder, parsley, and black pepper before discarding it. 8. Arrange the salmon on the planks and cook until the internal temperature reaches 140°F. 9. Eliminate off the Pit Boss Wood Pellet Grill and set aside for 10 minutes before serving.

Serving Suggestions: Serve with grilled peaches.

Variation Tip: You can also use apple cider vinegar.

Nutritional Information per Serving: Calories: 319 | Fat: 15.1g | Sat Fat: 2.2g | Carbohydrates: 7.8g | Fiber: 0.2g | Sugar: 0.2g | Protein: 11g

Baked Tuna Noodle Peas Casserole

Prep Time: 30 minutes | Cook Time: 45 minutes | Serves: 4

Ingredients:

1 box whole wheat pasta (13.25oz)
2 cups whole milk yogurt
1 cup almond milk
1 tsp ground mustard
½ tsp celery salt

1 cup sliced button mushrooms
10 ounces tuna, Cooked
1 cup peas, canned
1 cup grated Colby and Monterey Jack cheese

Preparation:

1. Bring a large pot of salted water to a boil over high heat. Add the pasta and cook according to the manufacturer's instructions. Drain and set aside. 2. In a medium bowl, combine yogurt, milk, ground mustard and celery salt. Add the mushrooms, tuna, peas and cooked pasta. Fold in half the cheese. Pour the mixture into a greased 13x9-inch baking dish and top with remaining cheese. 3. When ready to cook, set the Pit Boss to 350°F and preheat, lid closed for 15 minutes. 4. Place casserole dish directly on the grill and cook for 45 minutes or until warmed through and cheese is melted. Enjoy!

Suggested Wood Pellet Flavor: Maple pellets.

Serving Suggestion: Serve baked tuna noodle casserole with salad.

Variation Tip: Use salmon.

Nutritional Information per Serving: Calories 457| Fat 27.9g |Sodium 113mg | Carbs 29.3g | Fiber 4.3g | Sugar 12.6g | Protein 30.7g

Juicy Teriyaki Salmon

Prep Time: 15 minutes | Cook Time: 20 minutes | Serves: 6

Ingredients:

1 cup soy sauce
6 tbsp brown sugar
4 cloves garlic
1 tbsp ginger, minced
2 whole oranges, juiced

4 pieces (5 oz.) salmon fillets
1 tbsp sesame seeds
Scallions, chopped
Toasted sesame seeds

Preparation:

1. Place the broccoli in a large resealable bag. 2. Combine orange juice, oil, garlic, salt and pepper, then drizzle over broccoli and turn to coat. Leave to rest for 30 minutes. 3. When ready to cook, set Pit boss temperature to 375°F and preheat, lid closed for 15 minutes. 4. Place the broccoli in a topper basket or sheet tray to prevent the broccoli from sticking or falling through the grill. 5. Roast 8 to 10 minutes or until crispy but tender. Remove and sprinkle with Parmesan. Enjoy!

Suggested Wood Pellet Flavor: Oak pellets.
Serving Suggestion: Serve roasted broccoli with Parmesan with soup.
Variation Tip: Use cauliflower instead of broccoli.
Nutritional Information per Serving: Calories 804| Fat 24.9g |Sodium 2113mg | Carbs 69.3g | Fiber 3.3g | Sugar 50.6g | Protein 80.7g

Delicious Grilled Togarashi Salmon

Prep Time: 5 minutes | Cook Time: 20 minutes | Serves: 3

Ingredients:

1 salmon fillet
¼ cup oil

½ tablespoons salt
1 tablespoon Togarashi seasoning

Preparation:

1. Preheat your Pit Boss Wood Pellet Grill to 400°F. 2. Place the salmon fillet on a sheet foil with the skin side down. 3. Rub oil then sprinkle salt and Togarashi seasoning on the fillet. 4. Bake in the preheated grill for 20 minutes or until the internal temperature reaches 145°F. 5. Serve immediately.

Serving suggestion: Serve Togarashi salmon with white rice.
Variation Tip: Adjust Togarashi seasoning to your liking.
Nutrition-Per Serving: Calories 119| Fat 10g |Sodium 433mg | Carbs 0g | Fiber 0g | Sugar 0g | Protein 6g

Classic Teriyaki Salmon

Prep Time: 10 minutes | Cook Time: 20 minutes | Serves: 4

Ingredients:

1 salmon fillet
⅛ cup oil
½ tablespoons salt
¼ tablespoons pepper

¼ tablespoons garlic salt
¼ cup butter, sliced
¼ cup teriyaki sauce
1 tablespoon sesame seeds

Preparation:

1. Preheat your Pit Boss Wood Pellet Grill to 400°F. 2. Place the salmon fillet in a foil sheet then drizzle it with oil then sprinkle the seasonings and place butter on top. 3. Place the foil sheet in the grill and cook for 8 minutes. 4. Open the grill and brush with sauce and continue to cook for an additional 5 minutes or until the internal temperature reaches 145°F. 5. Remove from the grill and sprinkle with sesame seeds. Serve.

Serving suggestion: serve teriyaki salmon with fried rice.
Variation Tip: add seasonings of choice.
Nutrition-Per Serving: Calories 296| Fat 25g |Sodium 1179mg | Carbs 3g | Fiber 0g | Sugar 3g | Protein 14g

Easy Grilled Prawn skewers

Prep Time: 10 minutes | Cook Time: 10 minutes | Serves: 6

Ingredients:

2 pounds prawns, clean
2 tablespoons oil

Salt and pepper to taste

Preparation:

1. Preheat your Pit Boss Wood Pellet Grill to 400°F. 2. Skewer the prawns on soaked skewers. Brush them with oil then sprinkle with salt and pepper. 3. Place the skewers on the grill grate and cook for 5 minutes per side. 4. Serve and enjoy.

Serving suggestion: serve prawn skewers with cooked veggies.
Variation Tip: Add cayenne pepper in place of pepper.
Nutrition-Per Serving: Calories 221| Fat 7g |Sodium 1481mg | Carbs 2g | Fiber 0g | Sugar 0g | Protein 34g

Bacon Wrapped Scallops

Prep Time: 15 minutes | Cook Time: 20 minutes | Serves: 8

Ingredients:

1 pound scallops
½ pounds bacon

Salt to taste

Preparation:

1. Preheat your Pit Boss Wood Pellet Grill to 350°F. 2. Pat your scallops with a paper towel until they don't have any moisture. 3. Wrap each scallop with a bacon piece and secure it with a toothpick. 4. Lay them on the grill with the bacon side down. Cook for 7 minutes while rotating them occasionally. 5. Serve and enjoy.

Serving suggestion: Serve these bacon-wrapped scallops with red pepper aioli.

Variation Tip: Use turkey bacon instead of regular bacon.

Nutrition-Per Serving: Calories 261| Fat 14g |Sodium 1238mg | Carbs 5g | Fiber 0g | Sugar 0g | Protein 28g

Grilled Spicy Lingcod

Prep Time: 10 minutes | Cook Time: 15 minutes | Serves: 6

Ingredients:

2 pounds lingcod fillets
½ tablespoons salt
½ tablespoons pepper

¼ tablespoons cayenne
Lemon slices

Preparation:

1. Preheat your Pit Boss Wood Pellet Grill to 375°F. 2. Place the lingcod fillet on a foil and season with salt, cayenne pepper, pepper, and top with lemon slices. 3. Place in the grill and cook for 15 minutes or until the internal temperature reaches 145°F. 4. Serve and enjoy.

Serving suggestion: serve grilled lingcod with roasted potatoes.

Variation Tip: Use ground ginger and cayenne pepper.

Nutrition-Per Serving: Calories 245| Fat 2g |Sodium 442mg | Carbs 2g | Fiber 1g | Sugar 1g | Protein 52g

White Wine–Braised Shrimp Scampi

Prep Time: 5 minutes | Cook Time: 10 minutes | Serves: 4

Ingredients:

½ cup melted butter
¼ cup dry white wine
½ tablespoons freshly chopped garlic
1 tablespoon lemon juice

1 pound shrimp, peeled and deveined
½ tablespoons garlic powder
½ tablespoons salt
Toppings: chopped parsley

Preparation:

1. Preheat your Pit Boss Wood Pellet Grill to 400°F. Set a pan on the grill. 2. Add butter, wine, chopped garlic and lemon juice to the pan and heat for 4 minutes. 3. Season the shrimp with garlic powder and salt then place them in the pan. 4. Cook the shrimp with the lid closed for 10 minutes. 5. Serve the shrimp and top with parsley.

Serving suggestion: Serve this grilled shrimp scampi with pasta.

Variation Tip: Use chopped shallots

Nutrition-Per Serving: Calories 298| Fat 24g |Sodium 1091mg | Carbs 2g | Fiber 0g | Sugar 0g | Protein 16g

Cajun Lemon Smoked Shrimp

Prep Time: 20 minutes | Cook Time: 5 minutes | Serves: 4

Ingredients:

¼ cup extra-virgin olive oil
1 lemon, juiced
2 clove garlic, minced

1 tbsp Cajun seasoning
1 tsp kosher salt
2 pound raw shrimp, peeled and deveined

Preparation:

1. Plan ahead as this will require marinating time. In a large resealable bag, combine all the ingredients together and toss gently to make sure all the shrimp are covered. The shrimp can be covered and marinated for 3 to 4 hours if desired. 2. When ready to cook, set Pit Boss Grill temperature to 500°F and preheat, lid closed for 15 minutes. 3. Thread the shrimp onto skewers and place directly on the hot grill grate. Cook for 3 to 4 minutes on each side until the flesh is opaque. Serve and enjoy!

Suggested Wood Pellet Flavor: Hickory pellets.

Serving Suggestion: Serve Cajun smoked shrimp with mayo dip.

Variation Tip: Use fish instead of shrimp.

Nutritional Information per Serving: Calories 387| Fat 16.9g |Sodium 1213mg | Carbs 5.3g | Fiber 0.3g | Sugar 0.6g | Protein 47g

Baked Salmon Celery Cakes

Prep Time:20 minutes | Cook Time: 30 minutes | Serves: 4

Ingredients:

2 (1 lb) salmon fillet
salt and pepper
½ small onion, diced
1 stalk celery, diced
1 medium red bell pepper, diced
1 tbsp dried dill

1 tsp fresh lemon zest
½ tsp black pepper
¼ tsp sea salt
1½ tbsp Italian seasoned breadcrumbs
2 large eggs
3 tbsp olive oil

Preparation:

1. Set the Pit Boss temperature to 275°F and preheat with the lid closed for 15 minutes. 2. Season the salmon fillets with salt and pepper. Then, place directly on the grill grate. Grill until the internal temperature reaches 120°F. Remove from the grill and set aside to cool. 3. Put the cooled salmon fillets in a large bowl and break up with a fork. Add onions, celery, bell pepper, dill, lemon zest, salt, pepper, bread crumbs and eggs. Mix well. 4. Shape the salmon mixture into 6 patties, roughly 2 inches wide. Increase Pit boss temperature to 375°F and preheat, lid closed for 15 minutes. 5. Place a cast-iron pan on the grill grate to preheat. Add olive oil to the preheated cast iron pan. 6. When the oil is hot, add the patties to the cast iron and cook in batches. Cook for 10 to 12 minutes, flipping once halfway through or until sides are golden brown. Enjoy!
Suggested Wood Pellet Flavor: Apple pellets
Serving Suggestion: Serve baked salmon cakes with salad
Variation Tip: Use tuna
Nutritional Information per Serving: Calories 453| Fat 27.9g |Sodium 313mg | Carbs 5.3g | Fiber 1g | Sugar 2.3g | Protein 48.7g

Smoked Citrus Seafood Ceviche

Prep Time: 20 minutes | Cook Time: 60 minutes | Serves: 4

Ingredients:

1-pound sea scallops, shucked
1-pound shrimp, peeled and deveined
1 tbsp canola oil
1 lime, zested and juiced
1 lemon juice
1 orange, juiced
1 tsp garlic powder

1 tsp onion powder
2 tsp salt
½ tsp black pepper
1 diced avocado
½ red onion, diced
1 tbsp cilantro, finely chopped
1 pinch red pepper flakes

Preparation:

1. In a bowl, combine the shrimp, scallops and canola oil. 2. When ready to cook, set the Pit Boss Grill temperature to 180°F and preheat, lid closed for 15 minutes. 3. Arrange the shrimp and scallops on the grill and smoke them for 45 minutes. While they are smoking, prepare all the other ingredients, and place them in a big mixing bowl. 4. When the shrimp and scallops are finished smoking, turn the grill up to 325°F and cook for 5 more minutes, to make sure they are fully cooked. 5. Let the scallops and shrimp cool, then cut in half width-wise and combine them with the ingredients in the bowl. 6. Refrigerate Ceviche for at least 2-3 hours to let the flavors combine. Serve.
Suggested Wood Pellet Flavor: Mesquite pellets.
Serving Suggestion: Serve smoked seafood ceviche with corn chips.
Variation Tip: Use fresh garlic instead of garlic powder.
Nutritional Information per Serving: Calories 408| Fat 17.9g |Sodium 1213mg | Carbs 19.3g | Fiber 5.3g | Sugar 6.1g | Protein 46.7g

BBQ Cheese Oysters

Prep Time:10 minutes | Cook Time: 6 minutes | Serves: 4

Ingredients:

1-pound unsalted butter, softened
1 tablespoon Pit Boss 11.0 ounces Texas BBQ Rub
1 bunch green onions, chopped
2 cloves garlic, minced

12 oysters
¼ cup seasoned breadcrumbs
8 ounces shredded Pepper jack cheese
Pit Boss Sweet Heat BBQ Sauce
½ bunch green onions, minced

Preparation:

1. When ready to cook, set Pit Boss Wood Pellet Grill temperature to 375°F and preheat, lid closed for 15 minutes. 2. To make the compound butter, thoroughly combine the butter, garlic, onion, and Texas BBQ Rub. 3. Place the butter on parchment paper or plastic wrap to keep it from sticking. Make a log out of it by rolling it up and tying each end with butcher's twine. To solidify, place in the freezer for an hour. This butter can be used to improve the flavour of any grilled meat. You can also replace the compound butter with high-quality butter. 4. Shuck the oysters, making sure to keep all of the fluid inside the shell. Breadcrumb the oysters and lay them right on the Pit Boss Wood Pellet Grill. 5 minutes in the grill You'll want to look for the oyster's edge to begin to curl slightly. 5. Place a teaspoon of compound butter in each oyster after 5 minutes. Add a pinch of pepper jack cheese when the butter has melted. 6. Remove the oysters after 6 minutes on the grill total. Top oysters with a squirt of Pit Boss Sweet and Heat BBQ Sauce and a few chopped onions. Allow to cool for 5 minutes, then enjoy!
Suggested Wood Pellet Flavour: Use Apple Pellets.
Serving Suggestion: Serve BBQ Oysters with salad.
Variation Tip: Use scallops.
Nutritional Information per Serving: Calories 1088 | Fat 106.2g | Sodium 1756mg | Carbs 13g | Fiber 0.4g | Sugar 2.5g | Protein 23.3g

Grilled Tuna Steaks

Prep Time: 5 minutes | Cook Time: 5 minutes | Serves: 2

Ingredients:

3 whole Tuna, steak
Olive oil
Salt and pepper

Soy sauce
Sriracha

Preparation:

1. Brush both sides of the Tuna steaks with olive oil and season with sea salt and ground pepper. 2. When ready to cook, turn Pit Boss Wood Pellet Grill temperature to High and preheat, lid closed, for 10 to 15 minutes. 3. Grill Tuna steaks for 2 to 2½ minutes on each side. 4. Remove the Tuna from the grill and set it aside to cool. 5. Cut into half-inch to ¾-inch pieces. Serve with a soy sauce and Sriracha sauce combo. Enjoy!
Suggested Wood Pellet Flavour: Use Mesquite Pellets.
Serving Suggestion: Serve the Tuna Steaks with sauce.
Variation Tip: Use chicken.
Nutritional Information per Serving: Calories 351 | Fat 9 g | Sodium 291 mg | Carbs 0.7g | Fiber 0g | Sugar 0.1g | Protein 63.2g

Grilled Halibut with Tartar Sauce

Prep Time: 60 minutes | Cook Time: 15 minutes | Serves: 2

Ingredients:

1 cup mayonnaise
½ cup chopped pickles
1 tablespoon chopped capers
½ tablespoon parsley, chopped
½ tablespoon Dijon mustard

½ medium lemon, juiced
6 pieces thick-cut Halibut fillets
Olive oil
Sea salt

Preparation:

1. To allow the flavours to blend, make the tartar sauce at least an hour ahead of time. Combine mayonnaise, dill pickles, capers, lemon juice, and mustard in a mixing bowl. Mix. Toss in the herbs and season to taste with salt. 2. Set the Pit Boss Wood Pellet Grill temperature to High and preheat for 15 minutes with the lid covered when ready to cook. Halibut fillets should be placed on a sheet tray. Drizzle with olive oil, season generously with sea salt, and then thoroughly coat the fillets in the olive oil with your hands. Allow for 5 minutes of resting time. 3. Place the fillets with the presentation side up directly on the grill grate. Cook on high heat until the fish becomes opaque (about 10 minutes). 4. Reduce temperature to 180°F and continue to cook fish for 3-5 minutes. Transfer the fish to a serving tray and serve with lemon wedges and the tartar sauce. Enjoy!
Suggested Wood Pellet Flavour: Use Hickory Pellets.
Serving Suggestion: Serve Roasted Halibut with Tartar Sauce with salad.
Variation Tip: Use Flounder.
Nutritional Information per Serving: Calories 891 | Fat 52.6g | Sodium 1890mg | Carbs 30.8g | Fiber 0.4g | Sugar 0.1g | Protein 78.7g

Grilled Sweet Salmon with Balsamic Glaze

Prep Time: 15 minutes | Cook Time: 30 minutes | Serves: 2

Ingredients:

1 tablespoon freshly ground black pepper
1 tablespoon sugar
2 cups Balsamic vinegar

1 tablespoon Grand Marnier
Salt
2 pieces (8 ounces) Salmon fillet

Preparation:

1. Set aside the sugar and freshly ground pepper. 2. In a small, heavy-bottomed sauce pan, pour the balsamic vinegar. Bring to a low boil over medium heat. Reduce the Balsamic vinegar until it resembles a syrup or coats the back of a spoon, adjusting the heat to maintain a constant simmer. Allow to cool. Toss in the Grand Marnier and season with a bit of salt to taste. 3. Set the thermostat to High and preheat the Pit Boss Wood Pellet Grill for 10 to 15 minutes when ready to cook. Season the salmon with the pepper and sugar mixture evenly and place flesh-side down on the hot grill, preferably at the front for a good sear. Move them to the centre of the grill once they've been seared and cook for 10-15 minutes, or until they reach an internal temperature of 145°F. Serve heated with a glaze drizzled on top.
Suggested Wood Pellet Flavour: Use Mesquite Pellets.
Serving Suggestion: Serve Pit Boss Salmon with Balsamic Glaze with salad.
Variation Tip: Use Halibut.
Nutritional Information per Serving: Calories 339 | Fat 11.1g | Sodium 754mg | Carbs 10.3g | Fiber 0.9g | Sugar 13g | Protein 34.9g

Chinese-Style Sriracha Salmon

Prep Time: 20 minutes | Cook Time: 15 minutes | Serves: 4

Ingredients:

¼ cup soy sauce
2 tablespoons brown sugar
1 tablespoon rice vinegar
1 tablespoon Sriracha
1 tablespoon freshly grated ginger
1 tablespoon minced garlic
¼ teaspoon chipotle chile powder
1 teaspoon Pit Boss 14.75 ounces Champion

Chicken Rub
1½ teaspoon sesame oil
4 (4 ounces) wild salmon fillets
2 tablespoons finely chopped scallions
2 teaspoons toasted sesame seeds
Cooked white rice, brown rice or quinoa, for serving
Grilled baby Bok choy, for serving

Preparation:

1. Combine the soy sauce, brown sugar, vinegar, Sriracha, ginger, garlic, chipotle chile powder, Champion Chicken Rub, and sesame oil in a large resalable bag. 2. Add the salmon, toss to coat evenly, and marinate for up to 1 hour in the refrigerator. 3. Take the salmon out of the bag. Remove the marinade and toss it out. 4. When ready to cook, set the Pit Boss Wood Pellet Grill temperature to 450°F and preheat, lid closed for 15 minutes. 5. Place the salmon directly on the grill grate, skin-side down, for 8 to 10 minutes for medium-well. 6. Remove from the Pit Boss Wood Pellet Grill, then sprinkle with scallions and toasted sesame seeds.

Suggested Wood Pellet Flavour: Use Mesquite Pellets.
Serving Suggestion: Serve Sweet and Spicy Sriracha Salmon with Lemon Pasta.
Variation Tip: Use Cod.
Nutritional Information per Serving: Calories 373 | Fat 6.2g | Sodium 356mg | Carbs 3g | Fiber 0.4g | Sugar 0.1g | Protein 78.7g

Spicy Asian BBQ Shrimp Skewers

Prep Time: 15 minutes | Cook Time: 25 minutes | Serves: 4

Ingredients:

1-pound jumbo shrimp, peeled and deveined
1 stalk green onions, minced
6 clove garlic, minced
2 teaspoons grated ginger
1 teaspoon jalapeño, minced
1 teaspoon Kosher salt
3 teaspoons canola oil
2 tablespoons ginger, minced

1 Jalapeño, minced
½ cup onion, diced
⅓ cup soy sauce
¼ cup brown sugar
1 tablespoon rice vinegar
2 tablespoons tomato paste
½ teaspoon sesame oil

Preparation:

1. Combine the shrimp, green onion, garlic, ginger, Jalapeño, oil, and salt in a large mixing basin. To coat the shrimp, properly combine all ingredients. While you're making the sauce, marinade the shrimp. 2. To make the sauce: In a saucepan, heat the canola oil over medium heat. Sauté for 3 minutes with the garlic, ginger, Jalapeno, and onion. Bring to a boil with the soy sauce and brown sugar. Cook for about 8 minutes, covered, over medium-low heat, or until onion is soft. Allow to cool slightly before transferring to a blender. Process in the remaining sauce components until a smooth purée emerges. 3. When ready to cook, set Pit Boss Wood Pellet Grill temperature to High and preheat, lid closed for 15 minutes. 4. Skewer the shrimp on metal skewers. Place shrimp skewers directly on the grill grate and cook the shrimp until they are pink and opaque, about 3 to 5 minutes per side. 5. Remove shrimp skewers from the grill and brush with the prepared sauce. Enjoy!

Suggested Wood Pellet Flavour: Use Pecan Pellets.
Serving Suggestion: Serve Spicy Asian BBQ Shrimp with mayo.
Variation Tip: Use crabmeat.
Nutritional Information per Serving: Calories 189 | Fat 4.2g | Sodium 3106mg | Carbs 15.8g | Fiber 1.1g | Sugar 13g | Protein 22.7g

Grilled Sea Scallops

Prep Time: 5 minutes | Cook Time: 15 minutes | Serves: 4

Ingredients:

2 pounds sea scallops
½ tablespoons garlic salt
1 tablespoon kosher salt

A dash of white pepper
4 tablespoons salted butter
1 lemon, juiced

Preparation:

1. Preheat your Pit Boss Wood Pellet Grill to 400°F with a pan inside. 2. Season the scallops with garlic salt, kosher salt, and pepper. 3. Add the butter and scallops to the pan and close the lid. 4. Cook the scallops for 15 minutes, flipping them halfway through cooking. 5. Remove the scallops from the grill and add the lemon juice. 6. Serve and enjoy.

Serving suggestion: serve these grilled scallops with basmati rice.
Variation Tip: Use black pepper or cayenne pepper in place of white pepper.
Nutrition-Per Serving: Calories 177 | Fat 7g | Sodium 1430mg | Carbs 6g | Fiber 0g | Sugar 0g | Protein 23g

Chapter 7 Snack and Appetizers Recipes

Buffalo Sriracha Chicken Wings

Prep Time:1 hour | Cook Time: 2 hours 40 minutes | Servings: 8

Ingredients:

2 tbsps. garlic powder
1 cup buffalo sauce
2½ tbsps. Pit Boos Sweet Heat rub, divided
6 lbs. chicken wings

1 tsp. salt
⅓ cup Sriracha Sauce, divided
1 tsp. pepper

Preparation:

1. Mingle ¼ cup Sriracha, Sweet Heat Rub, garlic powder, salt, and pepper in a 2-gallon plastic bag. After mixing everything together, add the chicken wings to the bag. 2. Seal the bag and massage the wings to coat them evenly. Refrigerate for 1 hour or more, up to overnight. Reserve the remaining sauce aside for the recipe. 3. Preheat your Pit Boss Wood Pellet Grill to 250°F with the Sear Slide open. Set the Pit Boss Wood Pellet Grill for MEDIUM-HIGH heat and direct heat if you are using a charcoal or gas grill. 4. Place the marinated wings directly on the grill grate and cook for 1 hour and 15 minutes. 5. After flipping the wings, slather each one with Sriracha sauce. Season with more Pit Boss Sweet Heat Rub, cover, and cook for another 1 hour 15 minutes on the Pit Boss Wood Pellet Grill. 6. Place the wings on a sheet tray after removing them from the grill. After basting with more sauce, open the Sear Slide and return the wings to the grill. Grill for 3-5 minutes, rotating frequently, until wings are lightly charred. 7. Dish out the wings in a serving platter and baste with the remaining sauce before serving.

Serving Suggestions: Serve with any dip containing honey.

Variation Tip: For a great sweet-heat flavor contrast, dip wings in honey mustard sauce.

Nutritional Information per Serving: Calories: 656 | Fat: 25.2g | Sat Fat: 6.9g | Carbohydrates: 2g | Fiber: 0.4g | Sugar: 0.5g | Protein: 98.8g

Buffalo Ranch Spicy Chicken Wings

Prep Time:10 minutes | Cook Time: 20 minutes | Servings: 6

Ingredients:

¼ tsp. cayenne pepper
1½ tbsps. apple cider vinegar
2 tsps. chives, minced
BBQ sweet rub, to taste
½ cup butter, unsalted, cubed

3 lbs. chicken wings, split
1 tbsp. ranch seasoning
⅔ cup hot pepper sauce
¼ tsp. Worcestershire Sauce
⅛ tsp. garlic, granulated

Preparation:

1. Preheat your Pit Boss Wood Pellet Grill to 425°F with the lid open. Set the Pit Boss Wood Pellet Grill for MEDIUM-HIGH heat and direct heat if you are using a charcoal or gas grill. 2. In a big bowl, assemble the chicken wings. Season with a dash of sweet heat. 3. Prepare the sauce: Preheat the Pit Boss Wood Pellet Grill and place a small cast iron skillet or saucepan on it. Whisk together the spicy pepper sauce, apple cider vinegar, Worcestershire sauce, sweet rub, cayenne pepper, and granulated garlic in a skillet. 4. Remove the skillet from the Pit Boss Wood Pellet Grill when the sauce begins to bubble and stir in the butter. Fill a mason jar halfway with the sauce. 5. Combine 1 cup buffalo sauce and ranch seasoning in a mixing bowl. Remove from the equation. 6. Cook the wings for 20 minutes on the Pit Boss Wood Pellet Grill, flipping and rotating every 3 to 5 minutes. 7. When the internal temperature of the wings reaches 165°F, remove them from the Pit Boss Wood Pellet Grill. 8. Pour the sauce over the chicken in a mixing bowl. Toss to coat evenly.

Serving Suggestions: Garnish with fresh chives and serve warm.

Variation Tip: Begin grilling the wings over indirect heat, away from the heat source. For best browning, go slowly towards the burn pot while turning and rotating.

Nutritional Information per Serving: Calories: 573 | Fat: 32.2g | Sat Fat: 14.4g | Carbohydrates: 0.2g | Fiber: 0g | Sugar: 0.1g | Protein: 65.8g

Thai–Style Chicken Wings with Peanuts

Prep Time:2 hours | Cook Time: 35 minutes | Servings: 8

Ingredients:

4 lbs. chicken wings, trimmed and patted dry
2 tsps. BBQ sweet rub
1 tsp. black peppercorns, ground
¼ cup peanut butter
½ cup strawberry preserves
2 tbsps. brown sugar

10 oz. peanuts, whole
1 tbsp. Thai Chili Sauce
¼ cup Worcestershire sauce
2 tbsps. honey
½ red onion, minced

Preparation:

1. In a baking dish, place the chicken wings. Refrigerate for 2 hours after pouring the mixture over the chicken and covering it with plastic wrap. 2. Preheat your Pit Boss Wood Pellet Grill to 400°F with the lid open. Set the Pit Boss Wood Pellet Grill for MEDIUM-HIGH heat and direct heat if you are using a charcoal or gas grill. 3. Cook for 25 minutes, rotating wings every 5 minutes, directly on the grill grate over indirect heat. 4. Meanwhile, lightly toast shelled peanuts on the griddle for 5 to 7 minutes, rotating regularly with a metal spatula. Eliminate the griddle from the heat and set it aside to cool. 5. Eliminate the wings from the Pit Boss Wood Pellet Grill and set aside for 5 minutes to rest. 6. Shell the peanuts and place them in a resealable plastic bag along with other ingredients while the wings are resting. 7. Crush the peanuts, then place them on top of the chicken wings. Warm the dish before serving.

Serving Suggestions: Serve your peanut butter and jelly chicken wings alongside roasted veggies.

Variation Tip: Use organic peanut butter for best blending. The extra creamy peanut butter makes whisking the other ingredients more difficult.

Nutritional Information per Serving: Calories: 773 | Fat: 38.4g | Sat Fat: 7.9g | Carbohydrates: 30.7g | Fiber: 4g | Sugar: 20.8g | Protein: 77g

Smoked Honey Chicken Kabobs

Prep Time:30 minutes | Cook Time: 15 minutes | Servings: 6

Ingredients:

2 garlic cloves, minced
3 chicken breasts, cut into 1 inch cubes
2 tbsps. honey
½ cup olive oil
1 green bell pepper, cut into large chunks
2 tbsps. soy sauce

1 lb. of button mushroom, destemmed and cut in half
1 red onion, cut into quarters
2 tbsps. Pit Boss Competition Smoked Seasoning

Preparation:

1. To create the marinade, whisk together the olive oil, soy sauce, honey, garlic, and Competition Smoked Seasoning in a big bowl. Mix in the chicken thoroughly. Allow the chicken to marinade for about 12 hours after it has been completely covered. 2. Soak the kabob skewers in a large, shallow baking dish for at least 2 hours and up to 12 hours. 3. Drain the water and take out the chicken from the marinade once the chicken has done marinating and the skewers have finished soaking. 4. Switch your Pit Boss Wood Pellet Grill to SMOKE mode. Heat up to 350°F once it's started. 5. Thread a piece of chicken, a piece of pepper, a mushroom, and an onion onto a thread. Repeat this until the skewers are completely filled. 6. Cook for 5 minutes per side, then flip and cook for 5 more minutes, or until the chicken acquires an internal temperature of 180°F. 7. Eliminate the skewers from the Pit Boss Wood Pellet Grill and place them on a serving platter.
Serving Suggestions: Serve with yogurt dip.
Variation Tip: You can also use chicken thighs.
Nutritional Information per Serving: Calories: 338 | Fat: 22.5g | Sat Fat: 3.9g | Carbohydrates: 12.2g | Fiber: 1.5g | Sugar: 8.9g | Protein: 24.3g

Loaded Cheese Chicken Nachos

Prep Time:10 minutes | Cook Time: 15 minutes | Servings: 8

Ingredients:

1 cup cheddar cheese, shredded
1 can corn kernels, drained
1 can black beans, rinsed and drained
2 cups chicken, diced

½ tbsp. Pit Boss Champion Chicken
½ cup salsa
½ red onion, diced
¼ cup sour cream

Preparation:

1. Put half of the tortilla chips on a big sheet pan, then top with half of the shredded cheese and one cup of chicken. 2. Half of the Champion Chicken Rub should be sprinkled on top. Finish with the remaining tortilla chips, cheese, chicken, and spice. 3. Preheat your Pit Boss Wood Pellet Grill to 350°F. 4. Grill for about 7 minutes until the cheese is melted and bubbling and the mixture is thoroughly warmed. 5. Eliminate the pan from the Pit Boss Wood Pellet Grill and set it aside.
Serving Suggestions: Top the nachos with the black beans, corn, diced red onion, sour cream, cilantro and pickled jalapenos.
Variation Tip: You can vary the toppings according to your choice.
Nutritional Information per Serving: Calories: 323 | Fat: 11.3g | Sat Fat: 5.9g | Carbohydrates: 32.2g | Fiber: 5.6g | Sugar: 3.1g | Protein: 25g

Smoked Beer Cream Cheese Dip

Prep Time:20 minutes | Cook Time: 10 minutes | Servings: 6

Ingredients:

8 oz. cream cheese
6 oz. beer, can
1 tsp. onion powder
½ tsp. pepper

2 cups cheese, shredded
½ tsp. salt
Fresh parsley

Preparation:

1. Preheat your Pit Boss Wood Pellet Grill to 350°F. Set the Pit Boss Wood Pellet Grill to MEDIUM-HIGH heat if you're using a gas or charcoal grill. Secure the lid and preheat for 15 minutes. 2. Blend beer, shredded cheese, onion powder, salt, and pepper in a cast iron skillet. 3. Preheat the Pit Boss Wood Pellet Grill to 350°F and place the cast iron skillet on it. Fry for about 10 minutes, then stir and cook for another 5-10 minutes. 4. Add extra shredded cheese and fresh parsley to the top.
Serving Suggestions: Serve with fresh baked pretzels.
Variation Tip: Use organic peanut butter for best blending. The extra creamy peanut butter makes whisking the other ingredients more difficult.
Nutritional Information per Serving: Calories: 298 | Fat: 25.7g | Sat Fat: 16.3g | Carbohydrates: 2.9g | Fiber: 0.1g | Sugar: 0.4g | Protein: 12.4g

Pit Boss Chex Party Snack Mix

Prep Time:15 minutes | Cook Time: 60 minutes | Serves: 8

Ingredients:

6 tbsp butter or margarine
2 tbsp Worcestershire sauce
1 ½ tsp seasoned salt
¾ tsp garlic powder
½ tsp onion powder
3 cups Corn Chex Cereal

3 cups Rice Chex Cereal
3 cups Wheat Chex Cereal
1 cup mixed nuts
1 cup bite-size pretzels
1 cup garlic or regular bagel chips, broken
into bite-sized pieces

Preparation:

1. When ready to cook, start the Pit Boss Grill and set the temperature to 375°F. Preheat with the lid closed for 10-15 minutes. 2. Melt butter in a large roasting pan on the grill. Stir in Worcestershire and seasonings. Slowly stir in the remaining ingredients until evenly coated. 3. Cook at 250°F for 1 hour, stirring every 15 minutes. 4. Spread onto a paper towel to cool. Store in a resalable bag or airtight container. Enjoy!
Suggested Wood Pellet Flavor: Hickory pellets.
Serving Suggestion: Serve chex party mix with juice.
Variation Tip: Use soy sauce instead of Worcestershire sauce.
Nutritional Information per Serving: Calories 391| Fat 19.7g |Sodium 813mg | Carbs 50.3g | Fiber 5.3g | Sugar 6g | Protein 8.7g

Sweet & Spicy Cashews

Prep Time: 05 minutes | Cook Time: 60 minutes | Serves: 6

Ingredients:

3 tbsp sambal oelek
1 tbsp maple syrup
1 lemon, zested
½ tbsp fresh chopped rosemary

1 tsp red pepper flakes
¼ tsp cayenne powder
1 pound cashews

Preparation:

1. Start the Pit Boss Grill and set the temperature to 225°F. Preheat with the lid closed, 10-15 minutes 2. Combine sambal oelek, maple syrup, lemon zest, rosemary, red pepper flakes, and cayenne in a small bowl. Toss the cashews in the mixture to coat them. 3. Spread cashews out on a sheet tray and place directly on the grill grate. Cook nuts for 1 hour, stirring occasionally. 4. Remove from grill and let cool. Enjoy!
Suggested Wood Pellet Flavor: Hickory pellets.
Serving Suggestion: Serve smoked sweet & spicy cashews with juice.
Variation Tip: Use walnuts.
Nutritional Information per Serving: Calories 336| Fat 25.9g |Sodium 47mg | Carbs 21.3g | Fiber 2.3g | Sugar 4.6g | Protein 8.7g

Crispy Kale Chips

Prep Time: 05 minutes | Cook Time: 20 minutes

Serves:4

Ingredients:

2 bunches kale, leaves washed and stems
removed

1 tbsp extra-virgin olive oil (as needed)
1 tsp sea salt to taste

Preparation:

1. Thoroughly dry the kale leaves and place them on a baking sheet. 2. Drizzle lightly with olive oil and sprinkle with sea salt. 3. Set the Pit Boss Grill temperature to 250°F and preheat, lid closed for 15 minutes. 4. Place the sheet tray directly on the grill grate and cook until kale is lightly browned and crispy, about 20 minutes. Enjoy!
Suggested Wood Pellet Flavor: Apple pellets.
Serving Suggestion: Serve with bread.
Variation Tip: Use spinach.
Nutritional Information per Serving: Calories 42| Fat 3.9g |Sodium 111mg | Carbs 3.3g | Fiber 0.5g | Sugar 0g | Protein 1g

Crispy Sweet Potatoes with Lime–Mayo Sauce

Prep Time: 15 minutes | Cook Time: 30 minutes | Serves: 4

Ingredients:

4 sweet potatoes, wedges
3 tablespoons oil
1 tablespoon salt
1 tablespoon black pepper

1 cup mayonnaise
2 chipotle peppers in adobo sauce
2 limes juice

Preparation:

1. Preheat your Pit Boss Wood Pellet Grill to 400°F for 15 minutes with the lid closed. 2. Toss the sweet potatoes with oil, salt, and pepper. Spread them on a sheet pan. 3. Place the sheet pan on the grill grate and cook for 30 minutes while stirring occasionally or until crispy. 4. Meanwhile, mix mayo, peppers, and juice in a blender. Blend until smooth. 5. Serve the sweet potato fries with the sauce.
Serving suggestion: Serve the roasted sweet potatoes with grilled chicken thighs.
Variation Tip: Use lemon juice in place of lime juice.
Nutrition-Per Serving: Calories 323 | Fat 30g |Sodium 1141mg | Carbs 15g | Fiber 3g | Sugar 4g | Protein 1g

Baked Bacon Wrapped Cheese Jalapeno Poppers

Prep Time: 10 minutes | Cook Time: 25 minutes | Serves: 4

Ingredients:

6 jalapenos
4 Oz. cream cheese
½ cup cheddar cheese, shredded

1 tablespoon veggie rub
12 slices thinly cut bacon

Preparation:

1. Preheat your Pit Boss Wood Pellet Grill to 375°F. 2. Slice the jalapenos lengthwise and scrape out the seeds and membrane. Set aside. 3. In a mixing bowl, mix the cheddar cheese, cream cheese, veggie rub until well mixed. 4. Fill the jalapeno halves with the mixture then wrap each with a bacon slice. 5. Grill for 20 minutes or until the jalapenos are soft and the bacon is crispy.
Serving suggestion: serve these bacon-wrapped jalapenos with ranch dressing.
Variation Tip: Add chopped mushrooms.
Nutrition-Per Serving: Calories 3231 | Fat 15g |Sodium 994mg | Carbs 5g | Fiber 0.7g | Sugar 2g | Protein 19g

Roasted Potatoes with Bacon

Prep Time:20 minutes | Cook Time:2 hours | Serves: 6

Ingredients:

1 pound sliced bacon
6 large russet potatoes
½ cup (1 stick) unsalted butter, cold, plus additional melted butter, as needed

Salt and pepper
1 cup shredded Cheddar cheese
3 scallions, thinly sliced

Directions:

1. Chill the bacon in the freezer for 30 minutes. 2. When you're ready to cook, preheat the Pit Boss Wood Pellet Grill to 350°F for 15 minutes with the lid closed. 3. Cut the potatoes in half. Place two wooden spoons on either side of the potato on a cutting board to keep your knife from cutting all the way through. Slice the potatoes into thin chips, leaving about ¼-inch on the bottom attached. Rep with the remaining potatoes. Take the bacon out of the freezer. Cut the bacon into 1-inch pieces, about the size of a stamp, with a sharp knife. Place the cold bacon between every other slice of potato in the cracks. Place thinly sliced cold butter between the other potato slices. Place the potatoes in a large cast iron skillet and season with salt and pepper to taste. 4. Close the grill and place the cast iron skillet directly on the grates. 5. Cook the potatoes for 2 hours, basting every 30 minutes with melted butter, until tender, cooked through, and golden brown. 6. Cook until the Cheddar cheese is melted over the potatoes, 5-10 minutes. 7. Remove the grilled potatoes from the grill and top with scallions. Enjoy!
Serving suggestion: Serve it with hot dogs.
Variation tip: Add grilled cheese over it.
Nutritional Value (Amount per Serving): Calories 405 | Fat 12g | Carbs 67g | Sugar 2g | Protein 9g

Grilled Rosemary Olives

Prep Time: 15 minutes | Cook Time: 2 hours | Serves: 6

Ingredients:

2 cup green olives
2 tablespoons oil
2 tablespoons white wine

2 minced garlic cloves
¾ tablespoons dried rosemary
¼ tablespoons red pepper flakes

Preparation:

1. Preheat your pit boss wood pellet grill to 220°F. 2. Mix all the ingredients in a heavy-duty aluminium foil that has been moulded into a tray. 3. Place the olives on the grill and cook for 2 hours. 4. Serve and enjoy.
Serving suggestion: Serve the grilled olives with your favourite cheese.
Variation Tip: Use more herbs of choice.
Nutrition-Per Serving: Calories 64 | Fat 6g |Sodium 15mg | Carbs 3g | Fiber 1g | Sugar 1g | Protein 1g

Roasted Sweet Cinnamon Almonds

Prep Time: 5 minutes | Cook Time: 60 minutes | Serves: 4

Ingredients:

1 whole egg white
½ cup granulated sugar
½ cup brown sugar

1 tbsp ground cinnamon
1 pinch salt
1 pound almonds

Preparation:

1. Put the egg white in a small bowl and beat until frothy. Add the sugar, cinnamon and salt. Mix the almonds with the egg white mixture and cover well. 2. Spread the almonds on a baking sheet lined with parchment paper, ensuring they are in an even layer 3. Set the Pit Boss Grill temperature to 225°F and preheat, lid closed for 15 minutes for optimal flavor. 4. Place the sheet tray directly on the grill grate and roast almonds for 90 minutes. Stir every 10 minutes or so until coating is dry. 5. Let them cool a bit before serving. Enjoy!
Suggested Wood Pellet Flavor: Hickory pellets.
Serving Suggestion: Serve roasted cinnamon almonds with blueberries.
Variation Tip: Use pecans.
Nutritional Information per Serving: Calories 596| Fat 35.9g |Sodium 62mg | Carbs 59.3g | Fiber 9.3g | Sugar 45.6g | Protein 16.7g

Spicy Lemony Cashew

Prep Time: 5 minutes | Cook Time: 1 hour | Serves: 6

Ingredients:

3 tablespoons sambal oelek
1 lemon, zested
½ tablespoons rosemary, chopped

1 tablespoon red pepper flakes
¼ tablespoons cayenne powder
1 pound cashews

Preparation:

1. Preheat your Pit Boss Wood Pellet Grill to 225°F for 15 minutes with the lid closed. 2. In a mixing bowl, mix sambal oelek, lemon zest, rosemary, pepper flakes, and cayenne powder. 3. Pour the mixture over cashews and mix well. 4. Spread the cashews on a sheet pan and place the sheet pan on the grill grates. 5. Cook for 1 hour while stirring occasionally. Let cool before serving.

Serving suggestion: Serve the smoked cashews with a cool drink.

Variation Tip: Use coriander and smoked paprika.

Nutrition-Per Serving: Calories 439 | Fat 35g |Sodium 6mg | Carbs 26g | Fiber 6g | Sugar 2g | Protein 12g

Smoked Cheese Popcorn

Prep Time: 15 minutes | Cook Time: 15 minutes | Serves: 2

Ingredients:

4 tbsp butter
2 tsp Italian seasoning, finely crumbled
1 tsp garlic powder

1 tsp salt
¼ cup popcorn kernels
½ cup Parmesan cheese, grated

Preparation:

1. When ready to cook, set the Pit boss to 250°F and preheat, lid closed for 15 minutes. 2. Melt the butter in a small saucepan over medium heat. Stir in the Italian seasoning, garlic powder, and salt until everything is well combined. Remove the pan from the heat and set it aside. 3. Add ¼ cup of popcorn to a brown paper lunch bag. Fold the top of the bag over twice to close. Then, place the bag in the microwave and microwave on high for 1 to 2 minutes, or until there are about 5 seconds between pops. Open the bag with care and dump into a large mixing bowl. 4. Toss the popcorn with the butter mixture in a mixing basin. Place popcorn on a baking pan and cook it. 5. Remove from the grill after 10 minutes of smoking. To serve, toss with parmesan cheese. Enjoy!

Suggested Wood Pellet Flavor: Cherry pellets.

Serving Suggestion: Serve smoked herb popcorn with juice.

Variation Tip: Use quinoa.

Nutritional Information per Serving: Calories 325| Fat 25.9g |Sodium 1213mg | Carbs 21.3g | Fiber 4.3g | Sugar 0.6g | Protein 5.7g

Simple Grilled Sweet Potato

Prep Time: 5 minutes | Cook Time: 20 minutes | Serves: 6

Ingredients:

5 large sweet potatoes
1 tbsp canola oil
1 tsp salt

1 tsp pepper
½ tsp onion powder

Preparation:

1. Wash and peel the sweet potatoes, then cut them into eighths lengthwise. 2. Mix them in the oil, salt, pepper and onion powder. 3. When ready to cook, set Pit Boss temperature to 500°F and preheat, lid closed for 15 minutes. 4. Place the sweet potatoes directly on the grill. Note: they will get a great sear by placing them in the very front and in the very back of the grill. 5. Once they have good grill marks, slide them down the center and continue cooking for about 15-20 minutes. Serve warm.

Suggested Wood Pellet Flavor: Maple pellets.

Serving Suggestion: Serve grilled sweet potato planks with sauce.

Variation Tip: Use normal potatoes.

Nutritional Information per Serving: Calories 172| Fat 2.9g |Sodium 399mg | Carbs 34.3g | Fiber 5.3g | Sugar 0.6g | Protein 2g

Seared Lemon Buttered Scallops

Prep Time: 05 minutes | Cook Time: 05 minutes | Serves: 4

Ingredients:

12 Scallops
Kosher salt
Black pepper
1 tablespoon butter
1 tablespoon olive oil

4 tablespoons butter, melted
1 clove garlic, minced
1 lemon, juiced
Chopped parsley, for garnish
Lemon zest, for garnish

Preparation:

1. When ready to cook, set Pit Boss Wood Pellet Grill temperature to 500°F and preheat, lid closed for 15 minutes. Place a cast iron skillet directly on the grill to preheat for 20 minutes. 2. If the frill is still intact, remove it. Using a paper towel, pat the Scallops dry. Season with a generous amount of salt and a pinch of black pepper. 3. Place the butter and olive oil in the skillet once the grill is hot. Place the Scallops on the griddle once the butter has melted. Close the lid and cook for about 2 minutes, or until one side is charred and browned. 4. Combine the melted butter and garlic in a small bowl while the Scallops are cooking. Cook for 1 minute more after flipping the scallops and spooning a couple tablespoons of garlic butter over the top. 5. Remove from the Pit Boss Wood Pellet Grill, top with parsley and lemon zest, and drizzle with a little extra garlic butter if preferred. Enjoy!

Suggested Wood Pellet Flavour: Use Pecan Pellets.
Serving Suggestion: Serve Seared Lemon Garlic Scallops.
Variation Tip: Use Lobster.
Nutritional Information per Serving: Calories 140 | Fat 7.1 g | Sodium 205mg | Carbs 3.7g | Fiber 0.4g | Sugar 0.4g | Protein 15.3g

Smoked Cheese Chicken Stuffed Jalapeño Poppers

Prep Time: 15 minutes | Cook Time: 60 minutes | Serves: 4

Ingredients:

12 medium Jalapeño
6 slices bacon, cut in half
8 ounces cream cheese

2 tablespoons Pit Boss 12.5 ounces Chicken and Poultry Rub
1 cup grated cheese

Preparation:

1. When ready to cook, set Pit Boss Wood Pellet Grill temperature to 180°F and preheat, lid closed for 15 minutes. For optimal flavour, use Super Smoke if available. 2. Cut the Jalapeños lengthwise in half. With a tiny spoon or paring knife, scrape off any seeds or ribs. Combine softened cream cheese, Pit Boss Chicken and Poultry Rub, and grated cheese in a mixing bowl. Fill each side of a jalapeño with the mixture. Wrap the bacon around the cheese and fasten with a toothpick. 3. Place the Jalapenos on a baking sheet with a rim. Place on the grill for 30 minutes to smoke. 4. Raise the grill temperature to 375°F and cook for another 30 minutes, or until the bacon is cooked to your liking. Warm it up and enjoy it!

Suggested Wood Pellet Flavour: Use Mesquite Pellets.
Serving Suggestion: Serve Smoked Jalapeno Poppers with mayo.
Variation Tip: Use Serrano chili.
Nutritional Information per Serving: Calories 479 | Fat 41.3g | Sodium 1690mg | Carbs 4.8g | Fiber 1.2g | Sugar 1.5g | Protein 22.4g

Artichoke Parmesan Stuffed Mushrooms

Prep Time: 15 minutes | Cook Time: 30 minutes | Serves: 8

Ingredients:

8 cremini mushroom caps
6½ ounces artichoke hearts
⅓ cup Parmesan cheese, grated
¼ cup mayonnaise

½ teaspoon garlic salt
Your favorite hot sauce
Paprika

Preparation:

1. Using a damp paper towel, wipe the mushrooms clean. Remove the stems and toss them out or preserve them for another project. 2. Scoop out the insides using a tiny spoon (gills, etc.). Mix together the artichoke hearts, mayonnaise, Parmesan cheese, garlic salt, and spicy sauce. 3. Fill the mushroom caps with the filling. Paprika should be sprinkled over the tops. 4. Arrange the mushrooms in a baking dish that can be used in the grill. 5. When ready to cook, set Pit Boss Wood Pellet Grill temperature to 350°F and preheat, lid closed for 15 minutes 6. Bake the mushrooms (uncovered) until the filling is bubbling and just beginning to brown, about 25 to 30 minutes. Serve immediately. 7. For a simple variation, stuff the mushrooms with your favorite bulk sausage and bake on your Pit Boss Wood Pellet Grill as directed above. Enjoy!

Suggested Wood Pellet Flavour: Use Pecan Pellets.
Serving Suggestion: Serve Baked Artichoke Parmesan Mushrooms with grilled chicken.
Variation Tip: Use zucchini.
Nutritional Information per Serving: Calories 64 | Fat 2.8g | Sodium 100mg | Carbs 7.5g | Fiber 1.4g | Sugar 1.8g | Protein 3.3g

Chapter 8 Dessert Recipes

Caramel Bourbon Bacon Brownies
Prep Time:15 minutes | Cook Time: 1 hour | Servings: 16

Ingredients:

1 cup brown sugar
2 cups all-purpose flour
1 cup caramel sauce
6 large eggs
4 tbsps. water
1 cup canola oil
2 tbsps. instant coffee

3 cups white sugar
1 tsp. sea salt
1 cup powdered sugar
¼ cup bourbon
1½ cups cocoa powder
6 slices bacon, raw

Preparation:

1. Get your Pit Boss Wood Pellet Grill up and running. Set the temperature to 400°F once it's preheated. 2. Merge the powdered sugar, cocoa, white sugar, flour, and instant coffee in a large mixing basin. 3. Stir the eggs, oil, and water into the flour mixture until just mixed. Lightly grease a 9x13 pan with cooking spray. 4. Drizzle half of the batter in the pan with caramel. Pour the remaining batter on top and sprinkle with caramel, then top with candied bacon. 5. Cook the brownies for 1 hour in the smoker, or until a toothpick inserted in the center comes out clean. 6. Eliminate the meat from the smoker and let it cool completely before slicing.
Serving Suggestions: Serve with vanilla ice cream.
Variation Tip: Are you a Bourbon sceptic? As an alternative, use non-alcoholic vanilla extract.
Nutritional Information per Serving: Calories: 525 | Fat: 19.7g | Sat Fat: 3.2g | Carbohydrates: 84g | Fiber: 3g | Sugar: 54g | Protein: 8.4g

Blueberry Cheesecake Skillet Brownie
Prep Time:10 minutes | Cook Time: 30 minutes | Servings: 6

Ingredients:

2 eggs
1 tsp. vanilla
1 box brownie mix
1 can blueberry, pie filling

1 package cream cheese
½ cup sugar
½ cup oil
¼ cup water, warm

Preparation:

1. Mix up all of the brownie ingredients. 2. Merge cream cheese, sugar, egg, and vanilla in a separate dish and beat until smooth. 3. Pour brownie batter into greased skillets. 4. Top with cheesecake and cherry pie filling, blending with a knife to create a marbled effect. 5. Bake for around 30 minutes at 350°F in your Pit Boss Wood Pellet Grill. 6. Allow to cool for about 10 minutes before serving.
Serving Suggestions: Serve with blueberry ice cream.
Variation Tip: You can also use natural sweetener if you don't want to have sugar.
Nutritional Information per Serving: Calories: 751 | Fat: 39.8g | Sat Fat: 8.5g | Carbohydrates: 98.6g |
Fiber: 0.6g | Sugar: 19.3g | Protein: 7.2g

Smoked Bourbon Pumpkin Pie
Prep Time:10 minutes | Cook Time: 1 hour | Servings: 8

Ingredients:

1 can (14 oz.) sweetened condensed milk
1 can (14 oz.) pumpkin puree
1 cup evaporated milk
2 eggs

1 pie crust
2 tsps. pumpkin spice rub
1 oz. bourbon

Preparation:

1. Preheat your Pit Boss Wood Pellet Grill to 400°F by setting it to SMOKE and letting it run for 10 minutes with the lid open. 2. Carefully push the pie crust into the corners of the pie pan. Fold the crust's edges over the edge of the pie pan. Remove any excess crust with a knife. 3. Merge the remaining ingredients, except the eggs, in a mixing dish. 4. Once everything is completely incorporated, whisk in the eggs until they are barely combined. 5. Put the pie filling into the pie pan. Cook for 15 minutes on the smoker. 6. Reduce the oven temperature to 350°F. Bake for another 45 minutes, or until the middle of the pie is completely set. 7. Cool for 2 hours before serving!
Serving Suggestions: Serve topped with whipped cream.
Variation Tip: Beat eggs before adding into pie filling for ease of mixing.
Nutritional Information per Serving: Calories: 348 | Fat: 14.3g | Sat Fat: 5.5g | Carbohydrates: 46.2g | Fiber: 1.4g | Sugar: 36.6g | Protein: 8.2g

Grilled Cinnamon Peaches

Prep Time:1 minute | Cook Time: 8 minutes | Servings: 3

Ingredients:

½ tbsp. cinnamon, ground
3 tbsps. brown sugar

3 full peach, halved and pitted
1 tbsp. butter, melted

Preparation:

1. Preheat your Pit Boss Wood Pellet Grill on SMOKE with the lid open until a fire in the burn pot is started (3-7 minutes). 2. Preheat the grill to 400°F. 3. In a small mixing dish, incorporate brown sugar and cinnamon. Drizzle melted butter over peach halves. 4. Arrange the peach halves on the grates, cut side down after the grill is ready. 5. Cook for 7 minutes on each side, or until grill marks appear. Sprinkle cinnamon sugar on top of peaches. 6. Grill for another 3 minutes, until the sugar mixture begins to caramelize. 7. Serve immediately.

Serving Suggestions: Serve topped with maple syrup.

Variation Tip: You can also use apples for this recipe.

Nutritional Information per Serving: Calories: 130 | Fat: 4.3g | Sat Fat: 2.4g | Carbohydrates: 23.7g | Fiber: 2.9g | Sugar: 22.8g | Protein: 1.5g

Tasty Pimento Cheese Cornbread

Prep Time:15 minutes | Cook Time: 30 minutes | Servings: 4

Ingredients:

½ cup cornmeal, yellow
2 tsps. baking powder
1½ cups flour, all-purpose
¼ cup sugar
2 eggs

Smoked salt and cracked pepper rub, to taste
2 tbsps. Pit Boss Bacon Cheddar Seasoning
2 cups buttermilk, low fat
16 oz. Pimento Cheese Spread

Preparation:

1. Preheat the Pit Boss Wood Pellet Grill to 350°F. Warm up a cast iron skillet on the Pit Boss Wood Pellet Grill. 2. Blend the eggs, buttermilk, Pit Boss Bacon Cheddar Seasoning, and pimento cheese spread in a mixing basin. Combine the sugar, baking powder, cornmeal, salt, pepper and flour in a bowl. Mix until everything is well blended. 3. Carefully take the cast iron skillet from the Pit Boss Wood Pellet Grill, oil it, and pour in the cornbread batter while using cooking gloves. 4. Grill for 30 minutes until golden brown.

Serving Suggestions: Serve alongside a simmering cup of tea.

Variation Tip: For even more bacon flavor, sprinkle a little diced crispy bacon on top!

Nutritional Information per Serving: Calories: 809 | Fat: 45.9g | Sat Fat: 18.5g | Carbohydrates: 71g | Fiber: 2.4g | Sugar: 22.6g | Protein: 31.8g

Homemade Strawberry Rhubarb Pie

Prep Time:20 minutes | Cook Time: 30 minutes | Servings: 8

Ingredients:

1 prepared pie shell, deep
⅓ cup flour
2½ cups strawberry, sliced into small pieces

3 stalks rhubarb, sliced into small pieces
1 tbsp. lemon, zest
1 cup sugar

Preparation:

1. Preheat the Pit Boss Wood Pellet Grill to 400°F. 2. Merge the rhubarb and strawberries with the sugar, flour, and lemon zest. 3. Pour into the pie crust that has been made. Place the top crust on top. 4. Bake for 1 hour in the Pit Boss Wood Pellet Grill and immediately serve.

Serving Suggestions: Serve topped with additional strawberries.

Variation Tip: You can also use raspberries instead of strawberries.

Nutritional Information per Serving: Calories: 142 | Fat: 0.7g | Sat Fat: 0.2g | Carbohydrates: 34.7g | Fiber: 1.4g | Sugar: 27.5g | Protein: 1.2g

Smoked S´mores Marshmallow Cake Bars

Prep Time:20 minutes | Cook Time: 1 hour | Servings: 8

Ingredients:

7 oz. marshmallow cream
2 cups graham cracker crumbs
1½ cups mini marshmallows
1 egg

1 stick butter, melted
1 box yellow cake mix
2 cups chocolate chips

Preparation:

1. Preheat the Pit Boss Wood Pellet Grill to 250°F by turning it on SMOKE mode and letting it run with the lid open for 10 minutes. If you're going to use a charcoal or gas grill, make sure it's set to low, indirect heat. 2. Use aluminum foil to line a 9x13" metal pan. 3. Combine the cake mix, egg, butter, and graham cracker crumbs with a hand mixer in a large bowl. 4. Set aside 2 cups of the graham cracker mixture, then press the remaining graham cracker mixture into the prepared pan. Dollop the marshmallow crème over the chocolate chips, then sprinkle the chocolate chips on top. 5. Sprinkle mini marshmallows on top and spread into a uniform layer. Top with the graham cracker mixture that was set aside. 6. Place on the Pit Boss Wood Pellet Grill for 50 minutes to SMOKE. Before cutting into bars, allow it cool fully.

Serving Suggestions: Serve with a crunchy graham topping.

Variation Tip: You can also use white chocolate chips.

Nutritional Information per Serving: Calories: 807 | Fat: 34.1g | Sat Fat: 17.3g | Carbohydrates: 117.2g | Fiber: 3.5g | Sugar: 68.9g | Protein: 8.6g

Maple Bacon Donuts

Prep Time: 5 minutes | Cook Time: 15 minutes | Serves: 8

Ingredients:

1½ cup powdered sugar
¼ cup maple syrup
2 tablespoons maple extract

2 tablespoons heavy cream
2 bacon strips
12 glazed yeast doughnuts

Preparation:

1. Preheat your Pit Boss Wood Pellet Grill to 500°F. 2. Add sugar, maple syrup, maple extract to a saucepan and cook on a stovetop at medium-high heat until the mixture comes to a boil. 3. Reduce the heat to low and stir in the heavy cream to the sugar mixture. 4. Place the bacon on the grill grate and grill for 7 minutes. 5. Remove the bacon from the grill and let it cool. Chop into small pieces. 6. Place the doughnuts on the grill and grill them for 5 minutes on each side. 7. Transfer the doughnuts to a serving platter, pour over the glaze, and sprinkle them with bacon. 8. Serve and enjoy.

Serving suggestion: serve maple bacon donuts with a cup of hot chocolate.
Variation Tip: use Greek yogurt in place of heavy cream.
Nutrition-Per Serving: Calories 491 | Fat 22g |Sodium 321mg | Carbs 69g | Fiber 2g | Sugar 48g | Protein 6g

Baked Coconut Chocolate Cookies

Prep Time: 5 minutes | Cook Time: 15 minutes | Serves: 8

Ingredients:

4 eggs
4 tablespoons brown sugar
1 cup coconut flakes
1 pinch salt

½ cup chocolate, chopped
5 tablespoons butter, melted
Salt for serving

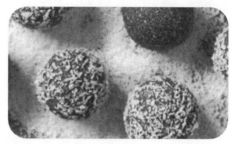

Preparation:

1. Preheat your Pit Boss Wood Pellet Grill to 375°F for 15 minutes with the lid closed. 2. Line a baking tray with foil. 3. In a mixing bowl, mix eggs, sugar, coconut flakes, salt, chocolate, and butter until well combined. 4. Let the mixture rest for 20 minutes. Spoon the mixture onto a tray and shape them like a circle. 5. Bake in the grill for 15 minutes or until the top is golden brown. 6. Sprinkle it with salt and grated coconut. 7. Enjoy.

Serving suggestion: Serve the coconut cookie with caramel apple dip.
Variation Tip: Use granulated sugar in place of brown sugar.
Nutrition-Per Serving: Calories 209 | Fat 16g |Sodium 152mg | Carbs 14g | Fiber 1g | Sugar 10g | Protein 4g

Grilled Peaches with Cream Cheese

Prep Time: 15 minutes | Cook Time: 8 minutes | Serves: 8

Ingredients:

4 peaches, halved
2 tablespoons honey

1 cup cream cheese
1 tablespoon oil

Preparation:

1. Preheat your Pit Boss Wood Pellet Grill to medium heat. 2. Brush the peaches halves with a light coating of oil. 3. Place the peaches on the grill grates with the cut side down. Grill for 5 minutes. 4. Turn the peaches, drizzle with honey and place a dollop of cream cheese on top. 5. Grill for an additional 3 minutes. 6. Serve immediately.

Serving suggestion: Serve grilled peaches with fresh berries toppings.
Variation Tip: Brown sugar and cinnamon can be added before grilling.
Nutrition-Per Serving: Calories 139 | Fat 10g |Sodium 135mg | Carbs 12 g | Fiber 1g | Sugar 10g | Protein 2g

Honey Cornbread Cake

Prep Time: 10 minutes | Cook Time: 40 minutes | Serves: 8

Ingredients:

⅔ cup oil
2½ cup buttermilk
4 eggs, beaten
6 tablespoons melted butter
½ cup mayonnaise
2 tablespoons honey

3 cup all-purpose flour
2 tablespoons baking powder
1 tablespoon salt
1 cup cornmeal
1½ cup granulated sugar

Preparation:

1. Preheat your Pit Boss Wood Pellet Grill to 350°F. 2. In a bowl mix oil, buttermilk, eggs, 5 tablespoons butter, mayonnaise, and honey until well combined. 3. In a separate bowl, mix the flour, salt, baking powder, cornmeal, and sugar. 4. Stir in the flour mixture into the egg mixture until a smooth batter is formed. 5. Pour the batter into a baking dish that has been greased with 1 tablespoon of butter. 6. Place the baking dish on the grill grate and cook for 40 minutes. 7. Let the cake rest for 10 minutes before slicing. 8. Serve and enjoy.

Serving suggestion: Serve cornbread cake with honey.
Variation Tip: Use breadcrumbs in place of cornmeal.
Nutrition-Per Serving: Calories 701 | Fat 37g |Sodium 1256mg | Carbs 79g | Fiber 2g | Sugar 27g | Protein 14g

Lemon Bars

Prep Time: 30 minutes | Cook Time: 60 minutes | Serves: 8

Ingredients:

¾ cup lemon juice
1½ cup sugar
2 eggs
3 egg yolk
1½ tsp corn-starch
Sea salt
4 tbsp unsalted butter

¼ cup olive oil
1 tbsp lemon zest
1 ¼ cups flour
¼ cup granulated sugar
3 tbsp powdered sugar
¼ tsp fine sea salt
10 tbsp unsalted butter, cubed

Preparation:

1. When ready to cook, start the Pit Boss Grill and set the temperature to 180°F. Preheat lid closed, 10-15 minutes. 2. Whisk together lemon juice, sugar, eggs and yolks, corn-starch, and fine sea salt in a small mixing dish. Pour into a sheet tray or cake pan and place on grill 3. Smoke for 30 minutes, whisking mixture halfway through smoking. Remove from grill and set aside. Pour mixture into a small saucepan. Place on stove top set to medium heat until boiling. Once boiling, boil for 60 seconds. Remove from heat and strain through a mesh strainer into a bowl. Whisk in cold butter, olive oil, and lemon zest. 4. Combine the flour, granulated sugar, confectioners' sugar, lemon zest, and salt in a food processor to make the crust. Pulse in the butter until it becomes a crumbly dough. 5. When ready to cook, set the Pit Boss to 350°F and preheat, lid closed for 15 minutes. 6. Bake until crust is very lightly golden brown, about 30 to 35 minutes. 7. Remove from the grill and pour the lemon garnish over the crust. Return to the grill and continue cooking until the topping is cooked through for 15 to 20 minutes. 8. Let cool to room temperature and refrigerate until chilled before cutting into bars. Sprinkle with powdered sugar and sea salt flakes just before serving. Enjoy!

Suggested Wood Pellet Flavor: Apple pellets.
Serving Suggestion: Serve Smoked Lemon Bars with chips.
Variation Tip: Use brown sugar.
Nutritional Information per Serving: Calories 376| Fat 15.9g |Sodium 123mg | Carbs 56.3g | Fiber 0.3g | Sugar 41.6g | Protein 4.7g

Grilled Honey Apricot with Gelato

Prep Time: 5 minutes | Cook Time: 5 minutes | Serves: 2

Ingredients:

2 apricots, halved
¼ cup honey

3 tablespoons white sugar
Gelato for serving

Preparation:

1. Preheat your Pit Boss Wood Pellet Grill to 450°F for 15 minutes with the lid closed. 2. Brush the apricot halves with honey then sprinkle with sugar. 3. Place the apricots, cut side down on the grill grates and cook until you see the grill marks. 4. Serve with a scoop of gelato and drizzle with more honey if you like.

Serving suggestion: Serve the grilled apricot with ham and arugula.
Variation Tip: Use black sugar in place of white sugar.
Nutrition-Per Serving: Calories 213 | Fat 0.2g |Sodium 15mg | Carbs 57g | Fiber 4g | Sugar 49g | Protein 0.1g

Baked Molten Chocolate Butter Cake

Prep Time: 20 minutes | Cook Time: 20 minutes | Serves: 4

Ingredients:

1 cup all-purpose flour
¼ cup butter
4 ounces butter
6 ounces bittersweet chocolate, finely chopped

2 eggs
2 egg yolk
½ cup sugar
1 pinch salt

Preparation:

1. When ready to cook, set the Pit Boss Wood Pellet Grill temperature to 450°F and preheat, lid closed for 15 minutes. 2. 4 (6 ounces) ramekins, butter and flour Remove any extra flour with a rag. Reserve the ramekins on a baking sheet. 3. In a double boiler, melt the butter and chocolate over low heat. In a medium mixing bowl, whisk together the eggs, yolks, sugar, and salt on high speed until thick and pale. 4. Whisk in the chocolate until smooth, then fold in the flour and egg mixture quickly. 5. Bake for 20 minutes, or until the sides are firm but the centres are soft, after spooning the mixture into the prepared ramekins. 6. Allow 1 minute to cool before covering each with an inverted dessert dish. Turn each over carefully, then set aside for 10 seconds before unmoulding. 7. Serve and Enjoy!

Suggested Wood Pellet Flavour: Use Apple Pellets.
Serving Suggestion: Serve Baked Molten Chocolate Cake with vanilla ice cream.
Variation Tip: Use almond flour.
Nutritional Information per Serving: Calories 502 | Fat 18.3g | Sodium 115 mg | Carbs 74.3g | Fiber 2.3g | Sugar 47.2g | Protein 10.2g

Apple Tarte Tatin

Prep Time:20 minutes | Cook Time: 60 minutes | Serves: 6

Ingredients:

2 cups all-purpose flour
1 tsp salt
1 cup butter
5 tbsp cold water

¼ cup unsalted butter
¾ cup granulated sugar
10 Granny Smith apples, cut into wedges

Preparation:

1. When ready to cook, start the Pit Boss Grill and set the temperature to 350°F. Preheat with lid closed, 10-15 minutes. 2. To make the crust, blend the flour and salt together in a food processor until well combined. Pulse in a small amount of butter at a time. 3. When it resembles cornmeal, add the water and stir until the dough comes together. Form a ballout of the dough, wrap it with plastic wrap, and chill it. 4. Place a pie dish or a 10-inch round cake pan on the grill while the dough cools; butter and sugar the pie dish. Allow it to caramelise. 5. Remove the sugar from the grill after it has caramelised and turned a dark amber color. Cover the caramel with apple slices in a fan shape. 6. Oil the pie crust into a large circle that will cover the pan. Cover the pan with the pie dough after pricking it with a fork. 7. Place on the grill and bake for 55 minutes until apples are soft. Let sit for 3 minutes. While the pan is still hot, place a plate over the pie and flip it over. 8. Serve warm.
Suggested Wood Pellet Flavor: Cherry pellets.
Serving Suggestion: Serve tarte tatin with ice cream or whipped cream.
Variation Tip: Use pears.
Nutritional Information per Serving: Calories 710| Fat 31.9g |Sodium 647mg | Carbs 101.3g | Fiber 10.3g | Sugar 64.6g | Protein 5.7g

Caramel Pecan Brownie

Prep Time:15 minutes | Cook Time: 55 minutes | Serves: 6

Ingredients:

¾ cup pecans, halves
¼ cup butter
1 cup brown sugar
¾ cup heavy cream
1 cup all-purpose flour
½ cup cocoa powder

¾ tsp baking soda
½ tsp salt
6 tbsp butter, melted
3 large eggs
6-ounce chocolate, chopped

Preparation:

1. To make the Pecan-Caramel Sauce, roast the pecans in a 9-inch cast-iron skillet over medium-high heat. Pecans should be toasted for 5 minutes, stirring occasionally. 2. Toss the pecans with ¼ cup butter and ½ cup brown sugar. Stir until the brown sugar and butter have melted and mixed. 3. Remove the pecans from the heat and slowly pour in ½ cup heavy cream. Return to the heat and stir until all of the cream is incorporated. Remove the pan from the heat and set it aside. 4. For Brownies: Combine the brown sugar, flour, baking soda, cocoa powder, and salt in a large mixing basin. Mix in the melted butter, eggs, and cream well. Fold in the milk chocolate chunks. Pour the brownie batter over the caramel pecan mixture. 5. When ready to cook, set the Pit Boss to 325°F and preheat, lid closed for 15 minutes. Put the brownies into the Pit boss and cook for 35-40 minutes or until the center comes out clean when checked with a toothpick. 6. Place the cast iron pan directly on the grill grate and cook for 35-40 minutes or until a toothpick comes out clean when inserted into the center. 7. Remove from grill and let cool for at least 10 minutes.
Suggested Wood Pellet Flavor: Cherry pellets.
Serving Suggestion: Serve baked caramel pecan brownie with ice cream.
Variation Tip: Use walnuts.
Nutritional Information per Serving: Calories 579| Fat 26.9g |Sodium 478mg | Carbs 80.3g | Fiber 3.3g | Sugar 46g | Protein 9.7g

Baked Brownie Bread Pudding with Candied Walnuts

Prep Time: 10 minutess | Cook Time: 45 minutes | Serves: 6

Ingredients:

4 egg
3 teaspoons vanilla extract
1 pinch salt
½ cup bittersweet chocolate chips
4 cups leftover brownies, cut into 1" cubes
1 cup heavy cream
½ cup sugar

¼ cup dried coconut flakes
2 sticks butter
2 cup brown sugar
½ teaspoon salt
1 teaspoon baking soda
Whipped cream
¼ candied walnuts or pecans

Preparation:

1. When ready to cook, set the Pit Boss Wood Pellet Grill temperature to 350°F and preheat 15 minutes, lid closed. 2. To make the bread pudding, whisk together heavy cream, sugar, eggs, vanilla, and salt in a small mixing basin. Whisk everything together thoroughly. Combine brownies and chocolate chips in a mixing bowl. 3. Fill a greased 9x13 baking pan halfway with the mixture and sprinkle with coconut flakes. 4. Cook for 45 minutes, or until the edges are gently browned and puffed and the centre is barely set, by placing the baking pan directly on the grill grate. 5. To make the caramel sauce, combine butter, salt, and sugar in a medium saucepan over medium-high heat. 6. Bring the mixture to a boil, then reduce the heat to a low and continue to cook until an instant-read thermometer registers 275°F. Remove the pan from the heat and stir in the vanilla and baking soda. Because it will bubble up and generate steam, proceed with caution. 7. Serve with caramel sauce, whipped cream, and candied walnuts on top of the brownie bread pudding. Enjoy!
Suggested Wood Pellet Flavour: Use Cherry Pellets.
Serving Suggestion: Serve Baked Brownie Bread Pudding with vanilla ice cream.
Variation Tip: Use macadamia nuts.
Nutritional Information per Serving: Calories 948 | Fat 59.8 g | Sodium 638 mg | Carbs 100.3g | Fiber 0.9g | Sugar 71.6g | Protein 8.2g

Chocolate Chip Walnuts Cookies

Prep Time: 10 minutes | Cook Time: 20 minutes | Serves: 4

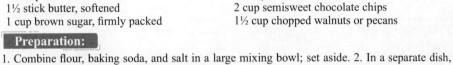

Ingredients:

2½ cups flour
1 teaspoon baking soda
½ teaspoon salt
1½ stick butter, softened
1 cup brown sugar, firmly packed

½ cup sugar
2 whole eggs
1 teaspoon vanilla extract
2 cup semisweet chocolate chips
1½ cup chopped walnuts or pecans

Preparation:

1. Combine flour, baking soda, and salt in a large mixing bowl; set aside. 2. In a separate dish, cream the butter until light and fluffy. Combine brown sugar, sugar, eggs, and vanilla extract in a mixing bowl. 3. Gradually incorporate the flour mixture. Fold the chocolate chips and nuts into the dough gently. 4. Drop spoonfuls of dough onto an aluminium foil sheet. 5. Preheat the grill to 350° F when ready to cook. 17 minutes in the grill to avoid sticking, start with a fresh piece of foil for each batch of cookies. Enjoy!

Suggested Wood Pellet Flavour: Use Apple Pellets.
Serving Suggestion: Serve Chocolate Chip cookies with juice.
Variation Tip: Use almond flour.
Nutritional Information per Serving: Calories 725 | Fat 36.6 g | Sodium 449 mg | Carbs 96.7g | Fiber 4.3g | Sugar 58.4g | Protein 5.9g

Smoked Cinnamon Apple Pie

Prep Time: 20 minutes | Cook Time: 60 minutes | Serves: 6

Ingredients:

8 cups apples, peeled, cored and thinly sliced
1 tablespoon lemon juice
¾ cup sugar
1 teaspoon cinnamon

¼ teaspoon nutmeg
2 whole frozen pie crust, thawed
¼ cup apple jelly
2 tablespoons heavy whipping cream

Preparation:

1. In a large mixing bowl, combine the apples, lemon juice, sugar, cinnamon, and nutmeg. 2. Make two 11-inch rounds out of the pie crust dough. Fit one circle into a 9" pie plate, ideally glass (try not to stretch the dough). Apply the apple jelly on the surface. Toss in the apple mixture. 3. Apply apple juice to the crust's edge. Seal the edges of the top crust by pressing them together. If desired, trim the pastry and flute the edges. Using a paring knife, make numerous small slices in the top crust. Lightly coat the top of the pie with the cream with a pastry brush. 4. Preheat the grill to high for 15 minutes when you're ready to cook. Bake for 50–60 minutes, or until the apples are soft and the crust is golden brown. Allow to cool on a wire rack. Warm or at room temperature is fine. Enjoy!

Suggested Wood Pellet Flavour: Use Apple Pellets.
Serving Suggestion: Serve Smoked Roasted Apple Pie with green tea.
Variation Tip: Use peaches.
Nutritional Information per Serving: Calories 521 | Fat 16.3g | Sodium 282mg | Carbs 96.3g | Fiber 8g | Sugar 64.6g | Protein 2.9g

Classic Red Velvet Cake

Prep Time: 10 minutes | Cook Time: 40 minutes | Serves: 8

Ingredients:

3½ cups all-purpose flour, plus more as needed
1 tsp baking soda
1 tsp baking powder
2 tbsp unsweetened cocoa powder
½ tsp salt
2 cups sugar
1 cup grapeseed oil
2 eggs

1½ cups buttermilk
2 tsp vanilla extract
2-ounce red food coloring
½ cup cold coffee
1 tsp apple cider vinegar
5 tbsp butter, softened
5 ounces cream cheese, room temperature
½ tsp vanilla
2 cups powdered sugar

1 tbsp milk, plus more as needed

Preparation:

1. When ready to cook, start the Pit Boss Grill and set the temperature to 325°F. Preheat lid closed, 10-15 minutes. 2. In a bowl, whisk together the flour, baking powder, baking soda, cocoa powder and salt. Set aside. 3. In a big bowl, combine sugar and vegetable oil. Mix in the eggs, buttermilk, vanilla and red food colouring until combined. Stir in the coffee and vinegar. 4. Combine the wet ingredients with the dry ingredients, a small amount at a time, mixing after each addition. Mix just until combined. 5. Using shortening and flour, oil and flour two 9-inch round cake pans. Pour the batter into each pan evenly. 6. Place cake pans on the grill grate and bake for 30 to 40 minutes, or until a toothpick inserted in the center comes out clean. 7. Cool the pans on a cooling rack until they are warm to the touch. Remove the cakes from the pans and set aside to cool fully. 8. To make the icing, follow these instructions. In a mixing dish, cream together the butter and cream cheese until smooth. 9. On a low speed, whip in the vanilla extract, then gradually add the powdered sugar. The mixture will have a tiny stiffness to it. 10. Add 1 tbsp of milk and beat on high speed, adding milk a tsp at a time as needed to achieve an icing with a spreadable consistency. 11. When the cake is cool, sprinkle with cream cheese frosting, doing a layer of frosting between both cakes. Enjoy!

Suggested Wood Pellet Flavor: Cherry pellets.
Serving Suggestion: Serve red velvet cake with juice.
Variation Tip: Use almond flour.
Nutritional Information per Serving: Calories 912| Fat 42.9g |Sodium 474mg | Carbs 125.3g | Fiber 1.3g | Sugar 84.6g | Protein 10.7g

Conclusion

To put it simply, the Pit Boss pellet grill is the greatest choice for a family with a small backyard and an average budget. Familiarize yourself with your grill by trying simple dishes and utilizing all of its cooking features before progressively honing your grilling skills. Have a good time barbecuing. Try all the juicy steaks, pork tenderloins, chops, lamb, rib racks, chicken, seafood, turkey, and vegetable recipes given in this cookbook, and let us know about your whole Pit Boss Grill experience. I hope you will have the time of your life while grilling with this smoker and grill.

Appendix 1 Measurement Conversion Chart

VOLUME EQUIVALENTS (LIQUID)

US STANDARD	US STANDARD (OUNCES)	METRIC (APPROXIMATE)
2 tablespoons	1 fl.oz	30 mL
¼ cup	2 fl.oz	60 mL
½ cup	4 fl.oz	120 mL
1 cup	8 fl.oz	240 mL
1½ cup	12 fl.oz	355 mL
2 cups or 1 pint	16 fl.oz	475 mL
4 cups or 1 quart	32 fl.oz	1 L
1 gallon	128 fl.oz	4 L

TEMPERATURES EQUIVALENTS

FAHRENHEIT(F)	CELSIUS© (APPROXIMATE)
225 °F	107 °C
250 °F	120 °C
275 °F	135 °C
300 °F	150 °C
325 °F	160 °C
350 °F	180 °C
375 °F	190 °C
400 °F	205 °C
425 °F	220 °C
450 °F	235 °C
475 °F	245 °C
500 °F	260 °C

VOLUME EQUIVALENTS (DRY)

US STANDARD	METRIC (APPROXIMATE)
⅛ teaspoon	0.5 mL
¼ teaspoon	1 mL
½ teaspoon	2 mL
¾ teaspoon	4 mL
1 teaspoon	5 mL
1 tablespoon	15 mL
¼ cup	59 mL
½ cup	118 mL
¾ cup	177 mL
1 cup	235 mL
2 cups	475 mL
3 cups	700 mL
4 cups	1 L

WEIGHT EQUIVALENTS

US STANDARD	METRIC (APPROXINATE)
1 ounce	28 g
2 ounces	57 g
5 ounces	142 g
10 ounces	284 g
15 ounces	425 g
16 ounces (1 pound)	455 g
1.5pounds	680 g
2pounds	907 g

Appendix 2 Recipes Index

Made in United States
Orlando, FL
29 September 2024

52092819R00062